Talking To Black People

An Exploration of Black Culture & Everything You Wish You Knew

Tunde Gbotosho

CONNECTING BRIDGES PUBLISHING

Connecting the world one conversation at a time

TALKING TO BLACK PEOPLE

An Exploration of Black Culture & Everything You Wish You Knew

Copyright © 2023, Tunde Gbotosho

Hardcover: 979-8-9891766-0-1
Paperback: 979-8-9891766-3-2
eBook: 979-8-9891766-7-0
Large Print: 979-8-9891766-6-3

Audiobook: 979-8-9891766-9-4

Front cover image: Alexandar Liang
Illustration art: Tunde × DALL·E
Book design: Tunde Gbotosho

Library of Congress Control Number: 2023921304

First printing edition 2023
Printed in the United States of America

Connecting Bridges Publishing
5830 E. 2nd Street, Ste 7000
Casper WY, 82609
www.connectingbridgespublishing.com

For The Culture

James 1:17

Author's Disclaimer About This Book:

I am not the spokesperson for Black people.

Though we may have shared experiences, Black people (all

people for that matter) are living and having very human, but

different experiences every single day.

Therefore, the contents of this book are an **objective** reflection

of my experiences, the experiences of other Black people around

me, and stories that have been shared with me, backed by a

substantial amount of qualitative and quantitative research.

Thank you

Contents

Preface

Hello. Welcome to my TED talk; please bear with me as we get started.

- Tunde

I have a professional background in strategy consulting, which means that I've developed a habit of putting an executive summary at the start of every project I do. Essentially, an executive summary is exactly what it sounds like – a high-level summary (usually meant for executives) of what you're about to read and talk about. I've found that executive summaries help "set the scene" or "set the mood," so to speak, because they provide an opportunity for the author to give a preview and answer any early questions people might have about the topic(s) at hand. For those wondering, *Talking to Black People* was a massive personal project of mine that went down many unexpected roads. What was meant to be a quick three-month project/challenge to myself ended up taking me almost three years to complete.

Why did this book end up taking me so long to complete? Well, for one, life happened, which took me away from this project, and two, a background in consulting means I've also developed a bad (or good) habit of being a perfectionist. While writing this book, I wanted to make sure I gave each chapter the due diligence and attention it truly deserved. I honestly would have felt guilty about putting something out into the world that I didn't love. So, three years later, here we are. Since this was my project, I know where everything is, and hopefully, the table of contents helped provide you with some guidance as to how I organized this book. If it didn't, then without further ado, here is my 'executive summary' of what to expect and things to keep in mind as you begin reading *Talking to Black People*.

Part One: Talking to Black People

Part One of this book is focused on how to talk to and interact with us (Black people) in ways that may not be known or fully understood. People come from different places, and due to social, cultural, and sometimes religious differences, things don't always translate well or the way they were intended when people interact with one another. This is even more true when two or more people interact and there are obvious differences between them. With how quickly social norms continue to change and with how politically correct (PC) things are and continue to become, it's often hard to know what's still okay to say or do and what's no longer okay to say or do. The rules seem to be constantly changing, and since nobody wants to look stupid, ignorant, out of touch, or be called out for being insensitive. People either choose to try and learn as much as possible, stay away from things they don't fully understand completely, or they're somewhere in between. Then, unless there is existing internal bias, people generally don't want to unintentionally offend someone, especially someone in a community they know nothing about. Now when it comes to us (Black people), some things are just the standard across the board - like a person not being Black, and it not being okay for them to say nigger, nigga, or any variation of it, and don't worry, we discuss why later; there's a whole chapter dedicated to this.

Personally, I believe that understanding the 'why' behind different norms when interacting with people of different backgrounds than yours is as important, if not more important, than just knowing the 'what.' Think about it: if you went about life doing every single thing you do every single day without understanding WHY you did it, how frustrating would that be? Even with little kids, as soon as they get over their "no" stage, their next favorite word to use towards you is "why." Why do I have to brush my teeth? Why do I have to go to bed so early? Why do I have to eat my veggies? Even as adults, when you're at work, and you are given a task, especially a task, you don't want to do and/or don't see the value in it, what's the first thing you ask the person who gave you the task? Exactly, if you're comfortable enough with them, you're going to ask them, "Why." Why do I have to do X?

So, as we can see, understanding the "why" behind norms is an important context to have. I know when it comes to Black people, there are **seemingly** many rules that exist when it comes to interacting with us. The truth is, there really aren't, but I've been asked specific questions enough times and have observed certain interactions being repeated enough times that I felt a conversation was warranted. So, the focus of Part One is to help guide people on how to interact with us more easily. Hopefully, the topics we will talk about in this section will help alleviate any currently existing discomfort or awkwardness felt when interacting with us in the future.

Part Two: An Exploration of Black Culture
I continue to receive many interesting questions from my Black and non-Black friends regarding different topics either related to or about Black culture. In Part Two, we will explore some of the questions I've discussed and explored the most, with some added commentary from me, of course. It's important to note that this section is AN exploration of Black culture. This is because culture, whether it's Black, White, Asian, Middle Eastern, Latinx, or everything in between and beyond, constantly evolves, expands, and changes. Therefore, capturing everything related to any particular culture would also be impossible. The best happy medium, in my opinion, is to pick the pieces of any culture you want to explore, which is precisely why this section is, as the section title describes it to be – an exploration of Black culture. Even over the course of time, it took me to write this book, I had to constantly go back and update parts of the book that I had already written because there were things that constantly either needed to be updated or

added. While sections of this book may not cover *everything* related to Black culture, I try to explore the pieces that socially seem to constantly cause the most confusion, disagreements, and discomfort. I really enjoyed writing the chapters in this section because so many of the topics we'll discuss, I have my own experiences with, and at times, controversial perspectives on, and I promise I kept my biases at bay when researching this book. Topics where I had minimal to no exposure to were then an opportunity for me to learn a tremendous amount. I was honestly surprised by some of the things I ended up discovering when writing the chapters in this section (more to come!).

As you read this section, I hope you will take away new understandings about things that might have eluded you before. As I said, culture is constantly changing and evolving, and what's "in" is always completely different on a decade-by-decade basis. The 70s were different from the 80s, the 80s were different from the 90s, the 90s were different from the early 2000s, the early 2000s were different from the 2010s, the 2010s were different from what we are currently experiencing in the 2020s, and the 2030's are sure to bring with it a whirlwind of issues, challenges, and changes. Thankfully, I started writing this book in 2020, so hopefully, I still have another 8 - 9 years of relevancy left before this book will need some major updating.

Part Three: Everything You Wish You Knew
Just as the section title implies, this part of the book is focused on providing you with additional details and resources on everything you probably wish you knew about Black culture. The chapter titles in this section of the book are pretty self-explanatory. If it will help, and while I'm not in love with this expression, you can almost think of this section as a "Black Guide," so to speak. Again, Black culture is expansive and constantly changing, so this section likely doesn't have everything you may be looking for, but what I provide is a pretty broad range. The list of

recommendations in this section was pulled together with a completely objective perspective, which means that I kept my bias out of it while putting this section together. Additionally, I'm not getting paid for including something over another. I just wanted to provide the best mix of things possible so that regardless of your interests or identity, there's something in here for you.

My following words may offend some people, but fuck it. I know I cannot control anyone or their actions or what they choose to do with information, but please do not use the resources in this section to try and seem like something you're not. As you explore some of the resources I provide in this section in real life, please act like you're entering someone else's home and be respectful. You don't know what you don't know, which might be one of the reasons you decided to buy this book in the first place, so don't think that exploring the chapters in this section (or this book, for that matter) will absolve you of the responsibility of continued self-learning.

Things To Keep in Mind as You Read This Book
The Book Order → The order in which this book is written is intentional. There are teachings in each chapter that are sometimes built upon in subsequent chapters. This makes the later chapters a bit easier to understand. While I did my best to make each chapter stand independently without context being required from a previous chapter, some chapters are just easier to understand if an earlier chapter has been read. Where this is the case, I've made sure to include a note at the top (and occasionally in the middle) of these chapters to please go back and read a specific previous chapter. While I strongly recommend, and hope, that you read this book in order of the chapters I have provided, you don't need to for this book to be enjoyable. Each chapter can stand on its own, so if there are chapters you want to dive right into based on the chapter title, go right ahead. Jump around if you want to;

after all, it's your book now. That being said, below are some key things I wanted to call out before you begin to read this book.

The Stories → All of the stories I start most of the chapters in this book with are 100% true. Some of these stories my own close friends have never heard before, some of them they were there for, and some of them they instigated (LOL). I want this book to feel like a personal conversation between you and me, so what better way to do that than to put a bit of myself in here, right?

Language Used → As you may be picking up by now, the language used in this book will be largely informal because personal conversations are informal. There are different parts of the book where I'm formal when required, but I wasn't about to spend almost three years writing a book that would be super stiff and hard to read. That would really suck, for both you and me, especially a book on Black culture, a culture that's known for being innovative, creative, and fun.

Lastly, I wanted to quickly speak to my word choice for groups of people who come up throughout the book.

- **Latinx** → I am aware there is currently a split view within the Latinx community of this word being used to represent the Latinx community over Hispanic, Chicano/Chicana, or Latino/Latina. I watched stand-up comedian Gabriel Iglesias's (also known as Fluffy) Netflix show *Mr. Iglesias,* which has a whole episode that goes back and forth on the argument (Season 1, Episode 6), which I thought was really informative. I ended up using Latinx because I felt that while Hispanic, Chicano/Chicana, or Latino/Latina would have been appropriate, Latinx seemed more 'current' to use. I could be wrong, and I'd be more than happy to talk to any of you who identify as Hispanic, Chicano/Chicana, or Latino/Latina about your word choice preference for identification over Latinx. We can have an open dialogue about your views on it; I'm always down to learn new things.

- **Other Marginalized Minority Groups** ➔ The official definition of this word has a long list of individuals who would fit into this category. Due to the focus of this book, whenever I use this term, I'm talking specifically about anybody in the United States who is a person of color: A person who is Black, Hispanic, Latino/Latina or Chicano/Chicana, Latinx, Asian, Pacific Islander, American Indian or Native American, Alaskan Native, or Other, a person who is part of a religious minority, a non-White identifying immigrant, a refugee, a member of the LGBTQ+ community, or a person with disabilities.

- **Non-Black** ➔ Contrary to what some of you may be thinking, this term and its usage throughout this book is not implying nor specifically calling out White people. When I use this term, I am talking about anybody who doesn't identify as Black, African, or African American. So, when this term is used, know that I'm referencing anyone who identifies as White, Hispanic, Latino/Latina or Chicano/Chicana, Latinx, Asian, Pacific Islander, American Indian, Native American, Alaskan Native, Other, or any combination of the above.

- **Black Community:** When I use this term, I am referring to all Black people in America and, when required, contextually the world. It just depends on the context of what topic we're talking about. Don't worry; the times when I mean it from a global perspective, I call it out.

Well, that's it for all our required prep work before you start reading this book. I thoroughly enjoyed writing about all of it, and I hope you enjoy reading what I have to say.

Authors note: Other than specifically this book, I do not own the rights to any song, movie, TV show, clip, book, podcast, website, link, social media site, content, business, or other that I recommend or reference in this book.

Introduction

"Hey! You - yeah, the person currently reading this book. I just wanted to say hi, and thanks for buying my book. I appreciate you"

- Tunde

"Hey, is it okay if I ask you something?"
"I didn't know if I could ask you that"
"I didn't want to look stupid"
"I just didn't want to sound dumb"
"Am I allowed to say this?"
"OMG, was I allowed to say that?"
"It felt uncomfortable asking you about that"
"I thought it would be an awkward conversation to have"
"I'm not racist, I swear"
"Fuck"

Thinking back to many of the conversations I have had with my non-Black friends, these were some of the responses they gave for being nervous to ask me questions about Black people, the Black community, and Black culture. This was always surprising to me because some of these responses came from people whom I had already had plenty of "awkward" conversations with about race, ethnicity, and culture. I eventually came to realize that part of the reason for the constant nervousness, or fear had nothing to do with the closeness of our friendship but with our society and how social norms sometimes make it extremely uncomfortable and awkward, if not outright impossible, for anyone to talk about, or even ask questions about a race and culture that is not their own. There is this air that exists now that "you are just supposed to know" and "shame on you if you don't." Well, that doesn't make any sense, does it? If anything, it's a little bit ridiculous. How are you; matter of fact, how is anyone supposed to know what they don't know if they're not allowed to freely ask questions about what they don't know? I've been in this situation plenty of times before, and not only is it annoying, but sometimes it's really frustrating. No one should be ostracized for not knowing what they don't know, especially when there is an honest curiosity and a genuine interest in learning.

I often reflect to try and figure out how we, as a generation and society, have somehow gotten to a place where things that have been, and should be, super easy to talk about, are now risky or taboo topics. If you ask enough people the exact same question about their identity or cultural heritage, I can guarantee you are bound to find at least one person who will be offended by the question being asked. What makes things so tricky these days is that you never know who will be offended or what will offend someone. As of late, it's started to feel like everything is either offensive or can be considered offensive. Shoot, even me writing this book will probably offend some, if not many, people. It's life, and part of why I decided to write the book anyway is because you, within reason of course, can't go around living life doing or not doing things simply because of the fears of "what will people say/do."

So, how did we get here as a society where things are risky and taboo? Well, one of the things I personally blame is how rampant politically correct (PC) culture has become. For those who don't know, political correctness (PC) is the term used to describe language and sometimes policies used to prevent the accidental offense of a particular group of people's race, gender, culture, or sexual orientation. While this, in theory, is a good idea, how it's played out and the effects it's had on how we now interact with one another is undeniable. As an example, it's why jokes you would see on TV ten, even five years ago, you would never see today. Some of the changes in jokes and content have been amazing because some stuff was offensive, but some changes have been excessive. In fact, political correctness is probably a key contributing factor to the perspective that our generation today is "sensitive." There are many good and bad things you can say about PC culture, but one thing I think we can all agree on is that, for better or worse, PC culture can be *restrictive*. This is even more true when it comes to the topics of race and culture. In my experience, every time I google something that has to do with race or culture, I never find exactly what I'm looking for. I'm always open to learning more about how to respect or interact with another culture, but rarely do I ever find resources that provide a non-watered down, blunt perspective on how to *interact* better with someone of a different racial identity or culture than mine. Then, whenever I do, it's always surface-level stuff at best, and again, it's usually pretty watered down.

During my research for this book, I realized that the same struggle I had been having with finding resources I could use to interact better with people of different racial identities and their cultures is the same for our culture (Black people). Most internet searches you do on the topic of "Black people" will generally lead you to articles and videos on how to be an ally, Black Lives Matter, recognizing privilege, systematic oppression, racism, etc., and the list goes on and on. These are all great topics and I encourage you to read up on them to further your own understanding because they are important, but these weren't the only things I was personally looking for. These topics probably weren't the only things you were looking for either when you googled "how to talk to Black [insert descriptive adjective here]." You probably were not looking for another article to tell you that you are a fucked-up person for enjoying benefits and privileges that you probably didn't even know you had. You probably were not looking for another video that gave you superficial information that did not really answer any of your questions. Most of all, you probably were not looking for something that would confuse you with more questions than answers.

You were probably looking for something that can answer all your questions or, at minimum, gave you the baseline you felt you needed to be able to talk to and interact better with Black people and/or Black culture. Feeling lost or confused when talking to or interacting with someone from a different culture or background than you when you are earnestly trying to connect is discouraging. If this is true for you, then you, my non-Black friends, and Black friends who have felt disconnected from the Black community are all in the same boat. My friends are lucky in the sense that I can be, and I'm happy to be a resource for them and provide guidance wherever I can. They do their own research and do the work when they truly want to learn something new, and I help fill in the gaps, if and where any may be. Thankfully, I've always been open and happy to talk about Black people and Black culture and answer many of their questions (I mean, I did write a whole book about it - LOL).

Unfortunately, not everyone has a friend who is not only a Black person who continuously interacts with Black culture (no offense intended to any Black people who don't) but is also willing and patient enough to have these types of conversations (and no offense to those of you who aren't/don't want to have these conversations). It's part of why I decided to write this book. It's to give you, and all my other confused friends, something to fall back on whenever you are feeling lost or confused about something, for however long this book stays relevant. I also recognize that not everybody has Black friends they even feel comfortable enough to have certain conversations with or ask certain questions with. After all, no one wants to look stupid or ignorant, especially to their friends. That being said, I do want to say that talking about race, ethnicity, and culture does not and should not have to be this thing people try to avoid for the sake of "not looking dumb or ignorant." It can and honestly should be a super relaxed conversation; it just sometimes depends on who you are able to talk to. I get it because

I've been there before. I've been in situations where friends from different cultural backgrounds than mine called me out for not knowing about things that they expected me to "just know," and I didn't like it. I can't be faulted for not knowing about things I've never been exposed to, and because I've been there before, I can, at times, empathize with the struggle that non-Black people and even some Black people have when it comes to being confused when interacting with Black people and Black culture. It can be hard to know how to talk to and respectfully interact with Black people and Black culture when a good chunk of America, and some parts of the world, can manage to go most of their lives growing up with limited, if any, interactions at all with Black people.

I look back at my freshman year of college and remember the time one of the non-Black guys on my floor eventually told me that I was his first Black friend after we became good friends. Listen, as someone who grew up in NY, went to pretty much an all-Black high school, and was constantly surrounded by Black and Nigerian influences, this was a huge shock to me. When he said this, the very first thing that came to mind was, "How could someone manage to go 18 years of life without ever having to interact with Black people personally?" but then he explained it. He grew up in an all-White neighborhood; all his family members were White, and due to his neighborhood, all his classmates and friends up until college, were also White. His only exposure to Black people before college were the Black athletes on the opposing high schools' sports teams they had to play against, social media, and the news... great, lol. Through the constant expansion of my friend group, I've come to realize that this friend of mine's experiences was not unique to just him, and I'm not just talking about my White friends either. Depending on where they were from, my friends from other cultural backgrounds and other parts of the world had similar experiences, which in turn shaped their perspective on Black people, Black culture, and, by extension, race.

Why I Wrote This Book

So, I want to help shape those experiences and perspectives and make sure they are as positive as possible. In the spirit of all that, this book is an exploration of the different yet most asked questions about Black people and Black culture that I have received from the different groups of people I have had the privilege of interacting with. This book explores all those conversations and attempts to summarize some of the key takeaways. Due to this, this book does not explore every possible thing that can be talked about within the focus of each chapter, but the things my friends and you guys who bought this book probably want to know the most about. I believe the foundation of communication is understanding. If there is no understanding, then communication is difficult, and if communication is difficult, then we eventually stop talking, and when we stop talking, chaos ensues. That is what has been happening a lot in the world, and it's really disheartening to see.

So, now that you know my motivations behind writing this book. I also want to state clearly that this book is for everyone. Whether you are a non-Black person trying to learn more about Black culture and Black people, a Black person who feels disconnected from the Black community, someone who is just curious about Black people and Black culture, or a Black person already connected to Black culture and the Black community, wondering what I wrote about, this book is for you. This book is intended to be funny, light-hearted, relaxed, and, most of all, informative. My hope is that after you finish reading this book, you will be more informed and feel more comfortable talking to and interacting with your Black [insert descriptive adjective here] without feeling like you have to walk on eggshells. I want you, and urge you, to have more conversations with people who do not look like you nor have had the same experiences you have had. Things don't have to be awkward, stressful, or uncomfortable, and hopefully, if you don't believe me now, you will come to believe me by the end of this book.

What This Book Is NOT

Politically correct! In case you haven't noticed by now, this book is in no way, shape, or form going to be PC. I hate that acronym because it suggests you are talking about something that needs to be somehow restricted or censored. Why can't we just be two or more people having an informative but engaging back-and-forth conversation? Sure, some conversations can get spicy, but that just shows the people having the conversation care about what's being talked about. I learn from you, and you learn from me. We don't have to agree on everything, but we can discuss those differences and still respect each other. Conversations, dialogues, etc., shouldn't be a zero-sum game where one person has to win and one person has to lose. Let's learn from one another and do better for one another.

This book will not be a history lesson on the Black community or Black culture. It is not going to provide you with a super detailed overview on things like systemic racism, racial discrimination, oppression, etc. We will touch on these topics throughout the book, but this book is not going to tell you everything you should know about these topics. There is already **plenty** of literature that currently exists where these topics are the focus of discussion. If that is what you're looking for, then as I mentioned earlier, I suggest reading those books in addition to this book. If that is what you were looking for, I provide a pretty good list in Part Three of this book of some suggested readings focused on those topics.

This book is also not meant to be a be-all, end-all. This book is only going to provide you with a pretty good overview, with some additional details where necessary, on topics I felt were important to talk about and some of the most common points of confusion for non-Black and disconnected Black people when talking to and interacting with the Black community and Black culture. This book will give you enough knowledge for you to understand and interact better with us, but your work doesn't just stop with this book. My end goal is for you, the readers, to take the knowledge gained from this book to feel informed and confident enough to start or continue to have more conversations with us and other people who may not look like you. This book should be, at most, a starting point for your continued education and learning. It does not and should not stop with this book. Keep having more conversations, reading, talking, interacting, and most of all, learning.

Lastly, reading this book is NOT a free pass. Please do not think that by reading this book, you will know everything you need to know... not true. Even over the course of writing this book, I learned new things about topics I already knew about and gained a much better understanding of things I thought I knew about but then realized I clearly did not know enough about. Again, this book should, at most, be a starting point and can be referenced when doing additional reading. I want this book to supplement literature that already exists for you, not to be the core of it.

Now that we have the introductions out of the way, let's dive right in! As you read this book, I hope you'll laugh with me, learn with me, and grow with me. I hope this book will teach you at least one new thing, but more than anything, help you feel more comfortable to start having more conversations. So, here's to the current you for getting this book and the future you for finishing it.

It's lit.

- Tunde

Part One - Talking to Black People

We're Not All the Same

"Black is Brilliant, Black is Creative, Black is Beautiful, Black is Diverse"

- Tunde

Black people are not all the same. Contrary to the image that some media outlets try to push about us, we really aren't all the same. Not all of us are criminals, uneducated, poor, gangbangers, thieves, rapists, killers, lazy, dumb, don't have our fathers, are baby mothers, are angry, or even like watermelon! These are some of the craziest stereotypes I have ever heard and seen being perpetuated about us, and honestly, it's a little bit ridiculous. It's bad enough that we are constantly being put in a box as to who we are and what we are capable of, but it's even worse that this box has nothing but bad things in it. We're often painted as being the lowest of the low, and the times when we are given positive traits and characteristics, it's only when we're playing a sport or are somehow involved with the entertainment industry... rapping, acting, singing, modeling, etc.

I'm not saying there aren't some Black people who can't be associated with some of the negative traits and characteristics I listed above, but none of those traits or characteristics are exclusive to just Black people. Growing up in not the best of circumstances and/or committing a crime is probably one of the few things in this world that are color blind; the color of someone's skin does not somehow increase or decrease the likelihood they will commit a crime. A person can be White, Latinx, Middle Eastern, Asian, other, and everywhere in between and still be associated with all of the negative traits I listed above, and some actually are. Let's be serious now; prison isn't full of just Black people. One Black person breaking the law does not mean that all Black people break the law. It's the exact same way how someone who is not Black not committing a crime, doesn't mean that all non-Black people

29

don't commit crimes. If a person thinks the world works this way, then they are indulging in an incredible amount of serious 'overgeneralization.'

The Dangers of Overgeneralizing

Overgeneralizing an entire population of people just because of the actions of one or a few members of that population is a slippery slope. If we lived in a world where we believed the actions of the few represented the actions of the many, then I could say:

- All White people are White supremacists
- All mass school shootings are done by White people
- Everyone who is Latinx is an illegal immigrant
- All Asians are racist
- All Muslims are terrorists
- All Christians are hypocrites
- All Catholic priests are pedophiles

OBVIOUSLY, NONE OF THESE STATEMENTS ARE TRUE, so why, then, should the actions of a few Black people represent all Black people as a whole? Anybody can be any of the things I just mentioned above, irrespective of the color of their skin or religion. So why is it there are so many negative beliefs held by non-Black people about Black people? One of the main functions of our society that I personally blame is the media, news reporting, and the portrayal of Black people in movies, TV shows, and films that often play on, if not outright sell, negative untrue stereotypes about Black people as truth. Overgeneralization is dangerous because it trains and reinforces untrue stereotypes and ideas about a group of people that aren't true as fact. What this causes is an involuntary, subconscious, and sometimes conscious response to a person we do not know simply because of the color of their skin and/or their religion.

An Example

Let's say I had no Muslim friends, and due to this, all I knew about Muslims was how the media portrayed them to be. Then, let's say that due to my limited exposure to Muslims, I take the media's portrayal of Muslims, which is usually nothing good, as the truth. I'll subconsciously start to internalize whatever potentially biased things I have heard about Muslims as being true and start to form my own internal biases against Muslims. Then, if I watch a bunch of different movies, and in all the movies I watched, all Muslims are depicted the same way (as an example, angry terrorists), then I'm even further inclined to believe that all Muslims are angry terrorists (stereotyping). Let's also say this happens over the course of my entire life, and because of where I'm from and/or where I work, I've never met or talked to a Muslim person before. Since all I've heard and seen about Muslims my whole life has been negative things, I'm unlikely to try and make a Muslim friend or even want to learn more about Muslims and/or the Islamic faith. All I will know will be limited to what I have seen or heard be reported and portrayed in the media. Then, let's say one day I'm catching a flight, and a family I am assuming is Muslim comes on board. Because all I know about Muslims is limited to only all the negative things I have seen or heard in the media, instead of maybe thinking, "Oh, another family," I might be thinking, "Oh shit, a Muslim family - I hope they don't try and bomb the plane," or something ludicrous like that. Thankfully, I personally have friends who are Muslims who have taught me much about the Islamic faith and the history behind it. Because of the conversations we've had, I know that many of the things I have seen or heard about Muslims through either news reporting or media portrayals are untrue. As for the aspects that are true, I was reminded again that the actions of the few do not represent the views of the many. That being said, do I discredit that some Muslims *can* be terrorists? Of course not. My friends who are Muslim also don't discredit that either, but anyone, irrespective of skin color or religion, can be a terrorist. It just depends on whether or not the media is willing to portray them as a terrorist or instead as a "person who was facing some challenges," "a person with a mental illness," or "a person who was acting in self-defense."

Unpopular Opinion -> White People Can Be Terrorists Too

I mean, let's think about it for a second. How many times have there been attacks on civilian peace, freedom, liberty, and lives, and instead of the media portraying the perpetrators of these attacks as terrorists because they were White, the media portray them as "challenged individuals." A 2011 study by Kimberly A. Powell, Ph.D., University of Georgia 1992, and professor of Communications and Women & Gender Studies at Luther College, found that media coverage for 11 U.S. based attacks between November 2001 and December 2009 suggests that Muslim perpetrators tend to be portrayed as linked to al-Qaeda and motivated by a war against the U.S.; but in contrast, non-Muslim U.S. citizens are more likely to be described as mentally unstable and coming from families who do not support violence. According to data from the Center for Strategic and International Studies, in 2020, White supremacists were responsible for 67% of terrorist plots and attacks in the United States. Crazy stats, huh?

By definition, a **terrorist** is "a person who uses unlawful violence and intimidation, especially against civilians, in the pursuit of political aims." The question I then had was, "What if the person who I think is a terrorist didn't have any political pursuits?" Then I realized that there are different types of terrorism, and I'm going to go into them below:

The FBI defines **domestic terrorism** as "the unlawful use, or threatened use, of force or violence by a group or individual based and operating entirely within the United States or Puerto Rico, without foreign direction, committed against persons or property, to intimidate or coerce a government, the civilian population, or any segment thereof in furtherance of political, [personal], or social objectives."

The FBI also defines a **terrorist incident** as "a violent act or an act dangerous to human life, in violation of the criminal laws of the United States, or of any state, to intimidate or coerce a government, the civilian population, or any segment thereof, in furtherance of political, [personal], or social objectives."

Under Federal Law, **domestic terrorism** is defined as "activities that involve acts dangerous to human life that are a violation of the criminal laws of the United States or of any state; appear to be intended to intimidate or coerce a civilian population, to influence the policy of a government by intimidation or coercion, or to affect the conduct of a government by mass destruction, assassination, or kidnapping; and occur primarily within the territorial jurisdiction of the United States."

What I found interesting during my research is that a review conducted by the White House to assess the threat of domestic terrorism found that "the two most lethal elements of today's domestic terrorism threat are (1) racially or ethnically motivated violent extremists who advocate for the superiority of the White race and (2) anti-government or anti-authority violent extremists, such as militia violent extremists."

What was your reaction to (1)? I want to say that I didn't expect this, but I and other Black people and marginalized minority groups have often looked at the many domestic attacks conducted by White people as not "attacks by a troubled, challenged, or mentally ill individual," but as by definition of what they really were, domestic terrorist attacks.

Here, to put things in perspective, I'll give you guys a couple of examples that, by the four definitions above, would count as acts of domestic terrorism carried out by White people.

We can agree to disagree, but:

- The **many** continued attacks committed by the Ku Klux Klan against Black people
- The 1963 16th Street Baptist Church bombing that killed four children and injured many more
- The 1995 bombing in Oklahoma City that killed 168 people – including 19 children and injured many more
- The 2015 mass shooting in a Charleston Church that killed nine people and injured many more
- The 2019 El Paso shooter who shot and killed 23 people and injured 23 people
- The xenophobia directed against Asian Americans before and during the COVID-19 pandemic. A couple of points on this one:
  - Contrary to media reporting and select viral videos, an analysis conducted by Janelle Wong, a professor of American Studies at the University of Maryland, found that across official crime statistics and other studies, **more than 75% of offenders of anti-Asian hate crimes and incidents, from both before and during the pandemic, have been White people**, not Black people
  - Wong conducted her analysis across nine sources and four different types of data about anti-Asian hate incidents, including the Stop AAPI Hate forum, Pew Research, as well as official law enforcement statistics
  - Wong believes that it is media sources misreading and frequently citing a study published in 2021 by the American

Journal of Criminal Justice that has helped push the narrative that it has been predominately Black people attacking Asian Americans and perpetuating xenophobia

- And last but probably not least, the January 6th, 2021, attack on the U.S. Capitol

There have been other incidents, but I'm not one to belabor a point. When these incidents were reported on the news, the perpetrators were called everything but terrorists. I'm also not using these examples to pick on White people, but talking about the reporting around White terrorism juxtaposed with the reporting around Islamic terrorism makes the point I was making with my example above with the hypothetical Muslim family more real. I'm sure I'm not the only one who believes that if the various acts of terrorism I listed above were committed by non-White people, the media would not have framed these individuals as "troubled, challenged, or mentally ill," but as they have often already referred to them as in the past, as domestic terrorists.

The Media Plays Favorites

Here's a fun fact for you:

- According to a PRRI American Values Study, 75% of White Americans report having social networks comprised entirely of White people, with no minority presence.

This statistic was surprising and concerning to me for many reasons. The main one being, if this many White people aren't interacting with Black people, then unless they try and learn things on their own or go out of their way to interact with Black people, then everything they see on TV, in movies, and the like, they will likely take as the truth about Black people and other marginalized minority groups. It's not just about White people either; this concern of mine also includes all non-Black people who aren't White. If you're not talking to and interacting with people of a different background from you, how are you really getting a diverse, if not global, exposure to different experiences and schools of thought? How are you developing an unbiased perspective on people, and where they may be from, and what experiences they may have gone through? TV and social media can't be your only exposure to people who don't look or sound like you. It's concerning if it is.

Here are a couple more stats for you as to why this is concerning. According to a study conducted by the Color of Change and Family Story:

- Black families represent 59% of the poor in the media but make up just 27% of the poor in the general population, while White families represent 17% of the poor in the media but make up 66% of the poor across the country.

- Black families represent 60% of welfare participants in news and opinion media, but according to government reports, they only make up 42% of welfare recipients. This media portrayal is interesting because, according to the Washington Post, in 2014, government assistance and tax credits lifted 6.2 million working-class White families out of poverty, more than any other racial group, making them the biggest beneficiaries of welfare.

- News and opinion media are 1.32x more likely to associate Black family members with criminality compared to White family members. However, in comparison with crime reports, while 37% of those represented as criminals in news and opinion media are Black family members, only 26% of Black family members are arrested for criminal activity. In contrast, while 28% of White family members are represented by news and opinion media as criminals, White family members constitute 77% of those arrested for criminal activity.

- News and opinion media are almost 1.5x more likely to represent a White family as an illustration of social stability than a Black family.

- Additionally, according to a 2015 Journal of Social Issues research study conducted by Hurley, R. J., Jensen, J., Weaver, A., Dixon, T., Black men tend to be overrepresented in the local media as criminal suspects while underrepresented as victims in news reporting.

    Did any of these statistics surprise you? The one that really had me scratching my head the most was the one about social stability. All the Black families I have been exposed to, while having some level of dysfunction (but let's be honest, whose family isn't a little bit dysfunctional), were pretty stable to me, even the ones where the fathers weren't present in the household. Thankfully, I have the data to back up this belief of mine. According to a 2013 report by the CDC:

- Black fathers who lived in the same home with at least one or more of their children were more likely to eat meals with or feed their children everyday (78%) than White fathers (74%) and Hispanic fathers (64%).
    - In contrast, Black fathers who did not live in the same home with at least one or more of their children were less likely to not have eaten a meal with or fed their children (31%) than White fathers (35%) and Hispanic fathers (58%).

- Black fathers who lived in the same home with at least one or more of their children were more likely to have bathed, dressed, diapered, or helped their children use the toilet everyday (70%) than White fathers (60%) and Hispanic fathers (45%).
    - In contrast, Black fathers who did not live in the same home with at least one or more of their children were less likely to not have bathed, dressed, or diapered their children in the last

four weeks (from when this study was taken) (34%) than White fathers (39%) and Hispanic Fathers (66%).

- Black fathers who lived at home with at least one or more of their children were more likely to take their children to and from activities everyday (27%) than White fathers (20%).
  - In contrast, Black fathers who did not live at home with at least one or more of their children were less likely to not take their children to and from activities (58%) than white fathers (70%) and Hispanic fathers (83%).

- Black fathers who lived at home with at least one or more of their children were more likely to help their children with homework every day in the last four weeks (from when this study was taken) (41%) than White fathers (28%) and Hispanic Fathers (29%).
  - In contrast, Black fathers who did not live at home with at least one or more of their children were less likely to not have helped their children with their homework in the last four weeks (from when this study was taken) (56%) than White fathers (70%) and Hispanic fathers (82%).

- Out of all the fathers involved in this study who did not live with at least one or more of their children:
  - (25%) of Black fathers had not played with their children in the last four weeks (from when this study was taken), compared to White fathers (30%) and Hispanic fathers (52%).
  - (21%) of Black fathers had not talked to their children about things that happened that day in the last four weeks (from when this study was taken), compared to White fathers (29%) and Hispanic fathers (63%).

Why are these statistics important? Well, remember the example I gave just a few pages ago on Muslim representation in news and in media? That's why. If there are no Black people in a non-Black person's social circles, and all you know about Black people is what comes from the news and media portrayal, then you're bound to think of us as being this group of people who are poor, dangerous criminals, who have no fathers, are uneducated, and are uncouth, rather than the **diverse, stable, and multi-faceted people that we are**.

Breaking Down Mental Boxes

I hope that by now, you see the problem with the media portrayal of people and how it often leads to the overgeneralization of an entire population of people. I'm sure many of the statistics I provided surprised many people. I hope that, at minimum, these statistics show you can't believe everything you hear about an entire population of people on the news, nor can you trust how they're depicted in movies, films, commercials, TV shows, or viral videos. When you do this, all you end up doing is looking at the world through a very narrow lens. Everyone is placed into a box based on the color of their skin or their religion, and that's a very hard way to live life. You end up missing out on so many amazing opportunities and experiences because everything and everyone is in a box.

The same way that, yes, one Black person can temporarily be a criminal (temporarily because criminality is an act that can be forgiven once time is served and reforms have happened), as only one aspect of their identity, is the same way that another Black person can be anything else. Identity is super complex. Other than being Black, a Black person can be mixed with another ethnicity and have more than one culture they identify with, can be in the LGBTQ+ community, can be a person with disabilities, can practice any religion (or not), can come from the upper class, middle class, or lower class, have gone to any university (or not), can be of any age, talk in any way, have any profession, and any combination of all the above. Just because a person is Black does not mean they must fit into this "one size fits all" box the media constantly tries to put us into. Don't let media portrayal and the news influence how you think about people. Take responsibility for your own education and do your part to get as much information as possible. We already know the news can't be fully trusted all the time, so if we know that, why let that be your only source of information? Black people are not all the same; we are multi-faceted and extremely talented. We all have different perspectives, opinions, experiences, and thought processes. We are all individuals with our own dreams, ambitions, hopes, and aspirations. No single one of us represents the whole.

To those of you who may currently be saying, "**Well, I've personally interacted with Black people, and it was a terrible experience. They were rude, obnoxious, and aggressive.**" That's a fair statement. Nobody deserves to be disrespected by anybody. What is not fair is taking those experiences and using them to say that is how all Black people are. It's an unfair blanket statement and one hell of an overgeneralization. I've met and interacted with plenty of non-Black people (and even some Black people) who were rude, obnoxious, and aggressive, but I didn't then go and say this is how all people from these groups of people are like. Those are personality traits that have nothing to do with the color of someone's skin. As an example, I have personally been in situations involving White, Middle Eastern, Asian, and Latinx individuals who were racist towards me. They were rude, obnoxious, and aggressive. Some of those interactions were even a little bit terrifying because there were times when I felt like my life might have been in danger. While some of these experiences were traumatic, I still have White, Middle Eastern, Asian, and Latinx friends, close friends at that. I didn't say that because of the actions and words of a small handful of White, Middle Eastern, Asian, and Latinx individuals that I had come across, that all White, Middle Eastern, Asian, and Latinx people are racist. Did these experiences at times make me cautious when I would later interact with people who were White, Asian, or Latinx? Of course, but I have always kept it in the back of my mind that not all White, Middle Eastern, Asian, and Latinx people are racist. To judge the character of someone I had never met before based on the past actions of someone with the same skin tone as them would have been messed up. I'm not saying that people can't or aren't allowed to do this and think this way, but I am saying that it is unfair. So, if you have ever had interactions with Black people who were rude, obnoxious, or aggressive towards you, please do not assume this is how all Black people are. It's a very limiting way to live your life, don't you think?

The color of a person's skin is only one aspect of a person's unique and complex identity. I have met amazing people with the most surprising skills and talents I never would have expected. I have had the privilege of being told the most captivating stories that came from the personal experiences of people whom I know and have met in passing. I have visited awe-inspiring and breathtaking places, tried unique and memorable foods, been exposed to diverse music, cultures, and traditions, and overall have had experiences that I otherwise never would have had, had I allowed myself to keep people in boxes. We should not limit our exposure to people and, by extension, potentially new experiences because of a few unpleasant interactions with a group of people or what was seen and/or heard on TV. The world is extremely expansive and has the most interesting and complex of individuals within it. Explore it all safely, of course, and don't allow fears and/or preconceived notions to prevent you from making new connections with people who are different from you. No matter what ethnic group you look at (Black, White, Middle Eastern, Asian, Latinx, and everyone in between), there will be rude people, and there will be kind people. Don't let the rude ones prevent you from getting to know the cool ones.

"Black is only one aspect of a Black person's unique and complex Identity"

Black Excellence

Black is Brilliant, Black is beautiful, Black is creative, Black is diverse.

Across America and the world, we (Black people) are:

- Authors (you're reading a book by one right now)
- Actors & Actresses
- Athletes
- Biologists
- College Graduates
- Directors
- Fashion Designers
- Governors
- Judges
- Mechanics
- News Reports
- Pilots
- Professors
- Surgeons
- Veterans

- Ambassadors
- Bankers
- Business Owners
- Consultants
- Doctors
- Filmmakers
- Hair Stylists
- Lawyers
- Millionaires
- Nurses
- Police Officers
- Psychologists
- Teachers
- Veterinarians

- Accountants
- Architects
- Barbers
- Chefs
- Dancers
- Editors
- Firefighters
- Innovators
- Managers
- Models
- Olympians
- Politicians
- Scientists
- Therapists
- Youtubers

- Activists
- Artists
- Billionaires
- Coaches
- Dentists
- Engineers
- Geniuses
- Journalists
- Mayors
- Musicians
- Photographers
- Presidents
- Software Developers
- Trendsetters
- Zoologists

And we are so, so, so, so, soooooooooo, much more

👏

Final Thoughts

I hope I gave you a great deal to think about, but we still have much more to discuss. I think the conversation around race, when specifically focused on Black people, is such an interesting one because we are equally loved for the things that we create, as we are hated just for being, well, Black. There is no data that exists or will ever exist that can statistically prove that we're a criminal and violence-loving population of people because we're not; if anything, as I presented above, the data proves otherwise. Only media narratives, media portrayals, and the news, depending on which news network you listen to, will try to and continue to portray us in a negative light.

We, as Black people, are incredibly diverse. We are more than what we are portrayed as. We are global, we are impactful, we are leaders, we are innovators, and we are so much more. We're part of every walk of life and can be found anywhere in the world. We influence cultures and make things fun for everyone (I give examples of this in the "Black Twitter" chapter). We love everyone, even our brothers and sisters from different Latinx cultures and heritages who sometimes don't claim us, and that includes the ones who don't even think they're Black (no shade to any Afro–Caribbean or Afro-Latinx people who this applies to).

Another thing, if you respect us and give us reason to respect you, then we're going to respect you right back, it's that simple. Respect is huge in the Black community and is what we base many of our interpersonal interactions and relationships on. We generally respect everybody else; it's everyone else who usually doesn't respect us, and quite frankly, **we're tired of being disrespected.**

Lastly, this is a personal pet peeve of mine that I know many of my Black friends have shared with me they also have. Don't assume that because a Black person says they are from a specific city, country, or even university, they happen to know the other black person/people who you know from that same city, country, or university. I can't tell you how many times I've told non-Black people I was Nigerian, and they hit me with the "OMG, you're from Nigeria, do you know _____?" No, the person asking me this question, Nigeria is a whole country, not a small high school, I do not know the person whom you are talking about. That's like a non-Black person telling me they're from either France, Japan, or the Dominican Republic, and I ask them if they know the one other French, Japanese, or Dominican person who I know. Come on now, let's be serious.

And to everyone in the Black community, regardless of how you may identify:

"I love us, for real"

- **Monique Angela Hicks**

(Also popularly known as "Ms. Parker from the hit show "The Parkers")

Do I Say Black, African American, or Person of Color?

"https://www.youtube.com/watch?v=rZHwGnGrm_k"

- Tunde

We've all been there before. You're in a situation where you're trying to describe someone or a group of people you know or met, and there's this tendency to want to use race and any other obvious physical traits to do so. We use things like gender, height, hair color, clothing, size, weight, and, most common of all, perceived race. What's interesting to me is that I've seen people easily say White, Asian, or Hispanic/Latinx when describing members of these communities, but when it comes to Black people, there is always a hesitancy by non-Black people to say either Black, African American or Person of Color. I always see the internal dilemma as people struggle to pick one of these terms because the discomfort is always apparent on their faces. It's understandable, though; in today's political climate, everyone wants to be politically correct, and no one wants to say the wrong thing or misidentify someone unintentionally.

Well, let me make it easy for you: the most 'politically correct' term to use to describe a Black person is, well, Black. I mean, I've been and will continue to call us Black throughout the entire book (lol). That being said, the only way to know for sure which term someone prefers you use when you are describing or referring to them is to ask them, but until you're sure, Black should be your default. This is important because racial identity is very complex and unique to everyone. A person may be Black but identify as African, Afro-Caribbean, Afro-Latino, Afro-Asians, or any other possible Afro-[insert place of origin here], or other that may exist. In today's day and age, the physical traits or characteristics you see when you look at someone may not be enough to describe the full spectrum of their identity. Plus, some people may take offense to it if

47

they feel you are only focusing on one part of their identity vs. their identity as a whole. Therefore, it's important that you always ask a person what they would prefer to be identified as after you've gotten to know them a bit. **An important thing to note is that you can't use the terms Black, African American, African, or Person of Color interchangeably**. There's a common misconception you can use them interchangeably. I used to think this, too, but you can't because each term means something very specific.

Breaking It Down

- **Black**
  - This is the correct term to use to describe all people who may have 'Black' skin tone. You would use the term Black because a person may have Black skin but not identify as being African and/or American. Black is the best term to use when describing people who are 'Black' because Black isn't about race; it's about culture and identity, and these two things are multifaceted. Remember, a person can be Afro-*anything*

  - A person can be Black, but they and their family can be from France, Italy, Korea, Germany, Jamaica, Haiti, Dominican Republic, Russia, Australia, India, Costa Rica, the UAE, Greece, or any other country in the world. I personally know plenty of Black people who aren't American and aren't from Africa. They identify with the country and culture they are from, as they should. Identity is a spectrum that cannot and should not be put into a box

  - But aren't all Black people originally from Africa? Yes, but if we really want to use that argument, then the same can be said for literally everybody in the world, so it's a weak argument to try and use

- Lastly, some people prefer to be referred to as Black over African American because they can't trace their ancestry to a specific country in Africa. They may not feel comfortable claiming African American, so Black is a good default. **Black is the correct term to use because it's inclusive regardless of where in the world a person may be from**

- **African American**

  - This term is a bit tricky. The technically correct way this term should be used should be to describe someone born in the U.S. and has African ancestry, with the key caveat being that their ancestors were slaves. Another way to put it is that this person is a descendant of slaves. This person may or may not identify with or know which country in Africa their ancestors were from. This person feels comfortable and/or prefers being called African American over Black

  - This term is tricky because it doesn't technically include Black people whose parents were immigrants from Africa and gave birth to them in America. This is where the gray area is because, technically, by definition, people born in America are American. They may want to be referred to as [*insert country of origin*]- American, African American (because this technically also wouldn't be incorrect), or they may want to be referred to strictly by their country of origin

  - As an example, my parents and I are immigrants from Africa (Nigerian), and even though my little brother was born in America and can technically identify as African American, he doesn't identify himself as African American. He should be referred to as either Black or African, specifically Nigerian, but not African American. Another way to look at it is that my little brother is an American-born Nigerian or Nigerian-American. I know it's a bit confusing because, by a broader definition, my little brother can be identified as African American, and it technically would not be incorrect, but because he still has a direct tie (our parents) to his African (Nigerian) heritage and identifies with it, he is more so African/Nigerian-American or Blackthan he is African American. He considers himself Nigerian before he considers himself African American. This is an example of why it is always important to ask someone their preference because, by definition, a person can technically be identified as one thing, but then, due to other factors, the person themselves may self-identify as something completely different

- o Think about it like this: all African and African American people are Black, but not all Black people are African or African American. Read that again, please.

- **African**

  - o This one is pretty easy. This term is the correct word to use when describing someone born in an African country living in America (or somewhere else in the world). This person may eventually consider themselves [insert African country of origin]-American over time, especially if they get their American citizenship, but calling them just African wouldn't be wrong.

  - o There is also another gray area here in the fact that the people in North Africa, while geographically in the continent of Africa, don't consider themselves "African" in the way East, West, and South Africa consider themselves "African." It's not just them either; most of the world has this perspective. Here's an example: would you consider someone from Algeria (North) "African" in the way you would consider someone from

Ethiopia(East), Ghana (West), or Zambia (South) "African?"
Anyway, this is a conversation for a different day

- **Person of Color (POC) or Black Indigenous Person of Color (BIPOC)**
    - **POC:** This is the correct term to describe anyone in the U.S. who isn't White. That's the only difference. If a person is in the U.S. and they're not White, then they can be described as a POC.
    - **BIPOC:** This is the correct term to describe anyone in the U.S. who is a Person of Color (POC) but is also specifically a Black or Indigenous person.

Terms That You Should Not Use to Identify a Black Person

I hope my examples helped, but this section wouldn't be complete if I told you what you could say but didn't tell you what you couldn't say. Language changes and evolves over time. This means the meaning of words and phrases can change with it. We see in our society today that things you could say 10+ years ago and not mean anything and be perfectly fine can now get you into much trouble today. So, let's make sure we don't get into any trouble, yeah? Here's your list.

Don't say:

- **The Blacks** → try this, and someone might hit you with a "wtf do you mean the Blacks?" and you may have an unnecessary confrontation you now have to deal with. It's pretty much the same as saying, "You people." As we learned in the very first chapter, "you people" is a microaggression that has a negative connotation implied by its usage

- **Negro** → This used to be an accepted term, but as language has evolved, it has been retired and can come off as offensive if you use it now. This is why there were eyebrows raised when Joe Biden used this expression when he was talking about Baseball legend Satchel Paige

- **Nigga** → There's an upcoming chapter about this one. Just don't say it!

- **Nigger** → This is a no-brainer; just don't. It's even worse than saying 'nigga.' If you do decide to say it, good luck with whatever consequences come your way

- **Colored People** → this is not to be confused with People/Persons of color. This word also used to be an accepted term that one could use, but as language has evolved, it, too, has been retired and can come off as offensive if you use it now.

Lastly, before anyone tries to call out the National Association for the Advancement of Colored People (NAACP) and the United Negro College Fund (UNCF) for their names as being 'offensive,' they actually get a pass. We, the Black community, know they are not trying to offend anyone with their names. These are organizations built during a different time when the language was different, and they have done nothing but continue to try and advance the Black cause. These organizations' names may have stayed the same, but their continued efforts are always duly noted and appreciated.

Final Thoughts

Please do not allow yourself to be uncomfortable saying Black or Black people in general. You're not going to get in trouble; it's not a bad word or some taboo word. Also, please don't use the term Person/People of Color (POC) or Black Indigenous Person of Color (BIPOC) when you're specifically talking about Black people to try and be 'politically correct.' Just say Black, it's okay to describe us as we are – Black & Proud.

As long as you're not saying "you people" when you're describing a Black person, a group of Black people, or other marginalized minority groups, then you will be okay. Just in case there is still any confusion about why saying "you people" is offensive and why the conversation can go left very quickly, let me give a brief explanation. "You people" can be perceived to be an attempt to overgeneralize a whole population of people as something they are not, which is usually something negative. Besides, in social settings, the only instances where people really use the expression "you people" is when they're trying to be offensive. Language in today's PC culture is already tricky enough without you unknowingly using expressions that will get you into an unwanted confrontation with someone. So, just to be safe, avoid using the expression "you people" in public social gatherings.

Other than that, just say Black. It's cool, I promise.

How to Talk to Black People

"I don't like being insulted, and as much as I may want to, I can't really blame you if you insult me but didn't even realize that it was an insult"

- Tunde

I have been in many situations, both professionally and personally, where I was with a group of people who weren't Black (sometimes I was the only Black person present), and someone unintentionally offended me. I'm not even being sensitive or screaming PC culture either because I know that when it happened, the offense was never maliciously intended; it was often a subtle action, question, or comment gone astray. Truth is, some of the interactions I have had with non-Black people have honestly left me anywhere from flabbergasted to confused, sad, uncomfortable, annoyed, angry, and at times, spiteful. The sad truth is that these types of interactions happen to me and other Black people and other marginalized minority groups so frequently that I (we) no longer get surprised when they occur.

Storytime: When I was in my freshman year of college, I had a White roommate. Not only did I have a White roommate, but almost every guy on my floor was White, with a very small handful being neither Black nor White. I realized this fact after everybody finished moving in, and it was at that moment, I knew I was completely out of my element. Before going to college, I was used to being a Black face in a Black space. Aside from the few Catholic school stints I did in elementary school, I went to a predominately Black middle and high school. When looking at my parents' friends, while there was some diversity, most of them were also Black. This meant that growing up, most of my classmates were Black, most of my friends were Black, and most of our family friends were also Black. My entire environment was pretty much as Black as it could have gotten. Now, this doesn't mean I didn't have non-Black friends or non-Black related exposure to culture and people; it's just that being a Black face in a Black space was an everyday occurrence for me. It was "normal" for me. Going to a PWI (Predominately White Institution) as opposed to an HBCU (Historically Black College or University), I knew I was going to be around and living with mostly White and other non-Black individuals. I knew it, but when it actually happened, it was still a huge change; in fact, it was a bit of a culture shock for me. It can be super intimidating to go from an environment where everyone looks like you, sounds like you, and talks like you to an environment where almost none of that is true. What do I say? What do I do? How should I act? How should I carry myself? How much of myself can I be? These were only some of the questions I asked myself. Realizing that I was a Black face in a White space for the first time in my young adult life was intimidating indeed, but I adapted.

I gave house music a try (Levels by Avicii (RIP) is a great song), I tried foods I never had before (meatloaf and shepherd's pie are actually pretty good if well made), I tried sports I'd never played before (I still suck at hacky sack, but I just might beat you in cornhole), and I made genuine connections with really good people who aren't Black. It was an amazing first year of college, and everyone on my floor was cool with each other. So cool, in fact, that I visited Philadelphia, PA (Philly), for the first time ever, through the invite of one of my White friends who lived on my floor. There was a group of us going, and this friend of mine let me know beforehand that his dad liked to joke around a lot but that sometimes his jokes could go too far, and he was apologizing in advance. I told my friend not to worry about it because I had thick skin, plus a pretty much free weekend trip to Philly with the opportunity to try an authentic Philly Cheesesteak for the very first time was not one I was going to pass up. I am a lover of great food. We get to Philly, and my friend's dad picks us up. As my friend had rightfully predicted, his dad was making jokes the whole car ride back to their house. Some of the jokes were funny, and some of the jokes were slightly cringe-worthy, but nothing too crazy, typical dad joke stuff. I'm in the back of the car thinking my friend overexaggerated and that there was nothing to worry about. We're pulling up to the house, I'm thinking things are going really well, and I could already see myself with the Philly Cheesesteak with double meat and extra cheese (I told you I loved food), and boom, then it happens...

As we're walking in, his dad jokingly yells to his wife, "**Honey! hide all the silverware and Fine China we have; there's a Black guy in the house.**" Whoa... I remember letting out a nervous chuckle but not really knowing how to react and not knowing if my friend's dad was really kidding or if he subtly meant it. I don't know what prompted the joke, but I didn't like it, I very quickly became uncomfortable. I started thinking to myself, "Great, what am I supposed to do now? We just got here; we're supposed to be here all weekend, and just because I'm Black, this guy's dad might think I'm a **thief**? At this point, fuck the Philly Cheesesteak, I just want to go home." After what seemed like an eternal internal debate, I chose to just let it go and move past it. I knew his dad wasn't trying to be malicious and insinuate that I was a thief (I hoped), but he did marginalize the hell out of Black people by using an untrue stereotype to try and be funny.

I would learn later in life that the uncomfortable feeling I got when my friend's dad made the joke is a feeling that many Black people often have to process every single day. Most of them opt to do what I did and move past it; other times, someone is sick of it and decides to face whatever caused the uncomfortable feeling head-on. In my friend's dad's case, me facing it head-on would have been me asking my friend's dad, "What did you mean by that joke? Are you trying to call me a thief?" The honest truth is, for the most part, whenever Black people are in a situation where we've been unintentionally offended by either an action, question, statement, or comment sent our way by a non-Black person, we often choose to move past it the way I did with my friend's dad. I think my friend's dad might have realized that his joke went too far because I remember him being extra nice to me for the rest of that weekend. I'm not mad at this friend of mine's dad; in fact, I never was. I was a little bit disappointed, but I was never upset with him. By the time this particular incident occurred, I'd already been in other similar uncomfortable situations and was beginning to come to terms with the fact that as long as I was a Black face in a White space, these types of situations would continue to occur.

Microaggressions

I didn't understand it at the moment, but the joke that my friend's dad made and the reason why it made me feel the way I did wasn't because I was being too sensitive or "couldn't take a joke," but because the joke he made, while likely innocently made, was a **microaggression**. It would have been one thing if we were in a setting where this type of joke would have been okay (like a comedy club or something) or if his dad knew me well enough to feel comfortable even making that kind of joke (I met him an hour prior and had said maybe 20 words to him), but we weren't at a comedy club or standup show, and he didn't know me that well, so it wasn't funny. If anything, it came off as a little bit mean and completely out of left field. I hate to admit this, but I can assure you that we have all unintentionally committed a micro-aggressive act towards someone at least once. In fact, some people may even commit microaggressions daily and have no idea.

For further clarity, Merriam-Webster defines a **microaggression** as "a comment or action that subtly and often subconsciously or unintentionally expresses a prejudiced attitude toward a member of a marginalized group," such as a racial minority. Another good definition of a microaggression defined by psychologist and professor of psychology and education at Teachers College, Columbia University, and author of "Microaggressions in Everyday Life: Race, Gender, and Sexual Orientation, Dr. Derald Wing Sue, is "the everyday slights, indignities, put-downs and insults that people of color, women, LGBT+ populations, or those who are marginalized experiences in their day-to-day interactions with well-intentioned individuals who are unaware that they are engaging in an offensive or demeaning form of behavior." Sue also explains that "microaggressions often appear to be a compliment or a joke, but contain a hidden insult about a group of people." As we can see, microaggressions can affect a wide range of people, but when specifically focused on Black people, some examples of racial microaggressions include, but are not limited to:

- Assuming all Black people come from the same part of the world

- Assuming Black people are "dangerous," "deviants," "threats," or "law-breakers"

- Assuming Black people are less intelligent and/or less capable than non-Black people

- Criticizing the cultural values of Black people, such as how we communicate, behave, and/or dress

- Treating Black people like objects and second-class citizens

- ….and so on

Okay, so microaggressions are bad, but what causes them exactly? A whole bunch of factors! In my experience, the two main common ones are the stereotypical depictions of Black people in popular literature, film, television, and media reporting and the passing down of perspectives and beliefs by an older generation who may have views from a more intolerant time in society.

Types of Microaggressions

Microaggressions are similar too, but are different from blatantly racist, sexist, or homophobic actions or comments. This is because microaggressions usually lack the negative or hostile intent that racism usually contains. Simply put, microaggressions are convert while racism is overt. While microaggressions may not always be intentionally malicious, they can still be used to target a person's:

- Race or Ethnicity
- Gender Identity
- Sexual Orientation
- Social Class or Income Level
- Disability or Health Status
- Religious Faith

Though microaggressions can target various aspects of a person's identity, not all microaggressions are the same in nature. In fact, there are three different types of microaggressions:

- Micro Assaults
- Micro Insults
- Micro Invalidations

Let's dive into each one for a bit more detail on the three different types of microaggressions.

1. Micro Assaults

Micro assaults occur when people behave in a discriminatory manner but are not explicitly trying to offend someone. The person may believe that other people do not notice their actions or that their actions are not harmful because they did not intend to be racist. Unfortunately for them, the people receiving the micro assault will almost certainly notice it.

Some examples of micro assaults against Black people include, but are not limited to:

- A group of Black children enter a public park and start playing. A non-Black parent watching by the benches immediately stands up and calls, "Kids! Time to go! Come over here, RIGHT NOW!"
  - **Hidden Meaning:** This reaction could imply a lot of things. Some include fear that the Black children will somehow hurt their children based off the fact that the children are Black (which is pretty messed up), or beliefs that the Black children are "dirty" or "uncouth" and not wanting their children to interact with the Black children.

- A Black person going to a grocery store and being followed by a store clerk/associate
  - **Hidden Meaning:** This assumes that a person, just because they are Black, will steal and therefore needs to be monitored and followed around to prevent any potential thefts (Because I am a 6'3, 250lb Black male, I experience this one regularly).

- Discouraging romantic interracial relationships when one of the partners is Black
  - **Hidden Meaning:** The basis of this one is that Black people are lower-class or second-class citizens and shouldn't marry anyone who isn't Black, especially if they're White. These views also stem from a more intolerant time in American history.

- Telling a racist joke and ending with "I'm just kidding / I was just kidding" before even seeing the reaction of the people who heard the joke.

- **Hidden Meaning:** The joke probably wasn't really a joke. Behind every "just kidding" is a little bit of truth.

- Wearing clothing of or celebrating the Confederate flag
  - **Hidden Meaning:** We all know the history of the Confederate flag and what it came to represent (White power, White Supremacy, hate, etc.). To the people who try to mask their real intent of why they wear and show the Confederate flag behind "Southern pride," I say this -- there are plenty of other amazing things that exist in the South that can represent Southern pride, that isn't the Confederate flag.

2. Micro Insults

Micro Insults are another type of subtle microaggression where people unintentionally communicate discriminatory messages to members of a targeted group. Compared to micro assaults, micro insults are much less obvious but just as harmful. These verbal and behavioral micro insults are ironically harmful because people mean them to be complimentary. However, unpacking micro insults generally reveals bias, cultural insensitivity, and false assumptions or beliefs. In my experience, micro insults are the most common type of microaggression. You can usually recognize a micro insult because it praises one member of a marginalized group while putting down the group as a whole.

Some examples of micro insults against Black people include, but are not limited to:

- Complimenting a Black person by telling them they are 'articulate' or 'well-spoken.'
  - **Hidden Meaning:** Implying that Black people, in general, are not articulate and that the Black person who was speaking is an anomaly or is "different," or somehow "better than" for being well-spoken/articulate.

- Complimenting a Black woman by telling her, "Wow, you're so pretty for a Black woman"
  - **Hidden Meaning:** Implying that Black women in general are ugly and unattractive and that the person being spoken to is an anomaly or is "different" for being attractive as a Black woman.

- Asking a Black person if they are on the right line/ in the right place when they are in line for VIP or the precheck line at the airport or, frankly, any other luxury/premium type of amenity and/or space. Ex., box seats, first class, frequent flyer lounge, Fast Pass, FastPass+, MaxPass lines at Disney, Country Club, Resort, etc.,
  - **Hidden Meaning:** Implying that Black people don't have the financial means to afford premium access to things such as VIP or other luxury amenities/spaces, so surely the Black person in question is in the wrong line / is accidentally in the wrong place.

- Asking a Black student on a college campus who is not wearing any paraphernalia to indicate that they play a sport (training gear, backpack, etc.), what sport they play, within the first few minutes of meeting them.
  - **Hidden Meaning:** Implying that Black people are uneducated/not intellectually gifted to make it to college and that the most likely way the Black person being spoken to could gain admission and attend the in-example university is through an "athletic backdoor."

3. Micro Invalidations

Micro invalidations deny the realities of what members of a particular population experience. Essentially, it aims to downplay the variety of factors that affect the realities of life for a person within a particular group. This could be age, race, gender, socio-economic background, and all of the other previously mentioned factors that a microaggression can target

Some examples of micro invalidations against Black people include, but are not limited to:

- Telling a Black person "I don't see color"
  - **Hidden Meaning:** This statement blatantly ignores the differences in treatment that Black people in America (and the world) experience as opposed to non-Black people. It can be well intended as in "I don't judge people based on the color of their skin," but this statement can also invalidate the different obstacles a Black person may have to overcome to reach the same level of success as a non-Black person simply because of the color of their skin.

- Telling a Black person, "If Black people would just simply comply with the police, then they wouldn't get killed so often"
  - **Hidden Meaning:** It's Black people's fault that we get harassed and killed by the police. This statement completely ignores the fact that even when Black people do comply with the police, which is almost all the time, we still get killed, not to mention all the unprovoked harassment towards Black people by the police. There are also statistics that prove all this, which I give examples of in the "What is Systemic Racism All About" chapter.

- Telling a Black person, "Racism is a thing of the past"
  - **Hidden Meaning:** This statement attempts to invalidate Black racial realities. Let's be honest; racism isn't over. While things in America have improved for everyone in a variety of ways, we've also seen a huge rise of racist incidents being recorded and shared on social media. This begs the question of whether

racism is really over or not. I personally think that Will Smith said it best, "**Racism is not getting worse, it's being filmed.**"

How Microaggressions Harm (Black) People

Many of the examples I provided in the previous section are examples of situations that many other Black people(including myself) have experienced before. The unfortunate thing about microaggressions is that many people who engage in them are usually people who think of themselves as good, moral, and decent individuals. Basically, the everyday person, and that's because very few people actually go out of their way to try and intentionally offend someone else (aka, being an asshole). Thankfully, a good number of people are usually willing to have a conversation about microaggressions and will try to understand what they are and how they affect the people who receive them.

The problem is the people who believe that microaggressions aren't serious and that this whole idea of microaggressions is just people making a big deal out of nothing. I've also heard arguments that people who are offended by these "so called microaggressions" are just being overly sensitive. Other pushback that other Black people and I have received whenever we've tried to educate people on microaggressions include, but are not limited to:

- "What? I meant it as a compliment"
- "Relax, I was just kidding, can't you take a joke?"
- "It was just a question, what's the big deal?"
- "OMG, you're so serious"
- "What? Isn't what I said true? All the Black people I've met except for you are [*insert any stereotype that targets Black people*]

I can understand where the pushback comes from because nobody wants to be called a racist or be insinuated as being racist. A comment, question, statement, or action being called out as a microaggression (an interaction that's rooted in racial bias) can invoke a defensive reaction from the person who committed the microaggression. I also acknowledge that microaggressions can be a gray area. Not all Black people are the same, so what may offend some Black people may not have offended other Black people who someone may know; so, it can sometimes be hard to know what's okay to say and what's not. I get it, but the baseline should always be this -> if someone is pointing out, most often in a non-aggressive way, that something was offensive or insensitive, then it's usually worth a listen. This is why it's important to remember that all Black people, and in actuality all people, are unique and complex in their own individual ways.

So, exactly, HOW do microaggressions harm Black people?

I'm glad you asked! There are many different ways (mentally, emotionally, financially, spiritually, and even physically) in which we're harmed by microaggressions, but I'll give you my perspective on what are the two biggest ways (again, these are personal perspectives):

1) Microaggressions suck to receive. Especially if they are received daily. It leads to us **policing ourselves and being hyper-aware of our identities in environments where we should just be able to go about our day**. As an example, I can't tell you how many times I've gone into a store and had to make sure my hands were in plain sight just so that I couldn't be accused of stealing when I notice I'm being followed around by a store employee. Or the times my neighbors have stopped to ask me in the elevator if I live in my building (especially at night)? Can you imagine going grocery shopping, or just shopping in general, and having to always make sure that you don't do anything out of the ordinary

so that people wouldn't think you were trying to steal? Or occasionally getting randomly stopped by people living in your building to ask if you live there? It's quite frustrating, and it's a cumbersome process to have to go through.

2) The second impactful way in which I believe microaggressions harm Black people is because we don't want to seem "sensitive" or "problematic" by calling out microaggressions when they occur. Most of us are taught to ignore microaggressions when they happen because there is no perfect solution to stop them from happening. Calling out a microaggression when it happens can either go really well or really poorly. Either the person who is being lightly reproached will be understanding and apologetic, or they will get defensive, and then it turns into an uncomfortable and unneeded confrontation. Unfortunately, there is no sure way for us to know what the response to calling out a microaggression might be. Many of us don't want to take the risk of it going poorly (it's not really a risk; more so, we don't want to have to deal with it) and will just choose to say nothing at all. This is problematic because **the cumulative effect of saying nothing negatively affects us mentally and emotionally**. Think about my situation with my friend's dad when he made the joke. What could you or would you have said or done in that situation if you were in my shoes? Remember, it's your freshman year of college, you just left campus, you're a solid three hours away, you don't know any other older adults in Philly, and are supposed to be there all weekend. How much peace would you have been able to have that weekend if you hadn't been able to move past the joke and just let it go?

While this is just what I think, I'm obviously going to validate the points I just made. Research has shown that the cumulative effect of microaggressions over time can have a significant adverse effect on the mental health of the people who receive them. Research has also shown your mental state can have an adverse effect on your physical health. Think about all the times when you may have been sad and didn't eat, and because you didn't eat, you got tired and possibly even sick. So, not only do microaggressions affect our mental health, but they can affect our physical health as well.

Microaggressions take a real psychological toll on us (Black people) because they can affect how we are able to interact with other people in our daily lives. Where we work, go to school, go to relax, shop for food, and all other environments stop being safe places for us. Microaggressions make these environments more hostile and less welcoming for us because we often don't want to **perpetuate stereotype threat,** which is "the fear of confirming existing stereotypes about one's group." Black people have often been called intimidating or confrontational in response to us calling out microaggressions, even when we're not being confrontational or aggressive! So, in order to not perpetuate the stereotype that Black people are aggressive and/or confrontational, I and so many other Black people who I know often choose not to say anything whenever a microaggression does occur.

Essentially, we hold it in, but that's also not good for our overall health either. When Black people receive microaggressions, the internal dilemma we go through in that moment (almost in order) include, but is not limited to:

- "Did they just say what I think they just said?"
- "What did they really mean by that?"
- "Should I say something? No. Saying something may make the situation worse; they'll probably think I'm being too sensitive and overreacting."
- "Speaking up is going to do more damage than good."

- And finally, the one most of us end up going with -- "Fuck it, I'm just not going to say anything; it's just not worth the potential argument or awkwardness"

Time and time again, Black people will go through this dilemma and will often choose to say nothing. Then, when we speak up and call out the microaggression that has occurred, our concerns are usually brushed off, and excuses are made for the person who committed the microaggression. Someone, or the group of people who usually try to mediate the situation, will then tell us comments like:

- "_____ didn't mean it like that" or
- "I'm sure _____ didn't intend it in that way" or
- "_____ is having an off day, and that's not their character," and
- "I hope you know that ___ isn't racist"

While these responses are valid, they are often said without reprimand to the person who committed the microaggression. This type of mediation has the underlying meaning that our feelings matter less than the person who committed the microaggression. This is not only a minimization of our experiences and realities but is a microaggression in and of itself. I have been in multiple situations where I have witnessed a microaggression occur; the person who received the microaggression said something about it, and the group of people present not only made excuses for the person who said the micro-aggressive statement but comforted the person who made the micro aggressive statement, and then turned around and confronted the person who received the microaggression for speaking up about receiving said microaggression. When this happens at work, sometimes things go a step further, and the person who was called out for said microaggression complains to HR about the person who called out the microaggression and claims that they felt 'threatened.' I wish you all could see how I put my hands on my forehead just now and shook my head in disappointment. It's like getting punched by somebody for no reason at all: you say something about it, and not only do the people you say something to make excuses for the person who punched you, but they then comfort the person who punched you and get mad at you for saying anything about being punched in the first place. This is often the reality of speaking up about microaggressions for Black people and other marginalized minority groups and why it weighs so heavily on us mentally and emotionally. It's why some of the mental and emotional long-term effects of receiving microaggressions include, but are not limited to:

- Anger
- Anxiety
- Depression
- Feelings of Helplessness
- Feelings of Self-doubt
- Feelings of Shame
- Feelings of Worthlessness
- Increased Stress
- Low self-esteem and self-confidence

As you can see, microaggressions can lead to a variety of adverse effects on Black people and other marginalized minority groups, so please, if someone ever points out a microaggression you likely accidentally committed, don't take offense. Try to take a step back to listen and learn. It will help keep you from repeating the same offense with someone else. If you are someone who witnesses a microaggression occur and wants to help mediate, do not make excuses for the person who committed the microaggression; it only makes the person who received the microaggression feel worse. Instead, diffuse the situation by acknowledging the feelings of the person who was offended, then, depending on the severity of the microaggression, gently reprimanding the individual who committed the microaggression, and finally, offer up a different time for the person who committed the microaggression and the person who received the microaggression to talk about what occurred. Emotions may be elevated at that moment in time, and conversations are always more effective when the parties involved are calm. This allows for a safe space of learning to occur where the person who was offended can speak to why they were offended, and ideally, the person who committed the microaggression will be able to speak to why the microaggression occurred, all while getting an opportunity to learn why what was said or done was a microaggression.

How to Avoid Committing Microaggressions

So, I provide a much more detailed step-by-step in my "How Can I Be an Ally To Black People & Other Marginalized Groups" chapter, but for the sake of this conversation, it made sense to add a really high-level summary here for all of you.

1. **Be self-aware and Examine Your Own Biases:** *Everyone* has biases. It literally comes with being human. But if you can actively identify and challenge these biases, you're less likely to have them slipping into what you say and how you act. The work starts with you.

2. **Be Open-Minded:** Don't be defensive. If someone is calling your attention to a microaggression, they're not trying to make you feel bad but simply bringing your attention to how something you said or did makes them, and likely others, feel. It's not always about you; communication followed by understanding is key in any relationship

3. **Self-Reflect:** Be open to discussing your own attitudes and biases and how they might have hurt others or, in some sense, revealed

bias on your part. This step can be hard because you'll have to look in the mirror and admit where you may have been wrong.

4. **Be Social and Take the Time to Learn About Others:** Seek out interaction with people who differ from you (in terms of race, culture, ethnicity, and other qualities). Spending time with people of different cultures, religions, and life experiences will be a key step in expanding your worldview. Challenge yourself to listen more than you speak. The more you learn, the easier it will be to know what can come off as a microaggression

5. **Consider your words carefully.** It never hurts to take an extra second or two to think about how what you say might come off before commenting on or questioning some aspect of another person's identity. Is what you want to ask any of your business? Will it further your relationship? Are you just being curious, or are you just simply being nosey?

6. **Be an ally:** When you notice a microaggression happening, speak up and say something. The more often you stand up for others, the easier it will be to spot microaggressions, and the more often you will notice them in yourself. Plus, you don't know just how much it will mean to the person receiving the microaggression.

Spotting A Microaggression

It was important to talk about microaggressions in the context of talking to Black people because it's not the white supremacist, KKK, or other racist groups that are committing them the most, but the educators, employers, and health care providers who are unaware of their biases that can affect our Black peoples' quality of life, and that's concerning. In reality, most people think they are good people, but unfortunately, even good people can commit microaggressions. Good people can be 'good' and still have no idea how microaggressions can be embedded into how they speak to Black people, think about Black people, and even make decisions when it comes to Black people and other marginalized minority groups. No person should be judged for anything other than who they are as a person and what they bring to the table, but even 'good people' may sometimes fail to do this. **Ignorance is bliss, but for whom?**

The stressful thing about microaggressions and trying not to commit them is that you often don't even know when you're committing one! Talk about a conundrum. So, in order to help with that, I've put together a list of different types of microaggressions that Black people, and sometimes other marginalized minority groups, receive and hope they can help you start to identify what they are and hopefully help you avoid committing them in the future.

Lastly, if you recognize any of these statements or actions as something that you've said or done before, it's okay. Don't go crazy trying to apologize to people for something you might have said or done weeks to months, if not years ago. Use the moment as a learning experience to self-reflect and examine why it happened, and figure out ways to make sure that it doesn't happen again. Growth is about learning, and maturing is all about taking accountability for our mistakes.

More Examples!

Additional Examples of Micro Aggressive Statements	Microaggression Type
"There is only one race, the human race"	Micro Invalidation
"You're the Whitest Black person I know"	Micro Insult
"What are you"	Micro Invalidation
"I'm not racist; I have Black friends"	Micro Invalidation
"You're so lucky to be Black; it must have been easy to get into college"	Micro Insult
"You People..."	Micro Assault
"Is that your real hair?" or "Your hair is unprofessional"	Micro Insult with undertones of a Micro Invalidation
"Is it okay if I say the n-word?"	Micro Invalidation
"You're one of the good ones"	Micro Insult
"White privilege doesn't exist"	Micro Invalidation
"Go Back to your own country"	Micro Assault
"Everyone can succeed in this society; they just need to work hard enough"	Micro Invalidation

Even More Examples!

Additional Examples of Micro Aggressive Actions	Microaggression Type
A non-Black woman crossing the street at night to avoid a Black man walking on the same side of the street, but wouldn't do the same if it was a non-Black man walking on the same side of the street	Micro Assault
A non-Black woman tightly clutching her purse / a non-Black man tightly holding his wallet when a Black person walks by them	Micro Assault
Assuming a Black person is a service worker in a store (luxury or non-luxury) and asking them for help without even checking to see if they work there.	Micro Assault with undertones of a Micro Insult
Going to a professional service (hospital, mechanic, vet, etc.) and specifically asking to see a non-Black professional (Doctor, Nurse, Mechanic, Vet.,)	Micro Insult
Constantly mispronouncing a Black Person's name or constantly calling a Black person the name of another Black person	Micro Invalidation
A Black person being pulled over in an affluential neighborhood for no justifiable reason, but no other non-Black person in the same affluential neighborhood is pulled over	Micro Assault with undertones of a Micro Invalidation
A black person having the police called on them while moving into an affluential neighborhood because the neighbors believed that the house was being robbed	Micro Assault with undertones of a Micro Invalidation
Calling the police on a Black person even though the Black person is breaking no laws	Micro Assault

Karen

"Don't Be a Karen. It's just not cool. If you do decide to be one, then that's on you. You can't blame anyone other than yourself for the consequences you'll face... especially if you end up going viral"

- Tunde

Disclaimer – this chapter is in no way attacking anyone whose birth name is Karen. I'm sure it sucks that the name Karen is now synonymous with privileged and sometimes racist behavior. To those of you with this name who do not act like a Karen, I feel for you.

What a world we live in where being a Karen is something someone can be. It's actually a little bit interesting if you think about it. This one word and all that comes with it has been impactful in the ways it has shaped and influenced our conversations around race and bias. That being said, if there were a list of things you probably wouldn't want to go viral for, being a Karen would likely be near the top of that list. Before we get into Karen and how this name came to be recognized the way it's used today, I want to first define what/who a Karen is in the context of this chapter.

Karen: A pejorative slang for an angry, rude, entitled, and/or selfish, (usually White) woman who uses her privilege to get her way and/or police other people's behaviors.

Essentially, a Karen is a person, usually a woman, who exhibits negative, sometimes racist, and often ludicrous behavior. Karens have been known to go on public rants and tirades against store employees and rock the "Can I speak to the manager" haircut, which is the short asymmetrical bob cut rocked by Kate Gosselin back in 2010.

Where Does the Name Karen Come From?

While the name Karen being used to describe a particular type of behavior is relatively new, the behavior isn't. Women who displayed Karen like behavior used to be referred to as "Miss Ann" from the pre-Civil War era to the Jim Crow era. Miss Ann was Black slang for "an unreasonable/problematic White woman." Similar behavior has also been popularly referred to by the Black community with other names like Stacy and Becky. This unreasonable behavior still continues to this day and has earned women across the internet different nicknames, such as:

- **BBQ Becky** – A White woman who called the police on a Black family for having a BBQ. The family was in the appropriate BBQ area to be in, but she called the police, said that they weren't, and then claimed that her life was in danger when things started to escalate as people called her out for being a Karen.

- **Permit Patty** – A White woman who basically called the police on an 8-year-old Black girl for selling water outside on the sidewalk while not having a permit to do so. This woman claimed that she did not have a problem with the little girl selling water but called the police because she wanted to know if selling water outside without a permit was legal. She also said that the little girl's constant heckling was preventing her from getting her work done as she was working from home, but later did apologize about the incident and "claimed" it had nothing to do with race.

- **Corner Store Caroline** – A White woman who falsely accused a 9-year-old Black boy of sexually assaulting her at a corner store. She claimed when she walked past him, he grabbed her butt, but later, surveillance video showed that the boy did not touch her, and it was likely that his backpack brushed past her. She later apologized to the boy, but the damage was already done.

- **Whitefish Karen** – A White woman who was not social distancing or wearing a mask in a grocery store and was asked to put one on by a Black couple inside the grocery store. An argument began because of this, but it didn't end inside the store. The altercation between the woman and the Black couple continued in the grocery store's parking lot. The woman continued to follow the Black couple while they were in the parking lot, and as they were recording her, the woman started intentionally coughing at them while yelling obscenities.

- **San Francisco Karen** – A White couple that threatened to call the police on a person of color for stenciling a #BLM chalk message on his property. The couple claimed they knew the owner of the house and that what the person of color was doing was vandalism. Unfortunately for them, the person of color they were speaking to happened to be the homeowner they were claiming they knew...

- ...and other creative alliterations.

These incidents, among others, increased the notoriety of the term 'Karen,' but the one that stands out the most is the infamous incident involving the Central Park Karen. This was the incident in 2020 where a White woman called the police on Christian Cooper, a Black birdwatcher who non-aggressively asked her to put a leash on her dog in a designated area where there were signs posted stating that dogs must be leashed at all times. During the incident, not only does the Central Park Karen tell Christian she's going to call the police and tell them that there's an African American man threatening her life, but she actually goes and does it! What caused this incident to make headlines the way it did and help propel the term Karen to the notoriety it's achieved today was that it was also the same day George Floyd was murdered at the hands of police brutality. Central Park Karen's act of calling the police on Christian Cooper while trying to use the fact that he is a Black man to try and escalate the urgency of the situation to the police was rooted in racism. Central Park Karen's actions during her confrontation with Christian showed that she, at minimum, subconsciously understood her privilege as a White woman and the history that Black people have had with the police in America, and then tried to use it to weaponize the police against Christian by victimizing herself. The underlying social constructs behind Central Park Karen's actions, coupled with the death of George Floyd occurring on the same day, are critical events that helped spark conversations and center national media attention on the tensions that exist between the Black community and the police. During this time, the term 'Karen' truly started to stand out as the term used to call out the type of behavior that Central Park Karen and others have shown.

What is Karen Behavior?

Karen behavior can usually be split into two different categories. The first category, which I'll call the "**Obnoxious Karen,**" involves acting in an unreasonable, entitled, or otherwise privileged manner. This includes but is not limited to, asking to speak to the manager when they feel as though they've received unsatisfactory service or acting like rules and regulations in public and private spaces do not apply to them. This type of Karen usually makes a scene with a food or retail employee because they are unhappy with the level of service they have received. They are often seen repeating and screaming obscenities and instructions at said workers. This type of Karen is a busybody and is generally very unpleasant to interact with. This is the type of Karen to call the cops on kids at the pool/park because they have more friends than the allotted pool/park slots. This type of Karen seems to have a vendetta against people having fun, has made children cry, and will usually try to ruin your day. This type of Karen is also known for their pandemic behavior, mainly refusing to wear a mask in places that require it. It's one thing if you don't agree with wearing a mask, but if a place requires it, either follow the rules or leave. They don't do this; they refuse to wear the mask, refuse to leave the establishment, and demand that they, nevertheless, receive service.

I have a funny movie reference that some of you may or may not remember. In the movie 'White Chicks,' there was a scene early in the movie where, after the Wilson sisters had been picked up from the airport, they were on their way to the Hamptons for a fabulous weekend extravaganza but ended up being involved in a minor car accident. One sister ended up having a minor scratched lip, while the other had a minor scratched nose. Remember the 'bitch fit' that one of the sisters had because they felt like they could no longer go to the event due to their minor scratches? Lol, yeah, that was a Karen moment; we all just didn't know it yet. Lastly, this is a question that I've gotten before a lot, and no, there's currently no male equivalent of the term 'Karen.' There have been several attempts to create a male equivalent version of the term Karen, which is in reference to the 'Obnoxious Karen.' Chad, Kyle, Ken, and Kevin are names that have often come up in conversation, but none of them have stuck. Perhaps there will eventually be one in the future; until then, Karen is the term to use. Similar to the next category of Karen we will be discussing, this type of Karen is usually quick to call the police and victimize themselves by embellishing the details of the interaction that's occurred to ensure they get their way.

The other category, which I'll call the **"Racist Karen,"** is usually a White woman who leverages racial stereotypes, racial tensions, and racial histories to their benefit. This type of Karen is socially destructive and chaotic because, at minimum, they subconsciously understand the underlying social constructs that exist within society, their standing as a White woman within these constructs, and they actively try to use that status to intentionally bring harm to, or disrupt the lives of people, usually people of color. This is the type of Karen that the Central Park

Karen, BBQ Becky, Permit Patty, Cornerstone Caroline, and all the other women who have involved the police during non-violent and non-threatening social interactions with people of color are. They are good at victimizing themselves to solicit help from strangers/bystanders and in front of the police when things are not going their way. They will cry on the spot, make things up, and file false reports if needed, which they often do. This type of Karen has strong racial bias and weaponizes the racial tensions that exist against the Black community and, at times, other marginalized minority groups with the police for their own selfish motives. This type of Karen not only wastes the police's time but also taxpayer dollars every time the police are called to a scene they didn't need to and should not even have been called to.

The frequency of this type of Karen calling the police on Black people just for doing everyday things has gotten so out of control that San Francisco politician, Shamann Walton, introduced the CAREN Act in 2020 to make it illegal to make racially biased 911 calls. The CAREN Act, which stands for "Caution Against Racially Exploitative Non-Emergencies," aims to punish people who exploit community resources, like the police, to perpetuate their own hate. The CAREN Act is very similar to Assembly Bill 1550 which was proposed by California Assemblymember Rob Bonta from Oakland, California. Assembly Bill 1550 is a statewide bill that labels discriminatory 911 calls as hate crimes and aims to dissuade people from weaponizing the police for racially motivated purposes. California is not the only state introducing bills like this. New York and Oregon are other states where bills have been passed to punish people who make racist 911 calls. It's unfortunate that we are still at a point in our progression as a society where laws like these must be put in place. The notion that these laws even had to be proposed in the first place is even almost a little bit depressing; like, come on, just be a good person.

Here is an interesting thought: David Dennis Jr., a journalist who has written about the downsides of giving nicknames to women who do malicious things, said that simply calling women like Central Park Karen a Karen or another creative alliterative nickname and not by their actual name "grants them a level of anonymity and belittles what they've done," and that "when a Karen commits a racist act, the public needs to remember their real names to ensure they can be held accountable in some way" because "these people go out into the world, they have jobs, they do things that impact people.....[and] we need to remove them from those positions." I think there's much truth to Dennis's words. It's concerning living in a society where the people in positions of authority and power who can dictate how your life can turn out are racist against you deep down inside, usually for no reason other than the color of your skin, and can use their hate against you. For example, imagine going to court and seeing a judge notoriously known for not liking people from your ethnic background? At that point being in court becomes even more nerve-racking than it already was. If you're on the defendant's side, it feels like you might as well just plead guilty because you'll likely get the guilty charge anyway, and if you're on the prosecution's side, you feel like you likely won't get the justice you deserve when the evidence is clear that you deserve it. Literally, almost every experience you will have in life, from dining out, to traveling, to shopping, to celebrating, even down to grieving, can be ruined at any moment in time by someone who does not fuck with you or the community you belong to simply because of the color of your skin. Then the most frustrating part is when these experiences are ruined, you're not expected to retaliate or complain but simply take it and say nothing. And why? All because you were unfortunate enough to have an encounter with someone who decided to be a Karen? Sigh... what an interesting world we live in.

Can Someone Who Isn't a White Woman Be A Karen?

I wanted to answer this question before we came to the end of this chapter. Honestly, anybody, regardless of how they choose to identify or what their ethnic identity is, can behave like the 'Obnoxious Karen' or 'Racist Karen' and, therefore, be a Karen. Nobody has a monopoly on bad behavior. However, since the term Karen is commonly used to describe the obnoxious or racist actions/behavior of a White woman, things can get confusing and social rules get 'broken,' so to speak, when the term Karen is used to describe the actions/behavior of someone being obnoxious or racist who isn't a White woman.

The Future of Karen

There have been rumblings of the term Karen now being considered as derogatory and sexist against women, but more specifically, White women. There's a school of thought that believes the term Karen is being used against White women to police and dictate their actions and that Karen is a woman-hating term. I think this is an interesting perspective. The truth is **nobody** wants to be shamed by society for an action/decision they did, especially if there's an unwanted nickname they can earn because of said action/decision. So, if there's a word with a negative connotation that someone can be 'crowned with' in response to an action/decision of theirs, it would cause second thoughts on said action/decision. Not wanting to be 'crowned' with that word can prevent someone from doing something they may really want to do. From that perspective, I can understand how the term Karen can seem derogatory and how it can seemingly be used to police the actions of women. That said, while I can understand it, I personally do not agree with this school of thought. For me, words should be associated with actions/decisions. Liking the associated word being used to describe said actions/decisions is a completely different conversation. Someone who steals is called a thief; someone who plays sports is called an athlete;

someone who sings is called a singer, and someone who is an angry, rude, entitled, selfish woman (person) who uses her (their) privilege to get her (their) way or police other people's behaviors is called a Karen.

How To Not Be a Karen

The best way to not be a Karen is just to be an objectively good person. Whether it's the 'Obnoxious Karen' or the 'Racist Karen,' both are prime examples of a person causing unneeded stress and potentially trauma to someone else simply because they have been triggered. Being triggered is fine, but lashing out, especially to the point where a scene is being caused, is an immature and entitled way to act, especially as an adult. It's childish behavior that shows a lack of maturity that when children do, they get disciplined for. I get it that people have off days, I get it that people have bad and/or stressful days, and I get it that people even have sad days, but none of that is an excuse to treat people poorly or with disrespect. Whether it's causing a scene and berating an employee because the quality of service wasn't as expected or calling the police on an innocent person and framing a situation out to be something it is not, simply because of an unsatisfactory interaction with said individual is shameful. So shameful, in fact, that the moniker 'Karen' had to be created to capture the shamefulness of it all. I often think about the Game of Thrones 'shame' scene where Cersei is walking through the crowd getting rotten food thrown at her, except instead of calling her obscenities, they call her a Karen. People are not punching bags, and if someone treats someone as such, they deserve whatever punishment comes their way because of it.

We, as people, always need to remember to interact with and treat people with kindness, empathy, and consideration. People with Karen like tendencies need to remember it is not always about them. You never know what type of day someone is having or what they're going through, and having to deal with someone being a Karen to them can be the straw that breaks the camel's back and pushes them over the edge.

Lastly, don't ask to speak to the manager if you don't actually have to speak to the manager, and most importantly, if you don't have any evidence of people doing any type of wrongdoing, especially people of color and specifically Black people, MIND YOUR OWN BUSINESS 😊.

Thanks

~~Nigga~~

"No, if you're not Black, you can't say nigga. No debate. No ifs, ands, or buts. Not even if you're Asian or part of the Latinx community"

- Tunde

Storytime: While I was in college, I had the opportunity to be a bouncer at one of the most, if not the most, popular college bars in town; shoutout to Trinity Irish Pub in Charlottesville, VA. Being a bouncer, you see a lot of shenanigans, hear a lot of shenanigans, have to stop a lot of shenanigans, and at times, you were part of the shenanigans. I look fondly at my time as a bouncer, not just because of the social perks I received, or because I had a great boss who always looked out for me (thank you, Kevin), or the people who I got to meet and can now call life-long friends... No, I look fondly at those times because of how much I learned about myself and how much I was able to learn about people. People are often their truest selves when drunk, and being a bouncer allowed me to see the best and often times worst in people.

I and pretty much the rest of the Black community know that non-Black people likely say, have said, or want to say the n-word. It's not some big secret; we all know it's true. In college, I heard people throw it around at frat parties. I've had non-Black friends 'accidentally' use it around me when rapping along to their favorite rap songs. I've had non-Black friends beg me for permission to say it. I've even had some non-Black people I know get a little too friendly and use it to me while drunk. I have a lot of memories of non-Black people using the n-word around me, but the one that sticks out the most to me, at no fault of the bar I worked at, is the one that happened while I was a bouncer.

It was a typical Friday night; most of the people at the bar were either slowly getting drunk, already drunk, or on their way to getting too drunk. I was on the third floor of the bar, making my rounds and walking around looking for people who were up to no good and those who were already way too drunk so I could kick them out. Sorry, not sorry if I ever kicked you out. The music was blasting, the bass was bumping, and the inhibitions of that night were so thick you could taste it in the air. I'm serious; people who wore glasses walked into the bar that night, and their glasses instantly fogged up. The music shifts, the DJ is doing his thing, and m.A.A.d City by Kendrick Lamar comes on.

The bar goes nuts!

Everybody starts rapping along, and the hook comes in just as hard as it always does;

> *"Every time I'm in the street I hear*
> *Yawk! Yawk! Yawk! Yawk!*
> *Man down*
> *Where you from, nigga?*
> *Fuck who you know, where you from, my nigga?*
> *Where your grandma stay, huh, my nigga?*
> *This m.A.A.d city I run, my nigga"*

I have never seen such a large gaggle of non-Black people yell out the n-word so confidently, so happily, and so consistently in a non-aggressive way. I was shocked, amused, unimpressed, and annoyed all at once, but at the core of it all, I wasn't surprised. Aside from the n-word, even if you don't know all the words to all his songs, Kendrick is pretty hard not to try to rap along to. This also wasn't the only time where I was in a social setting and something like that happened, but that night, in particular, has always stuck with me because of how in sync the whole floor was while rapping along to Kendrick while saying, "nigga" with everything they had in them. The real kicker to the story is that the DJ restarts the song shortly after the beat dropped! Imagine the befuddlement I experienced when the bargoers around me surrounded me to try and sing the song along with me like we were friends! Absolutely the fuck not. It was a whole bunch of non-Black people singing the n-word to me. I didn't know if I should have been amused or upset; I honestly think I landed somewhere in the middle.

Why You Can't Say The N-Word If You're Not Black?

"Why can Black people say the n-word, but I can't?" or "I can say the n-word because I'm not White, right?" or "What's the big deal with me saying the n-word? It's just a word." These are the questions and comments I have received the most from my non-Black friends regarding the n-word. My response to that question had always been, "You can't because you're not Black," and while this was my response, I never really had a good explanation of why, other than the origin of the word. As I've gotten older, my response to that question has started to become, **"Well, why do you care so much about being able to say it?"** and **"Why do you want to say it?"** The question of "Can I say the n-word?" has always struck me as a bit odd because there are so many other words that people use every day and don't even know how to say, yet there was this focus and/or fascination about this one word they weren't supposed to be saying. and for good reason, too. It sometimes felt like the more I told people they shouldn't say the n-word, the more they wanted to say it. It's almost like a little kid whose parents say, "Don't push that button," and now all the kid can think about is pushing that button.

The facts are as so, the word nigger was created to be used as a racial slur against Black people. It is a word that is rooted in a history of negativity, belittlement, and oppression. Even today, the word nigger is still used by some non-Black people to try to hurt and/or get a reaction from Black people. So, due to the history, origin, and ways in which the n-word is used to try and belittle Black people, the fact that "can I say the n-word" is still a question today is always so surprising to me. The n-word is not just another word, and to try and claim that it is and act like there's nothing wrong with saying it is intellectually dishonest.

Despite the environments where the n-word is currently being used in things like music, comedy, movies, and others, the history of the word itself is why non-Black people using the n-word is offensive, **even when the "er" gets dropped**. I'm also not saying that using the n-word makes you a racist, but it does make you ignorant by choice. Even non-Black people not from America understand the history behind the n-word, and not only do they not say it, but they also have no desire to say it, usually.

That being said, in America, you can pretty much say whatever you want, and nobody will stop you. Just know that in the same way, actions have consequences, so too do words. So, if you are a non-Black person and you decide to say "nigga", go ahead; just know that if you say it around the wrong (or right) group of people, there might be some consequences you are not going to like, but you just may have to face. On this point, I also want to add **there is no such thing as an n-word pass**. If you are a non-Black person, just because your Black friend is okay with you saying the word doesn't mean that all Black people will be okay with you saying the word. The truth is, your Black friend who gave you "permission" to say the n-word doesn't even have the right to give you "permission" to say it; nobody in the Black community does. Chances are that your Black friend(s) who told you they were okay with you saying the word might actually be super uncomfortable with you saying it. It's possible they did not know how to tell you "No," or they didn't know how to explain to you why you can't say the n-word. That, or they might not even understand the true weight of the word themselves and are therefore indifferent to a non-Black person saying it. So don't go out and say the n-word and then try to say your Black friend(s) are cool with you saying it. It's not going to work, and you're likely still going to have to deal with whatever consequences may come of you saying it. Also particularly important, dating someone who is Black or having Black family members also doesn't give you the right to say the n-word. You could have been around the n-word every day since the day you were born, but if you are not Black or mixed with black (we'll touch on the nuances of mixed people saying the n-word in the next section), you can't say the n-word.

Another reason why you can't say the n-word is respect; it's as simple as that. If I were your friend, or even if I was a stranger, and I tell you, "Hey friend/stranger, please do not say this word or use this word to me or around me because not only do I find it offensive, but it is offensive to my family and me" and your response is anything but "OK," then you are not really my friend or respectful because that shows how little you think of me and just how much respect you don't have for me. It's not wrong of you to later come to me and ask me why I asked you not to say or use a particular word to or around me or why I find it offensive **after** you've said OK. The problem is constantly challenging me as to why you can't say it, even after I've explained it to you, and then proceeding to use it behind my back anyway. Even if you didn't fully understand or agree with my explanation, out of respect for me as my friend, you would just not say it, even when I wasn't around you.

I'll use a completely different example to explain my point. If you are in a relationship with someone, then out of respect for that person and the relationship, you're not going to cheat on them, ideally. Even if your partner has to have a conversation with you about why you can't cheat, you're not going to ask your partner, "Well, why can't I cheat on you?" No, you're going to say "OK." You're not only going to be loyal to your partner when your partner is around; you're also going to be loyal to your partner even when they're not there, ideally. Obviously, it's a little bit different with the n-word because some Black people still say it, but you get my point.

I want to remind us of this. There is another word in American social history that we all used to say that has pretty much come under a socially accepted ban. I used to use this word a lot as a kid, not to be offensive or anything, but I also did not really understand the history or weight behind the word. This word was thrown around on the playground and used in various ways to imply a variety of things. That's right, I'm talking about the f-word -> faggot and its relation to the LGBTQ+ community. I can't recall the exact moment when it happened, but we all went from saying the faggot like it was nothing, with it being used repeatedly on TV (the show South Park used to abuse the use of this word), to us being criticized for saying it, to us now not even saying it at all. It's been a long time since I've actually heard the word used or of someone wanting to use it or challenging people on why they can't say it. I'll end this section with this question: If all of us can collectively stop using the faggot because we understood how it was offensive to the LGBTQ+ community and now have little to no desire to say it, why, then, do non-Black people still argue/question their right to use nigga despite the constant explanations provided by both Black and non-Black people as to why it's offensive to Black people and the Black community as a whole?

So Why Can Black People Say The N-word, but I Can't?

It's actually a really easy answer. I can say the n-word and call other Black people the n-word if I decide to, and other Black people can say the n-word and decide to call me the n-word if they want to because we're, well, Black. Okay, now that I've gotten that out of the way, let me explain the context behind it. If you think about the Black community as a family, then as a family, we have the right to call anybody in our family whatever we want, but if you're not in our family, you don't have the same right or privilege to do the same. I have a really close friend whom I still call either "fat ass" or "fat boy." He's not fat anymore, but he used to be. He's okay with the fact I still call him that because, as my friend, we have a shared history together of when he used to be fat and his transition in losing the weight, but if anybody else calls him "fat ass" or "fat boy," it is likely going to be a problem.

As a family, Black people have the same shared oppressive history with the origins of the n-word that nobody else in the world shares with us, and that is the key behind why Black people can say the word but other ethnicities can't. It doesn't matter if a Black person's ancestors were slaves; it doesn't matter where in the world a Black person is from; as long as you are Black in America and in certain parts of the world, you are liable to be a victim of systemic oppression that still exists in society, the same systemic oppression from which the n-word was born. If you don't go through the struggles of being Black, don't have the same fears related to being Black; if you have easier access to opportunities that Black people don't have access to, then why should you have the right or privilege to say the n-word, a word that comes from centuries of oppression against Black people? If you don't share the same types of relationships with the world specific to being Black or have to worry about going through certain experiences specific to being Black, then you can't say the n-word. The reality is that no one except for Black people has the exact same experiences and histories of being Black in the world, except for, well, Black people. In that same regard, no other ethnicity aside from Black people has the same shared history with the n-word, except for, well, Black people. The dynamics of existing interpersonal relationships affect the context within how words are used, perceived, and received.

It's not just the Black community either. Other interpersonal relationships and ethnicities also have words specific to that relationship or ethnicity that other people can't say. Otherwise, it can come off as rude, offensive, or disrespectful. I'll give you a couple of examples:

- I can call my significant other any type of endearing term (bae, baby, sweetheart, mine, honey, dinner 😊, etc.) that I want because she's my significant other. We've been through things together that made her my significant other, and we now have a relationship that gives me the right to call her any one of those endearing terms. I can call her these things, and no other man is allowed to call her any of those endearing terms, except for her male family members, nor should any other man ever call her any of those endearing terms because they don't have that type of relationship. If another man does try to do it, then it is going to be a problem. If my significant other and I ended up breaking up, and the dynamics of our relationship changed, then I no longer have the right nor privilege to call her any of those endearing terms, but she now has every right to accept being called that by anyone else.

- Women call their mom, sister(s), and best friends 'bitch' in an endearing way all the time. I'll never understand why, but even though I know they do it and have been around when they do it, I will never try to call any woman, regardless of my relationship with her, a bitch in an endearing way. I'm not a woman, so I know better than to try it, and if you're a man, you should know better too.

- Certain groups of White people call each other rednecks and crackers, and it's not offensive nor perceived as offensive. I, as a Black person, will never try to call a White person a redneck or a cracker because, well, I'm not White, nor do I belong to the group/class of White that refer to themselves as such.

- Some members of the Latinx community call each other Cholos, Cholas, and Cholitas. These are words that I don't use because I'm not a member of a Latinx community, nor do I try to use them. While I understand it is slang, hear them in songs, hear them in movies, and hear my friends who are Latinx use them, I stay away from using them because I don't share the same types of relationships with the world that the members of the Latinx community who use this word do. Mainly because I'm not Latinx.

I hope these examples helped. It's not due to a double standard, discrimination, or hypocrisy that Black people can say the n-word and other non-Black people can't. It's due to the pre-existing relationships that Black people share with one another and collectively with the world that gives us the right and privilege to say the n-word, while others who aren't Black can't and will never have. This is why the Asian community, the Latinx community, and all other non-Black minority communities in America can't say the n-word either. It is offensive when it happens. So, as I mentioned earlier, if you're not Black and decide to use the n-word, then you're crossing a boundary that shouldn't be crossed, and if you're going to cross that boundary, be prepared for whatever consequences you may have to face because of it.

Can You Say The N-Word If You're Mixed with Black?

I want to touch on the nuances of being mixed and saying the n-word. I have friends who have asked me this question because they come from an interracial family, and I'm sure others may also have this question. Essentially, if you're mixed with Black, you can say the n-word, but there's a catch. The things mentioned in this chapter as to why non-Black groups can't say the n-word can apply even if you're interracial. If you are mixed with Black but can pass as non-Black and/or go through life not embracing your Black identity, your 'Black side' so to speak, then chances are you're not going through the same struggles of being/looking Black or sharing the same experiences as others who are/look Black. So, if you're mixed but are not going through the struggles of being Black and can't or don't relate to Black culture, should you really be using a word that comes as a privilege to those who do? This isn't me questioning anyone's Blackness or saying what interracial people can and can't say; it's me simply giving a perspective that can be considered or ignored. Basically, if you're mixed, do whatever you want. Just understand what the perceptions of those around you who are non-Black might be when you do decide to use the n-word.

Lastly, I want to say that even if we ignored all the reasons I provided as to why non-Black people can't say the n-word, it's really weird when people who aren't Black try to use the n-word. It sounds forced, like a curse word you shouldn't be saying but decide to use anyway. Not only that, the n-word can also mean different things depending on *how* it's said and the context of *when* it's said. In the Black community, the n-word is more than just a word. It's now often used to express a variety of emotions and thoughts. So, including it being offensive, why use a word when you don't understand all the complexities that exist with its usage?

The English dictionary has thousands of words, many of which we don't even use. Instead of wanting to use the n-word, I wish people would try using one of them as an alternative. Black culture is not a cool menu you can go to and pick and choose which pieces you like and want and which pieces you don't like or want, the n-word included. **If you're not willing to take on everything it means to be Black in the world and Black in America, then you can't say the n-word.**

As I was putting this chapter together, I came across a pretty cool flowchart that summarizes what we discussed in this chapter. Here is my rendition of said flowchart. Enjoy!

HOW WOULD YOU DESCRIBE YOURSELF?

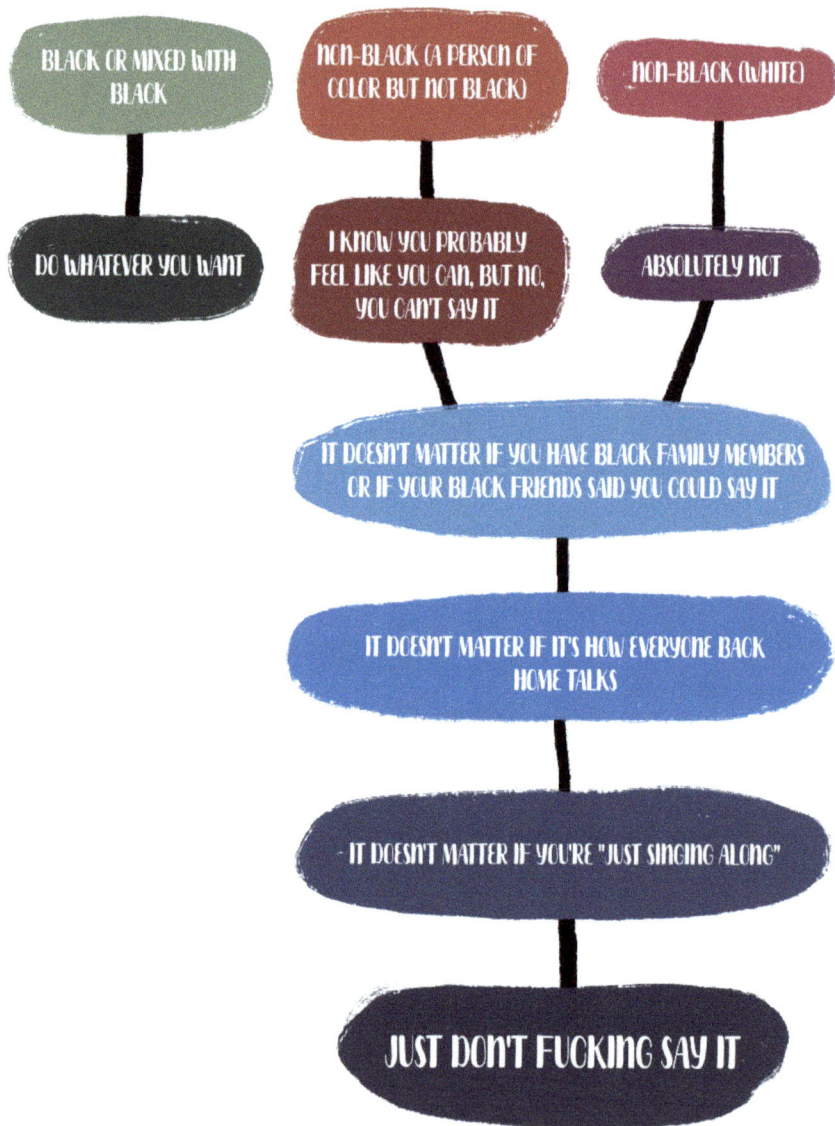

BLACK OR MIXED WITH BLACK

NON-BLACK (A PERSON OF COLOR BUT NOT BLACK)

NON-BLACK (WHITE)

DO WHATEVER YOU WANT

I KNOW YOU PROBABLY FEEL LIKE YOU CAN, BUT NO, YOU CAN'T SAY IT

ABSOLUTELY NOT

IT DOESN'T MATTER IF YOU HAVE BLACK FAMILY MEMBERS OR IF YOUR BLACK FRIENDS SAID YOU COULD SAY IT

IT DOESN'T MATTER IF IT'S HOW EVERYONE BACK HOME TALKS

IT DOESN'T MATTER IF YOU'RE "JUST SINGING ALONG"

JUST DON'T FUCKING SAY IT

Chart Visual Created by Uzo Njoku

My Thoughts on Black People Using The N-Word

There are two opposing views within the Black community on the use of the n-word. Some believe we can and should use the n-word. The rationale is that it is a way for the Black community to reclaim the power of the word. Others believe that due to the history of the word and its roots, we should not be saying or using it at all. There is an interview between Jay-Z and Oprah on the Black community's use of the n-word, with Jay-Z being for its use and Oprah being against it. Jay-Z explained, "People give words power, you know, and for our generation, what we did was, we took the word and took the power out of that word, you know, we turned a word that was very ugly and hurtful into a term of endearment." Jay-Z explained that if we remove the n-word, then a new word will just come and replace it, and we don't address the root of the problem. Oprah responded that for her generation and coming up in the civil rights movement, it was "a very hateful word," and for some Black people who were lynched, "it was the last word they heard." They both agreed to disagree and ended that piece of the interview there. It's a small piece of that conversation between Oprah and Jay-Z, but it does speak to the divide of how the Black community views the n-word and its usage.

Even though there are times when I personally say and use the word "nigga," I'm still on the side of the school of thought that is against the Black community using the n-word, so I'm with Oprah on this one. If we look at the history of the word, it is vulgar, and I have so many other words I can use in everyday language and with my friends to express the same sentiments that the n-word does. The problem is that the n-word is too rooted in Ebonics (for which there is a chapter on this in Part Three of this book). As I mentioned earlier, the n-word is no longer just a word but has now become a way to express thoughts and emotions depending on how and when it's used. It is why I still struggle with not using the word at times. The ironic thing is the NAACP tried to buy the word back in 2007 and had an actual funeral for the word! Unfortunately, it didn't work. In fact, if anything, it may have even backfired. Today, you can turn on almost any hip-hop song, new or old, by a Black artist and hear the n-word being used. Additionally, if you listen to a conversation between Black people, specifically Black men, for a long enough period of time, the word is bound to eventually be unintentionally or intentionally used.

I find it funny how life sometimes comes full circle for you. My thoughts on not using the n-word didn't start to occur until I heard the album version of "I" from Kendrick Lamar's 'To Pimp A Butterfly' album. Kendrick is not only attached to a core memory of mine where a gaggle of non-Black people were singing along to the n-word with joy, but he is also the reason why I've begun my journey of trying to un-learn using the word. In Kendrick's album version of the song 'I,' if you fast-forward to roughly the 4:52 minute mark, his freestyle references Oprah's conversations with rappers on the use of the n-word and his thoughts on it. In this song, he describes the word 'Negus' and its roots, and it was honestly the first time I had ever heard of the word Negus or heard the word being used. It's an interesting juxtaposition to be in, enjoying the use of a word while also knowing its history and roots. I will likely continue to struggle with not using the n-word for a while, but I'm well on my way to no longer using it.

Negus: A King – used as a title of the sovereign of Ethiopia

Plot Twist: We Know

I want to end this chapter by saying the Black community knows that non-Black people say the n-word behind closed doors. If you listen to rap or hip-hop music and have songs you like, chances are, you've sung along with the word either intentionally or unintentionally. I mean, think about all the videos that have been leaked of fraternities and sororities singing along with it or saying it during a pregame or a party. I have been to plenty of parties where the people in attendance were predominately non-Black, and I was the only Black person there; a song with the n-word comes on, and half the party says it, and the other half glances warily my way while the other half is saying it. I've seen groups of non-Black teenagers and young adults driving by, singing or rapping along to songs while saying it. I've seen plenty of drunk non-Black people get mad at other non-Black people and say it, and this one always confused me. I've seen the n-word used by non-Black people more times than I can count, so yes, we know that non-Black people not only use the word behind closed doors but abuse the fuck out of the word with how often they use it. In many ways, Black culture is pop culture, and due to that, the n-word has been popularized for a variety of different reasons. It's in songs, movies, TV shows, sketches, etc., it's everywhere. I know it's hard to get away from it, but even so, you still can't say it.

This chapter probably won't stop most people who aren't Black who currently say/use the n-word from saying/using it, especially behind closed doors, because, after all, it is free speech, right? But if you are going to say it, at least now you hopefully understand why I, being a Black person, can say nigga, and you being a non-Black person, can't.

Dating A Black Person When You're Not Black

"Interracial and intercultural dating is hard, but it's worth it and rewarding if you're willing to do the work and stick it out"

- Tunde

I write this chapter from the heart. Interracial dating should not be a problem or an issue, especially in 2023, but to most people today, it still is. I personally have no problems with people who date interracially/interculturally/interreligious or people who would be open to doing it. I have no issues with people currently in interracial, intercultural, or interreligious relationships because, truthfully, love is love. That stance is likely going to annoy many people, but "Kanye shrug." Personally, I have dated interracially and interculturally; I have friends in interracial, intercultural, and interreligious relationships and friends who have been in interracial, intercultural, and interreligious relationships. There were many mistakes made, lessons learned, and growth that happened.

Interracial/Intercultural/interreligious dating can be fun and rewarding and forces growth in many good ways, but it's not all fun and games, so if you are not ready for some of the things that it's going to come with, don't do it.

Before we head into the rest of the chapter, I'd like to add this note: While this chapter will be focused on what I believe are the most important topics a non-Black person who is interested in dating a Black man or woman should know, much of what I will be talking about can be applied to pretty much all interracial or intercultural relationships. Interreligious is a little bit more complex to apply some of these considerations, just given the nature of religion.

Things to Understand About Yourself Before You Date A Black Person

"OMG, I love Black guys"

"You're pretty for a Black girl"

"Is what they say about Black guys down there true?"

"My chocolate Nubian queen"

"I'm down for the swirl"

"I only date Black men"

"I only date Black women"

The list of overtly fetish-y and cringe-worthy comments and questions that I and other Black people have received when approached by non-Black people trying to flirt goes on and on. Let's start with this -- fetishes and kinks exist, and people like different things sexually, and that's why there's a whole industry that makes billions of dollars a year catering to all these different desires and another that makes billions providing toys and tools to cater to these desires. I'm not saying you shouldn't have the desires and the things you like to do and enjoy, but the moment it involves other people and a potentially emotional and/or life-changing attachment (i.e., a baby) from another person to fulfill these desires, check yourself. Dating is not a game, relationships are not a game, and getting emotionally involved with someone, *especially* when they are not from the same racial background as you, is not something that should be taken lightly.

It is okay if you're romantically interested in a Black person, and it's okay to act on those feelings of interest, but you first need to understand your motives for why that interest really exists. Plain and simple, is your interest a fetish, a preference, or did it 'just happen'? You need to answer that question honestly because your answer to that question will affect how successful or not the relationship you want to pursue is if you want a relationship that will last.

Fetish → If it is just a fetish, it's okay; you are who you are, and you like what you like. Everyone has fetishes. My advice to you is to treat this chapter as optional because most of what I'm going to talk about will probably not apply to you. What I'm going to explain is for those who fall in the 'preference' and 'it just happened' category. If your answer is fetish and you want to experiment or have a fling, be honest about it. You'd be surprised; there may be some Black men or women who will be fine with being your fling. Don't get me wrong, most people will not be fine with being your one-time experiment, but some people will. The honesty will allow everyone to know exactly what they are getting into and, ideally, end with nobody getting hurt. To start a whole relationship, and in some cases have children with someone over a fetish, is not only a waste of time, but is also disrespectful, dishonest, and honestly just fucked up. You never really liked the person; you just liked the fact that they were Black. There are much easier ways to get your 'kink off' and have it end up as a win-win for everybody involved.

It's A Preference → To those who answered that it's a preference - why? Understanding your reasons for this could be enlightening for you. You'll need to understand where your preference is coming from because your reasons could end up being pretty similar to, if not the exact same as, the people who fall into the fetish category. If you find your reasons all end up sounding like it is just a fetish, don't panic. The honesty with yourself has helped you learn something new about yourself and will prevent many unnecessary future heartaches and headaches. If the reasons for your preference are completely removed from fetish, then cool. It could be that you grew up around Black people and/or have been consistently exposed to Black culture, and that's where your preference is coming from. You could even be sapiosexual (attracted to someone based on intelligence) or demisexual (attracted to someone based on a strong emotional connection), and a Black person just so happened to be with whom you connected.

It Just Happened → If you're in the category of people where your romantic interest in a Black person 'just happened,' then cool. This category is rare, but sometimes it really does 'just happen.' I'm going to talk about many of the key things you'll need to understand if you decide to act on those feelings of interest. The first thing I'm going to ask you to do is reflect. Reflect on yourself, your past, your family, and your friends. Are there any racist people, elements, patterns, or events you have been to or were a part of? Do the people around you have any prejudice against Black people? If you notice anything, note what they are because a conversation about these things with the person you are interested in will need to eventually happen either before or after you've started dating. Believe me; it's better that it comes from you and for you and the person you're interested in to have a dialogue about whatever it is that you noted than for the person you're interested in to find out from someone else or through other means.

The other thing I'm going to ask you to do is to ask yourself how much exposure you currently have and how often you currently interact with Black culture and the Black community; aka, do you have any Black friends/family and/or feel comfortable in Black spaces? If you have never interacted with Black culture or with the Black community, then you are going to have to start. After all, for the person you are interested in, being Black is a piece of their identity and how the rest of the world looks at them. Please do not carry the mindset that "race doesn't exist" or that "you don't see color." Not only is this train of thought damaging and toxic to a relationship, but it undermines the feelings, identity, and realities of the Black person you're romantically interested in. The logic is this type of thinking could work in a utopian society, but unfortunately, ours is still one where Black people continue to get targeted, harassed, and killed simply because of the color of their skin.

If you are romantically interested in a Black person, the last thing I'm going to ask you to do is understand that 'Black' is an umbrella term that doesn't explain the complexity and diversity of identities that exist within being Black as we talked about in the very first chapter. Put it this way, you can be a White person but be any combination of Italian, German, Russian, Polish, French, English, Scottish, Christian, Jewish, Muslim, Buddhist, Atheist, Mormon, college-educated, non-college-educated, rich, poor, have blond hair, black hair, brown hair, red hair, green eyes, blue eyes, brown eyes, hazel eyes, can be in shape, a couch potato, have an accent, or not have an accent. The list goes on and on, and this was just a very small list of the different types of 'White' that a White person can exist within. The same is true for people who are Asian and Latinx. These are very diverse racial groupings. The same logic applies to Black people. We can be 'Black' but be from any country in Africa, be Afro-Latinx or Afro-Caribbean, Afro-Asian, be from any state in America, identify with any religion that we choose to, celebrate different holidays, eat different foods, talk and dress differently, and so many other things. The point is that a Black person being Black is just one small piece of who they are and how they chose to identify. They are a person, a complex one whom you like, who just so happens to be Black. Don't make any assumptions about how they identify, where they are from, or how they think. There is no 'correct' or 'official' way to approach a Black person either. The same way you would ask 1001 questions to someone you wanted to date who identifies with the same ethnic identity as you should be the same way you would with someone who happens to be Black. Whatever you may be confused about, ask, and if you find it uncomfortable to ask, be honest about that with the person you're interested in, and then ask. I promise you it will be okay. Irrespective of race-related conversations, being comfortable asking questions about things you're confused about or don't know about is going to be critically important for you to have a successful long-term relationship. Relationships are already hard enough, and choosing to date interracially will add complexities to the already complicated process of dating. Consistent, open, and honest conversations will be important to the foundation of your relationship.

Challenges A Black Person May Have to Overcome When They Decide To Be With A Non-Black Person

Through the honest conversations you will have with your Black partner, one of the first things you will learn is that they are likely dealing with backlash from the Black community and possibly their friends and family for dating you, especially if you are a non-Black person who is White, the same way you're possibly dealing with the backlash from whichever community you identify with for dating them. It's an unfortunate reality, and while views on it have started to become more accepting, we just haven't reached a place yet in our society where interracial couples don't have to deal with backlash for choosing to date outside their race.

The truth is this: views on interracial dating are so split within the Black community that some people may even look at your Black partner as a traitor to the race for dating you, while others may applaud them. There are a bunch of challenges a Black person who chooses to date outside the Black community may have to overcome when they decide to date a non-Black person. To get a better understanding of what some of these challenges are, we're going to do a deeper dive into some of them for the rest of this chapter's section.

1. **A "It's Us vs. Them" school of thought within the Black Community**

    Racial prejudice and systemic racism have and continue to cause harm to the Black community financially, emotionally, spiritually, mentally, and physically. This harm is inflicted upon individuals and, at times, groups of people through the form of various incidents. These incidents can range anywhere from microaggressions to racially motivated biased treatment or attacks to, at times, even loss of life. Those who have experienced these incidents first-hand or know people who have, know that these incidents are usually quite traumatic. The continuation/knowledge of these incidents can invoke a variety of negative feelings against all people who aren't Black. It's not intended, but for some, depending on what the prejudice or racism experienced was, it can create this mindset of "it's us vs them." These feelings then extend to the Black community as a whole and can create feelings of frustration when Black people are seen being romantically involved with someone who isn't Black. It's a viewpoint of "they are the enemy; they hurt and continue to hurt us, so why are you with them?" Think about it, if everyone but people who were part of whatever racial community you identify with treated you like shit, you're going to think poorly about everyone who doesn't identify with the racial community you identify with. People who hold these sentiments may approach your Black partner and disparage them, often even when you're present, for choosing to be with you. These people may try to put feelings of guilt into your Black partner and claim they are betraying their race by dating you. They'll claim your Black partner doesn't care about their culture or heritage or their Blackness. They may even question the authenticity of how "Black" your partner really is for being with you. After all, if they were 'really' Black, then they wouldn't be sleeping with the enemy.

2. **Media portrayal of interracial dating and its impacts within the Black Community**

Media portrayals of interracial dating continue to have a negative impact within the Black community and may influence how some Black people may react to finding out your Black partner is dating you, a non-Black person. (Please read the first chapter if you haven't already, as I give a more detailed breakdown of the damages media narratives can have on the Black community). While media narratives have been changing recently to be more inclusive and representative of all types of interracial relationships, this wasn't always the case. When focused on the Black community, the stereotypical interracial relationship shown has always been a successful Black man with a White woman, a non-Black woman who isn't White, or a Black woman who is lighter in skin complexion. Think of movies like Hitch, Focus, Birdbox, Man on Fire, Malcolm X, The Mountain Between Us; shit, even Save The Last Dance; I mean, the list goes on and on. Then, you sometimes get the occasional reverse with movies and shows like Spider-Man: No Way Home, You People, Guess Who, Something New, and Bridgeton.

There is this portrayal that the success of a Black man who has achieved some measure of status is only 'complete' when they become romantically involved with a White woman, a non-Black woman who isn't White, or a Black woman who is lighter in skin complexion. This portrayal has been damaging to the concept and image of a stable Black family and home. Let me explain: imagine growing up as a Black child and rarely seeing a successful Black family or home being shown in popular movies or TV shows. Then, the popular shows or movies you did watch that would depict these successful Black homes usually and often had a mother that was Black but was generally of a lighter skin complexion, or she wasn't Black at all. Some of these same shows and movies would then usually depict Black women who were of a darker skin complexion as loud, unruly, disrespectful, and aggressive. So, as a Black child, you're growing up with this consistent subliminal messaging of light-skinned Black women being 'better' and more desirable to be with than women of darker skin. This is the type of media narrative that many Black men grow up with and some follow through with.

Let's look at it from another perspective of how this has played out with a subset of successful Black men, specifically professional athletes. You can look at almost any league and look at the significant others of many of your favorite Black athletes. A good number of them have a significant other who is not Black. Then there's a small number of non-Black players across different leagues who have Black significant others. I have no data to back up my following statement, but over the last couple of years, the percentage of Black athletes with non-Black significant others seems to be rising, and if this is true, again, I mean no disrespect to anyone who this is true for, how do you think that influences the Black children who look up to these athletes? It's not just with sports either; this seemingly rising trend can be applied to successful Black men across all job types, from medical to political to legal and beyond; it's not just athletes.

Aside from the influence these media narratives have on how Black men view Black women, there's also damage done to the image and concept of what the 'traditional' Black home can/should look like. Black women and, by extension, Black homes are ultimately negatively affected. Black women, especially darker-skinned Black women, can grow up with negative opinions about themselves, which will then influence how they interact with the different aspects of whatever human experiences they are having, especially those related to dating and romantic relationships. I recognize and acknowledge there are some homes and families that exist where mom is Black and is lighter in skin complexion, and/or is Black mixed with something else, or is non-Black. I'm not saying anything is wrong with this; family dynamics are unique in their own ways. The problem is this subliminal rhetoric that exists in media, which seems to be trying to push the narrative of Black men being romantically involved with either a specific type of Black woman or a woman who is non-Black.

For Black women, especially Black women with darker skin tones, it's like being told they are not good enough, and for them to be able to be with a successful Black man, they must fit the European standard of beauty or be mixed with another ethnic identity. A study by the Journal of Black Sexuality and Relationships found that Black women are often pressured to conform to Eurocentric beauty standards. Essentially, they must be of a lighter skin complexion, have straighter hair, a narrower nose, and colored eyes; otherwise, they're not considered beautiful. The unfortunate truth is that the foundation of this rhetoric is rooted in **colorism**, "prejudice or discrimination, especially within a racial or ethnic group favoring people with lighter skin over those with darker skin." Sadly, colorism is not a new concept. It can be traced all the way back to pre-antebellum times in American history, where Black male and, more often, female slaves who were lighter in skin complexion were deemed 'more favorable' and were kept in the house to do domestic tasks while Black slaves who were darker in complexion were kept out outside and made to work in the fields with the more difficult tasks. Slave owners also favored lighter-skinned slaves because, over time, they were often the byproduct of an immoral union between slave owner and slave (lol, I know, that was a wild way to describe that). There is a dark history surrounding colorism in America which goes beyond the scope of this book. One such example of this history is the paper bag test that was used during the 1800s and 1900s when Black people were only allowed in certain spaces or considered for certain jobs if they were similar in skin complexion as a brown paper bag, if not lighter. Today, you can see aspects of colorism running rampant within the entertainment industry. Think about it for a second: aside from a few exceptions, many of the successful Black female entertainers (actresses, singers, artists, influencers, etc.) in America are lighter in skin complexion. The fight against colorism has been an ongoing battle that many Black men and women within and outside the entertainment industry have been fighting for a very long time. Thankfully, much progress has been made when it comes to representation, but more work still needs to be done.

The constant rhetoric that having European features and/or being mixed with another ethnic identity makes a Black woman more beautiful and more desirable and somehow 'better' has led to continued global controversy about colorism within the Black community. So, when Black men, especially successful Black men, enter into relationships with a woman who isn't Black or is 'exotic' looking due to being mixed, it's almost seen as a slap in the face to Black women and a disregard for one's own upbringing. I'm not saying this is the case, I'm just saying this is a perspective of what it can look like to a good number of Black people. This rhetoric also applies to Black women who date outside of the Black community and choose to be with non-Black men. The reactions and backlash towards your Black partner become "Oh, so we're not good enough for you," or "You couldn't find a Black person to love?" It's not a personal attack on you or your partner; it stems from issues much bigger than your relationship. In a nutshell, some Black people will look at your relationship and feel betrayed by the Black person dating you. They may feel that you, the non-Black person in the situation, "stole one of us" and attempt to disparage you or your partner for it verbally. That being said, your partner's motives for dating you, a non-Black person, should also be called into question. It would be quite the disappointment if one of the main motivations behind why your Black partner is with you is simply because you were non-Black or 'exotic' looking, wouldn't it?

3. **Your Partner Dealing With Being Treated as A Self-Hating Black Person**

Colorism, along with issues relating to racial prejudice, systemic racism, and media narratives, can often lead to self-hate and feelings of self-loathing within some Black people. These people may hate themselves for being Black and believe many of the stereotypes perpetuated about us, despite being Black themselves, are true. Honestly, this also applies to individuals in other marginalized minority groups who are affected by one or more of the things listed above. These people will intentionally date outside of the Black community and will then look down upon, talk badly about, and disparage those within the Black community. They will even take pride in the fact they're not dating a Black person. Some of these Black men or women will encourage those within the Black community to date outside the Black community while in the same breath, speak poorly on the topic of Black men or women as potential romantic partners. Some of them will see themselves as better for managing to date/be with someone who isn't Black. They'll make comments like, "I could never date/be with a Black bitch" or "I could never date/be with a Black man; they're criminals, thugs, disloyal, or that they are all cheaters." Due to the social rhetoric we previously discussed, the actions and opinions of these select individuals who date interracially have caused a bit of a divide within the Black community, and it rubs most people within the Black community the wrong way. Additionally, there are now seemingly double standards that exist today where it is okay for a Black man to date outside the race, due in part to media narratives, but it's not okay for a Black woman to do the same. Consequently, your Black partner may receive the negative backlash intended for these select individuals who are self-hating. Unless people in the Black community somehow know your partner, they may assume your partner is one of these self-hating Black people and take out their annoyances and anger out on them.

If you're confused as to what a self-hating Black person can sound like, the show "The Boondocks" does an amazing depiction with one of their characters, Uncle Ruckus. Here is a great video by Comedy Hype that explains more about Uncle Ruckus and the self-hating Black person that is depicted through him.

Here is the link → **youtube.com/watch?v=jOGz4p8pUVs**

(Alternatively, you can YouTube "Why Uncle Ruckus Hated Himself – CH News")

Perspective Is Everything

By this point, you might be thinking, "Well damn, why do all of those challenges exist? I should be able to date/be with whoever I want, and there shouldn't be so many issues for them to go through to be with me." Here's the thing: these aren't even all the potential challenges a Black person may have to face if they choose to date a non-Black person; these are just the ones that seemed to come up the most often. This is why perspective is everything. Understanding where people are coming from can help with connecting and empathizing better. Let me give you some perspectives you may not have considered before:

- According to 2020 data from the U.S. Census Bureau, nationally, there are only 100 Black male adults for every 113 Black women.
  - This is important because there is roughly an equal number of White men to White women, 93 Latinx men for every 100 Latinx women, and 107 Asian men for every 100 Asian woman

- A 2017 research study performed by Governing indicated that the single biggest driver behind the absence of many Black men within the general population is mass incarceration. We will talk more about this in the "What is Systemic Racism All About" chapter. There is also data that shows as the incarceration of Black men went up, the number of married Black women went down. So, while we can't prove causation while looking at these two data points, it would be intellectually dishonest, not at least to admit that these two stats could be related

- According to 2021 data from the U.S. Census Bureau:

- o Nationwide, there are only 93 Black men with full-time jobs for every 100 Black women. These numbers start to shrink even more when you go from blue-collar to white-collar jobs

- o 15% of married Black men are married to a non-Black woman, which is up from 11% back in 2010 and 8% back in 2000. As for married Black women, as of 2021, only 7% of them have a non-Black partner

- According to 2016 data provided by the Pew Research Center:
  - o While the rate of marriage for all races has been declining, the rate of decline within the Black community is especially steep. Only about 35% of Black adults 25 and older were married, compared with 60% of White adults; this is in contrast to 1970 when 60% of Black adults 25 and older were married and 76% of White adults 25 and older were married

- According to 2017 data provided by the Pew Research Center:
  - o In America, Intermarriage for Black people, where one partner is not Black, has more than doubled from 5% back in 1980 to 18% in 2015, while for White people, it also more than doubled from 4% to 11%, went from 26% to 27% for Latinx people and has decreased from 33% to 29% for Asian people

  - o In 2014, about 24% of recently married Black men had a non-Black spouse, compared to only 12% of Black women

  - o Among Black newlyweds, 17% of men vs. 10% of women with a high school diploma or less intermarried, while among those who have at least a bachelor's degree, 30% of men vs 13% of Black women intermarried

- According to 2018 data from the U.S. Bureau of Labor Statistics, families who are maintained by women (basically, there is no opposite-sex spouse present) accounted for 42% of Black families, compared to 25% of Latinx families, 15% of White families, and 12% Asian families

So, what does all this mean? Well, first, due to a plethora of reasons, the number of available Black men to Black women is not equal. There are literally fewer Black Men than Black women, which means that right now if every single Black man married a Black woman, there would still be a good number of Black women who wouldn't be able to get married to a Black man. This is even more true when looking at educated Black men with jobs. Then, these numbers only get worse the more educated and the better the job the Black man has. This is evident by the fact that, on a national level, despite the rate of marriage declining across all races, the percentage of Black men who are getting married outside the race, especially employed, educated Black men, is increasing. Then, these numbers change even more when accounting for the fact that not every Black man, or person for that matter, is trying to get married, is heterosexual, and finally, not every Black person is good spouse material. Anyway, enough about the men (lol). These statistics are also true, though, to a lesser degree, when looking at Black women who choose to date and marry non-Black men.

I hope the perspectives I provided with all these data points help explain why so many of these challenges exist. Whenever a Black person decides to marry a non-Black person, that is literally one less Black person who could have possibly gotten married to a Black person. The disparity of this problem doesn't really exist for White people and is not as prevalent for Latinx and Asian people in America. There are so many more views and things we could explore that go beyond the scope of this book, but the one takeaway I need you to have are the challenges your Black partner may face for being with you, especially if they're a highly educated, employed Black man or woman, are not baseless. Even if you don't believe me, do your own research; I'm pretty sure you'll be shocked by what you find.

Challenges A Non-Black Person May Have to Overcome When They Decide to Be with A Black Person

So, I talked about the challenges your Black partner may have for deciding to be with you, and I provided perspectives as to why; now, let's focus on you. The Black person who you're interested in dating likely won't be the only one who will face some challenges; you, the person interested in them, will also face some challenges. At the beginning of this chapter, I asked you to try to understand where your feelings of romantic interest in a Black person are coming from. This is mainly because the source and strength of your feelings will affect how much work and effort you are going to be willing to put into the relationship to make it successful and long-term. It's 2023, but even still, many people, even people you know and love, will not be okay with you dating a Black person.

1. Dealing With the Opinions Of Your Friends & Family

These are the people closest to you and the people who you want to approve of your relationship and your partner the most. In the most ideal cases, this is what happens, and everything is smooth; no judgmental or unintentionally offensive questions are asked, nothing. Unfortunately, this isn't always the case, especially if you're deciding to date a Black person as a non-Black person. If you come from a background where Black people are discriminated against, Black people are looked down on, or if your friends and family haven't really been exposed to Black culture or Black people, there are likely going to be many questions and potentially awkward if not outright chaotic introductions and family dinners.

It doesn't always happen, but be prepared for someone who you know to say or do something offensive to your Black partner when you bring them around. If this is your first time dating a Black person, it's also possible your friends and family may think it's just a phase and will not really respect your relationship or take your Black partner seriously. Your family could be racist or have a lot of prejudice towards Black people. These are going to be extremely difficult to overcome, and you may never be able to change how they think or feel about Black people. This is just something you may have to deal with for as long as you're with your Black partner. If this is your situation, then to prevent future uncomfortable interactions, you're going to have to educate your friends and family and set ground rules with them before they meet your Black partner. With your Black partner, you're going to have to be honest and let them know the type of treatment they may receive from your friends and family. I'm being serious here. Your Black partner obviously knows and, in some cases, will even expect their interactions with your friends and family not to go well. Due to these expectations, they may have feelings of discomfort, worry, anxiety, and even fear about meeting your family and friends. Don't try and hope through it and think a positive attitude will make things work out. That can work in other situations, but not this one. Talk through with your partner what fears and concerns they may have, if any before they start to meet your friends and family. Most of all, be honest about what they may have to face when meeting your friends and family. I would rather be prepared for what's to come, and nothing happens than not being prepared, and everything happens.

For your friends and family, start having conversations with them before the meeting and answer as many, if not all, the questions they might have so they don't come up in person with your partner later. Let them know what may or may not be appropriate to say or ask. Preparation is the key to success; the more prepared all parties involved are, the better things will go. Don't wing it and hope for the best because if you do that, I can promise you, in most cases, it won't.

2. Raising Black Children

Raising children is already difficult enough as is. Raising children with parents who have different religions, cultures, and/or ethnic backgrounds adds an extra layer of complexity that may make it even more difficult for parents to navigate and for the children to understand. As parents, you will have to decide how much of each parent's culture the children will learn and be exposed to. This will depend on how much the parents understand and identify with their culture. Something as basic as what the child's name should be can be a potential point of contention in the relationship. It is going to be a balance of traditions and customs and, likely, a very lively home to build.

If you have a child with a Black person, then your child will be Black and whatever the ethnic background of the non-Black parent is. Depending on what the ethnic background of the non-Black parent is, the child's Black features, skin tone, nose shape, lip size, hair, etc., may or may not be prominent. The world is not kind to Black people, and since your child will be Black, they will have to face and overcome all the challenges your Black partner had to and continues to have to overcome. Thankfully, the world is becoming more progressive, so hopefully, if you don't already have children, many of these challenges will no longer exist by the time you decide to have them. It's a strong hope, but let's not bank on that happening as quickly as we would like it to.

Your child may face racism, racial prejudice, and/or discrimination, if not outright bullied, simply for being Black, even if they're only half to a quarter Black. There will be some issues you, as the non-Black parent, will never be able to relate to, and that's okay. You're going to have to be comfortable with family members in your partner's family playing roles for your child in ways you are going to wish you could. An example is a non-Black father being unable to relate to his Black son's challenges being a Black man in America or a non-Black mother being unable to properly do or take care of her Black daughter's hair or even understanding what it's like being a Black woman in America. You, as the non-Black parent, can be empathetic with, sympathize with, and learn as many things as possible, but you won't be able to understand or relate to certain things fully, and that's okay. Lean into your Black partner's family and use them as resources as much as possible. Use them to help you and your child navigate things you may not be equipped to navigate. They are not the enemy; they want the same thing that you, the non-Black parent, will want for your child, which is hopefully to be as happy and as successful as possible.

3. Changes In How Society Begins to Treat You

Society and the many social interactions you will have with people as an interracial couple can ruin your relationship. We've talked a lot in this chapter about many of the things your Black partner will have to face while dating you and where some of those challenges are coming from. Your Black partner will have had a lifetime of experience dealing with many of these challenges, but you, as the non-Black partner, may not yet have these experiences. You may not even have been exposed to many things yet. If you are dating or decide to date a Black person, many of these challenges are now your challenges, too. After all, when you are with someone, their challenges are your challenges, and their problems are your problems, too, right? And obviously, vice versa; your challenges and problems are now their challenges and problems (within reason, of course). Depending on how you identify, the challenges and problems your Black partner has to overcome consistently will be shocking, heartbreaking, disappointing, and/or uncomfortable for you, and some of those experiences, maybe not so much. You will either see your partner experience systemic racism, racial prejudice, or discrimination and in some cases, you will experience it with them. Some harsh realities will be things like not getting approved for certain loans, your home valuation being lower than it's supposed to be, service at dinner or at private venues not being as good, business deals not going through, people not believing that either one of you is the biological parent of your child, getting stared at when you're in public together, people coming up to either one or both of you and giving you their unwanted negative opinion on the fact you are together. The list goes on and on, and they can eventually cause feelings of discomfort towards your Black partner and the relationship. The relationship will face both internal and external challenges, but if you genuinely want to be with this person, whether they are Black or not, you'll overcome any challenge together. This is why I asked you at the beginning to identify where your romantic interest in a Black person comes from. This is because there will be many more than just some of the challenges I listed here you're going to have to navigate. Ask yourself if this is really a journey you're ready to take.

Responsibilities A Non-Black Person Will Have If They Decide to Be with A Black Person

I'm going to start by saying that many, if not all, the responsibilities you will have being with a Black person are the exact same ones your Black partner will have being with you. So, anything discussed in this section can be internalized and reversed back to your Black partner for you.

While there are challenges a non-Black person is likely going to face being with a Black person, there are a couple of key responsibilities that exist that will help the relationship overcome many of those challenges. Relationships are different, and your responsibilities to your Black partner will change based on who your Black partner is and what is important to them. This isn't a one-way street; your partner will also have the same responsibilities towards you. Be flexible, talk about them with your Black partner, and understand the type of support you both will need. I hope some of the responsibilities I'm going to talk about help make your relationship stronger, even if by just a tiny bit.

1. **Accepting, Understanding, And Most Importantly, Integrating with Black Culture**

From my own experiences and what I have witnessed people close to me go through, this isn't talked about enough. All too often, I have seen Black people date interracially and have their partner accept them, but not Black culture. It's a little counter-productive and a little bit odd. How can you claim to love someone and everything about them but then not accept their culture and where they're from?

I have seen others accept their Black Partner and Black culture, but that's where the line is drawn; there are no efforts to understand it. That sucks and can cause friction and tension within the relationship. If I chose to date interracially or interculturally today, I would hope my partner would do her best to understand not just Black culture but Nigerian culture. I'm going to want to share things with her and talk to her about things that are a piece of who I am, and that will be difficult if my partner does not understand my culture and doesn't even try to understand it. Black culture is constantly evolving and changing. Keeping up can be hard, but luckily for you, you'll have your partner to help you and answer the questions about things you don't understand. After all, one of their responsibilities towards you is to help you understand. Just don't be afraid to ask, and always make an actual effort to try.

Accepting and understanding will lead you to one of the most important things you can do for your partner: **integrating with their culture**. It's not enough for you to accept or understand your partner's culture; you have to integrate with it as well. A harsh truth to remember is, the same way you're making some sacrifice, your Black partner is making some sacrifice to be with you. They're giving up being with someone who is Black and who will more naturally understand the intricacies and nuances of Black culture. Things such as 'the look' you'll be able to give each other with almost reflexive instinct when things are said or done around you in public that can be considered microaggressions, what dances to do to certain throwback songs, what foods are eaten at what specific festive events, and what traditions and customs have to be adhered to at family gatherings.

Many of these things can be learned; some will be easier than others, and some will take time to get used to and fully understand, and that's okay. The point is always to put in the effort and to integrate at a pace that works for you. After all, you're never going to get a seat at 'the cookout' if you don't not only understand but also integrate with Black culture. It's not just all on you either; your partner owes you the same in perfect reciprocity.

2. Understanding Social Issues & How They Affect Your Black Partner

Earlier, we talked about the challenges both you and your partner might face and where some of these challenges come from. The core of where these challenges come from is the fact your partner is Black and the history in America associated with that. While America has made great strides toward progress, many things still need to be changed. Understanding social issues and how they affect your Black partner will be critical if you want to be able to fully be there for your partner emotionally, mentally, physically, spiritually, and sometimes even financially. Things will happen in the world that will affect the reality your Black partner is living in and can instill a sense of sadness or hopelessness they may at times feel. Your Black partner is going to want to be able to rely on you and confide in you, but if you don't understand where they are coming from and why certain things affect them as negatively as they do, you may unintentionally be dismissive of their feelings. It will lead you to say things like, "Was it really that bad?" or "I'm sure you're just making a big deal out of things," or "I just don't get why it's such a big deal for you." Never say any of these statements or statements, even similar in message, because you may cause your partner to feel emotionally alienated and disconnected from you. If you have, apologize ASAP. If you're with someone, then their emotional well-being is partially your responsibility, the same way yours will be for them. Do it right.

The other piece of this particular responsibility is being comfortable having those uncomfortable conversations about race and social issues. Be okay with your partner challenging your thoughts and opinions about social issues, and be confident challenging your partner on their thoughts and opinions right back. Have open and honest conversations about these things. They're not arguments but discussions, so please don't turn them into arguments. Use unbiased data and statistics to explain your perspectives on things, not "I feel like" or "I just know" statements. Don't take things personally; try to understand where they're coming from and meet them halfway. This may be hard at first, but always remember, if your partner didn't love you, they wouldn't be with you, and likewise, you wouldn't be with them. If love and friendship are present, then though the work will be tough, the effort will always be worth it. Again, make sure that you do it right.

3. Allowing Your Black Partner to Be Their Most Authentic Self
No one likes a phony, and no one likes feeling like one. I have witnessed people acting one way with one group of friends and differently with another. I'm not talking about code-switching either, or

the way you act and carry yourself at work vs. with your friends. I'm talking about genuinely acting like a completely different person from a feeling or belief that it's the only way to be accepted by particular groups. People who struggle with this will hide parts of who they are or deny parts of themselves outright. As someone who struggled with this growing up, I can admit that it kills you a little bit on the inside every time you feel inclined to do this socially. Home should be where you can be your most real and authentic self. If you decide to be with a Black person, you now become that home for them the same way they will ideally become that home for you as well.

Empower, support, and encourage your Black partner always to show you who they are, chaos and all. Your Black partner should not have to feel like they need to hide any piece of their heritage, culture, traditions, and likes or dislikes about things. If your partner is African or Afro-Latin, Afro-Caribbean, or Afro-anything at all, there's another whole culture they will want to share with you that is not just Black culture. When it is introduced to you, welcome, embrace, integrate, and hopefully, enjoy it with them. Your Black partner will have a unique and complex identity that has helped shape who they are, and these complexities and how they are connected make them who they are. These complexities make them the person you want to be with or the person you already fell in love with. Support your Black partner to be their most real self around you, and I promise you, it will make the relationship so much better.

4. Protecting Your Black Partner & Sharing in Their Burdens with Them

The only thing worse than a partner who doesn't know they're supposed to protect their partner and share their burdens with them is a partner who knows they are supposed to do this and chooses not to. At the beginning of this chapter, I said that dating is not a game. Society will not always be kind to your Black partner, and sometimes it will be up to you to protect them. This means standing up for your Black partner both publicly and privately when people say things about or to them, being there to fight with and for them when they are being treated unjustly, and advocating for them every single chance you get. This means not being afraid to stand up for what is right, even when you feel uncomfortable doing so. There are plenty of responsibilities you're going to have when you decide to be with someone, even more so when the person you choose to be with comes from a background that's marginalized and discriminated against. If you're not ready to step up and overcome whatever challenges come with being with a Black person, then please, don't be with them at all. Call it a fling at the beginning of you guys getting together, and go your separate ways once the fling runs its course. My parents have always told me, don't start something you know you can't finish.

The responsibilities we went over together do not stop at your Black partner; they extend to your Black partner's family as well as the children you will eventually have if you choose to have children. Being an in-law and a parent will be hard, but the most important thing you can do is be there and be genuine. That's really the core message of these responsibilities, and that is to truly be there for each other.

My Advice to You, the Readers

I asked you at the beginning of this chapter to truly understand where your romantic interest in the Black person you are interested in is coming from. The purity, or honesty, of that answer will determine how much work you're going to be willing to put into the relationship and how much stress you'll be able to handle later in life as stressful situations start to occur. Love is great, and finding a partner who truly understands you the way you understand them is really a special thing. Relationships are amazing, but they take sacrifice and much communication to make them work long-term. The honest and sad truth is that love is never enough, and anyone who will tell you otherwise has never been in a serious relationship before. So much has to go into it that, truthfully, being with someone who comes from the same ethnic or cultural background as you really will make things easier. They will naturally understand things better, family and friends will generally be more supportive, and you won't have to deal with all the things that interracial dating, specifically the things that dating a Black person will bring. That being said, love is love, and you love who you love. Just understand your love's struggles and be ready to face those challenges with your partner.

Be there for each other, support each other, learn from each other, constantly communicate with each other, and grow with each other. Ask questions when you're confused about something, and love each other unconditionally. You're a team now, and it's you and them against the world, both figuratively and literally.

Part 2 – An Exploration of Black Culture

#BlackTwitter

"Black Twitter is lowkey wild, and I love it. Thank goodness it's not Facebook (Meta) – Facebook (Meta) is a whole different world"

- Tunde

Black Twitter. You may have heard this phrase being thrown around before, you may even know what it is, and that's great – but I figured, what better place to start this section of the book... than with Black Twitter?

One – because Black Twitter is sure to talk about this book if it ever reaches any measure of social clout (please be nice).

&

Two – because I actually love Black Twitter and all the humor, color, and education it brings into my everyday life. I've learned about things, laughed about things, cried about things, and shared a mutual love of things with complete strangers whom I have never met yet strangely feel connected with. One thing Black Twitter has taught me is that we are all not so different after all. We all share the same mutually cringe-worthy experiences, and we have all done the same weird things as kids at some point in time, and that thought is comforting in its own way.

So, here's to you, Black Twitter, for being the virtual home to all of us that you are.

What Is Black Twitter? (Now known as X)

If you ask 1000 different black people, "What is Black Twitter," you're bound to get 1000 different answers. This isn't because Black Twitter is hard to explain but because Black Twitter means something different to everybody. Black Twitter is experienced differently, related to differently, used differently, and even looked at differently. So, while 1000 different answers to "What is Black Twitter" may seem inconsistent, those 1000 different answers are exactly what makes Black Twitter, Black Twitter.

To me, Black Twitter is an ever-expanding, global digital consciousness. It is essentially the Black community digitally coming together on Twitter to share our collective experiences, often through satire, humor, and, when needed, information with one another. On the humor side, think of shows like Dear White People, The Simpsons, South Park, Family Guy, Modern Family, The Daily Show with Trevor Noah, Black Mirror, and Schitt's Creek. Now picture them being live, on all the time, while continuously getting bigger and better. The humor is shared through memes, videos, gifs, jokes, and relatable tweets. The satire humor covers all types of topics and is sometimes able to provide a comedic outlet to the collectively shared experiences of being Black. When things happen in America or the world in general, Black Twitter is used to share critical pieces of information with each other. You may be asking, "How is this any different from regular Twitter?" Well, it's different because the memes, videos, gifs, jokes, and information are usually rooted within or focused on Black culture, Black experiences and perspectives, and/or make references to Black-related events/history. These are tweets that, unless you are somehow in tune with the Black community or events/history specific to Black history and/or culture, you may not find funny, understand, or be able to relate to. This is not to say you cannot find the things that Black Twitter makes and shares funny or relatable; you just may not be able to relate to or understand everything, and that's okay. If you're not Black, it wasn't made for you anyway, and that's also okay.

A Quick History Lesson on Black Twitter

There are many different opinions on when Black Twitter really began, but the one that seems to be the most popular and accepted answer is dated August 10, 2010, when Farhad Manjoo wrote an article in *Slate* titled, 'How Black People Use Twitter.' There were many mixed reactions to this article, and a lot of people weren't happy. This eventually led to Kimberly C. Ellis publishing her own response to it titled, 'Why 'They' Don't Actually Understand What Black People Do On Twitter.' I bring these two up as examples to say that there are many notable individuals and events that have been important to the rise and attention that Black Twitter has received (shoutout to fellow Wahoo [University of Virginia], Meredith Clark; @meredithdclark on Twitter, who will soon be releasing a book on all things related to Black Twitter). There are so many, in fact, that in the process of writing this chapter, I discovered there are tons and tons of people who have done, are doing, and continue to do research on Black Twitter. It's a super interesting topic that has layers and depth that go way beyond the scope of this book.

The Growth of Black Twitter

So how do Black people continue to find each other on Twitter and continue to experience this virtual collective that is Black Twitter?

It's simple - #'s, also more popularly known as " 'hashtags.'

Before we get into hashtags and how they help virtually bring the Black community together, let's briefly talk about Twitter and the *network effect*. The *network effect* is the phenomenon that explains why the value of a good or service increases proportionally with the number of users that it has. Think of things like your cellphone, trains, Facebook, Instagram, LinkedIn, Google, Amazon, Tinder, Hinge, Uber, 2k on the PS5, the internet, the metaverse, and so forth. These are all things that become more fun and become more valuable the more people have and use them. So, with a quick analogy, Twitter is like an online multiplayer game – the more players, the more fun. Imagine how boring Twitter must have been when there were only 100 users or 1000 users TOTAL? Props to all of you early Twitter users who stayed on in no-man's land; you guys really helped change the game.

Back to the hashtags. Metcalfe's law states that the value of a network as a whole is proportional to the square of the number of participants, a.k.a. the more people in a network, the more valuable the network. Taking this definition and applying it to Twitter, this means the more people who use a particular hashtag, the more 'valuable' that hashtag becomes in Twitter's algorithm. Once a tipping point has been reached, that hashtag becomes a trending topic and a gateway to Black Twitter. The beautiful thing about hashtags is that even if a topic doesn't reach the tipping point to trend on Twitter, a space about a particular experience that Black people can relate to has been created. This is a space, a club if you will, that can always be found – you just have to know how to find it.

The Fun Side of Black Twitter

Jack Dorsey (well, now Elon Musk after that Twitter, now "X" purchase... lol), if you ever read this book, then I mean no disrespect with my following statement. Black Twitter made Twitter more fun, more popular, and more powerful. Let's start with a fun Twitter add-on that Black Twitter helped shape – Live Tweeting! Live Tweeting was already happening at different levels of engagement, but it wasn't until around the time Black Twitter started using it for the show #SCANDAL that live tweeting really took off. I personally never became an avid Scandal watcher, but from my friends who did, part of what made Scandal so fun and addicting to watch was being able to interact with other people's live tweets and reactions to the show. Thanks to the hashtag #SCANDAL, millions of people were able to watch, experience, and react to a show, *together*. It got to the point where if you had to miss that week's episode of Scandal, you couldn't even be on Twitter while it was on and then for at least one to two days after. If not, you would pretty much be able to 'watch' the episode and know what happened through tweets, reactions to tweets, and retweets without actually being able to watch it first. Scandal isn't the only show that has experienced the power and benefits of live tweeting from its viewers. Shows like The Bachelorette, Game of Thrones (I'm still disappointed by the last season), Power, BMF, Love is Blind, and others have all experienced it, and it's part of what helped these shows become so popular.

TV shows aren't the only things that Black Twitter has helped influence. Black Twitter has been instrumental to the rise of some of the viral challenges we've all watched or been a part of. Some viral challenges that Black Twitter has helped make viral and popular include the following:

- The "Do It Like Me" Challenge
- The "Don't Leave Me" Challenge
- The "Don't Rush" Challenge
- The "Flip the Switch" Challenge
- The "Harlem Shake" Challenge
- The "Hit the Quan" Challenge
- The "In My Feelings" Challenge
- The "June Bug" Challenge
- The Mannequin Challenge
- The Omarion Challenge
- The "Pass Me the Brush" Challenge
- The "Running Man" Challenge
- The "Sausage Rap" Challenge
- The "Juju on Da Beat" (TZ Anthem) Challenge
- The Whisper Challenge
- The "Wipe it Down" Challenge
- The "You Name It" Challenge

    ….and so much more

It's a short but eye-opening list of challenges that highlights some of the many different ways that Black Twitter, and by extension, Black culture and the Black community, has connected and creatively pushed us all out of our comfort zones. I've done almost all these challenges, and my friends likely have some pretty embarrassing videos of me doing some of them.

Beyond these challenges and others that Black Twitter helped make viral, Black Twitter has been a main driving force behind much of the internet pop culture buzz. It wouldn't be a stretch to say that Black culture drives a lot of pop culture. Aside from generating buzz, Black Twitter has been and is used as an outlet by the Black community to react to social events, express joy, celebrate successes, and have fun. Here are a couple:

- "Black Panther" ushering in the era of #WakandaForver (RIP Chadwick Boseman)
- All the memes that came from the Movie "Get Out"
- All the memes that were created when Obama won the presidential election
- Black people getting superpowers on Dec 21, 2020 (sadly, never happened)
- Creating and drawing attention to the term "Karen"
- Everyone singing along to Mo Bamba by Sheck Wes
- Giving Joe Biden the nickname "MoneyBagg Joe" because of the additional stimulus checks that Americans received
- Making "Salt Bae" viral and then famous

- Managing to create the noun *"Stimmy"* – short for stimulus checks
- The Bernie Sanders meme from the Joe Biden inauguration
- The Black community supporting other Black peoples' successes and achievements
- The memes that came out of the Navy accidentally tweeting "Nigger Navy" instead of "Bigger Navy"
- Usher being a menace to couples at his shows (lol, all jokes, please don't sue me)
- The 2023 Alabama River Brawl (aka "Fade in the Water Day)

    ...and so much more. It's a pretty expansive list, so I'll stop it here.

I can't even begin to count how many social events I have been to where a trending joke or topic from Black Twitter wasn't being shown or talked about. The different examples in this section are but a small fraction of how Black Twitter has helped us all express joy, celebrate successes, and have fun, hence, "The Fun Side of Twitter."

The Activist Side of Black Twitter

Twitter, as a platform, has helped shape and facilitate conversations across a variety of topics across the globe and is consistently leveraged as a driving force for change. It has given marginalized groups across the world a collective voice and continues to help bring national and global media attention to issues that otherwise might not have garnered the attention they have. So, as great as Black Twitter is and continues to be, it isn't just all fun and games. On one side of Black Twitter, you have the jokes, challenges, and fun; on the other, you have the activism, social work, and intellectual discourse. Black Twitter is actively discussing topics on issues such as systemic racism, racial injustice, police brutality, representation in various industries, and other social issues that affect the Black community. Discussions around these issues are usually centered around shared individual experiences that others have also experienced or can empathize with. The goal of these discussions is not just to vent but to try and figure out ways to change the things in place that cause these negative experiences to occur. As with any community, you can have fun together while also working to move forward together.

Twitter, as a platform, is great and innovative, but Twitter, as a tool, is powerful. Black Twitter has found and continues to find new ways to leverage Twitter as a tool to push social causes forward, with one such example being centered around the education of others. The learning opportunities that Black Twitter provides are immense. At any moment in time, users can find, engage with, share, and learn about different issues directly from the people who have experienced them. So, when Black Twitter uses hashtags in reference to different topics of discussion, those tweets become added to the archive of information that Twitter has on that topic. This archive of information is constantly growing, being updated, and is readily available.

Aside from information sharing, Black Twitter has also leveraged Twitter to increase the power of protests. Through Twitter, activists are able to reach millions of people worldwide, simultaneously coordinate the creation of protests across the country, sometimes the world, bring the media right to the heart of the protests and call attention to the issues behind the protests. A growing phenomenon that continues to aid Black Twitter's impact and reach is Hashtag Activism. **Hashtag Activism** is described as *internet activism,* or *the act of showing support for a cause through a like, share, comment, etc., on any social media platform, such as Instagram or Twitter.* Through the powers of hashtag activism, information about social issues is now being spread at a much faster rate than ever before. This process helps further increase the influence that Black Twitter has and, through it, increases the impact and reach of Black Twitter.

Looking back at American events related to the Black community over the last decade, it is easy to see how Black Twitter has been instrumental in centralizing the Black voice, empowering the variety of perspectives that exist and has ultimately helped change the narrative. Due to the lack of mainstream media coverage, the Black community and other marginalized minority groups have been plagued with issues that, for years, went unreported and, in some instances, were just dismissed. Well, with the growing power of social media and the increasing influence of Black Twitter, these issues are no longer quietly going away. Social media has connected the world in such a way that within seconds, anyone can join someone's livestream and experience events and situations with them as they happen. When this doesn't happen, thousands, if not millions, of other people and I can be very quickly updated on what's happening and immediately begin doing our part to help and spread the word (Hashtag Activism at work). Black Twitter has also been instrumental in bringing awareness to police brutality cases that might not have otherwise received the national media attention they did. We see instances of this happening with cases like:

Rest in Power:

Michael Brown -- Trayvon Martin -- Breonna Taylor -- Jamel Floyd -- Eric Garner -- Tamika Rice -- Sandra Bland – Rayshard Brooks -- Daniel Prude -- Atatiana Jefferson -- Aura Rosser -- Stephon Clark -- Botham Jean -- Philando Castille -- Alton Sterling -- Michelle Cusseaux -- Freddie Gray -- Janisha Fonville – Jonathan Price -- Akai Gurley -- Gabriella Nevarez -- Tamir Rice -- Tanisha Anderson -- Walter Scott -- Justin Howell -- George Floyd -- Daunte Wright – Mya Hall -- Elijah McClain -- Oscar Grant -- Leroy Browning -- Keith Childress, Jr

Unfortunately, this list does not represent all the victims of police brutality. It's a very small but sadly constantly growing list of lives lost but not forgotten.

The social media attention these cases generated became prominent to the point it became impossible for the mainstream media not to report on most, if not all, of them. The noise around these cases was so loud that the media finally started bringing more attention to the issues behind these lost lives and the change that still needs to happen in all communities, not just the Black one. The raw and unedited videos that have been uploaded to Twitter and other social media platforms have been able to provide the other side of stories and cases that often were not being told or wildly publicized before. These videos have helped change the narrative and, in some cases, but sadly not all, helped bring justice to the victims involved. There was even a situation once where one of the Jurors (Juror B37) from the Trayvon Martin case was trying to profit from the case and almost had a book deal to do a tell-all of the case. Well, it was brought to the attention of Black Twitter, and not long after that, the deal was off the table for Juror B37, and the deal ultimately fell through. Shoutout, Black Twitter.

The list of social causes that Black Twitter supports and continues to support is incredibly long and only continues to grow. This is because while Black Twitter might primarily focus on social issues related to the Black community, they are not the only issues it, or we, fight against. Black Twitter has admittedly helped keep me in the loop of the social ongoings in America and sometimes the world. Until I started paying more attention to the news, I can admit I was one of those people, and no shame or shade if you're currently one of them, who got their news updates on what was happening in America or the world through social media. Thankfully, Black Twitter has done an amazing job of supporting hashtags that made topics and events related to issues within the Black community trend on Twitter and, as a catalyst, captured national media attention. Within the universe of social-cause related hashtags that currently exist on Twitter, below is but a small fraction of those related to the Black community that Black Twitter has helped bring national attention to:

- #BlackLivesMatter → we'll talk about this once more in Part 2.5 of the book
- #BlackOnCampus → aims to raise awareness about the racism and discrimination that Black students face on college and university campus
- #HandsUpDontShoot → aims to raise awareness about police brutality against the Black community
- #ICantBreathe → aims also to raise awareness about police brutality against the Black community

- #OscarsSoWhite → aims to raise awareness about the lack of diversity (women, people of color, members of the LGBTQ+ community) in nominations for Oscars and Academy Awards
- #SayHerName → aims to raise awareness for Black female victims of police brutality and anti-Black violence
- #SolidarityIsForWhiteWomen → aims to raise awareness of the colorism that happens against Black women within the feminist movement
- #YouOKSis → aims to raise awareness about the harassment women face on the street, as well as a call to action for people of both genders to intervene if they see it occur

...the list of total hashtags is incredibly long, and I encourage you to do a bit of research on your own, see what else is out there, and try to understand the social issues affiliated with each hashtag

While Black Twitter does an amazing job of supporting social issues across America, it's reach isn't limited to just American related social issues. Time and time again, Black Twitter has shown support and brought attention to issues facing Black people across the world. It just goes to show that no matter where you are, Black Twitter, and by extension the Black community will always have your back. Some examples of international Black related social events that Black Twitter has helped bring attention to through hashtags are:

- #AfroLatinx – used internationally to celebrate and raise awareness about the experiences of Afro-Latinx individuals, who are often marginalized within Latin American communities

- #AmINext → used in 2019 to draw attention to the epidemic of gender-based violence and femicide, particularly against Black women in South Africa

- #BlackInCanada – used in Canada to highlight the experiences and perspectives of Black Canadians, who face systemic discrimination and underrepresentation in many sectors

- #BlackLivesMatter → because it's an international issue, not just an American one

- #BringBackOurGirls → aimed to bring awareness to the almost 300 schoolgirls that were kidnapped by the terrorist group Boko Haram in Nigeria

- #EndSars → aims to bring attention to the police brutality occurring in Nigeria

- #FeesMustFall → aimed to bring awareness to the increase of university fees in South Africa and a call to action for the government to increase the funding that went to universities

- #HijabisFightBack → used in South Africa to challenge Islamophobic and racists stereotypes about hijab women, particularly in the media and entertainment industries

- #SudanUprising → used to highlight the mass protests and civil unrest that took place in Sudan, where citizens were calling for democratic reforms and an end to authoritarian Rule

- #ZimbabweanLivesMatter – used in 2020 to draw attention to human rights abuses and government oppression in Zimbabwe, particularly against the country's Black Population

    …and many others!

Black Twitter has and will almost certainly continue to bring attention to issues in the Black community and other marginalized minority groups, aid in bringing justice to victims, and continue to help shape and change the narrative surrounding race. A big thank you to everyone for all the hard work that's happening behind the scenes of the various social issues hashtags have been created for. Your work does not go unnoticed - you have all helped make a difference.

Black Twitter and The News

While there may be differences in opinion about the role Black Twitter has played in bringing national media attention to issues that have been plaguing the Black community and other marginalized minority groups, there is no disagreement that it's had **a** role to play. With the growing influence of Black Twitter, it's no wonder it has started to become a more readily used source of information for mainstream news outlet stories and the like. Normally, this wouldn't be a problem if mainstream news outlets and journalists validated and engaged with Black Twitter more consistently to truly try to understand the information they are using to write on, or if mainstream news outlets and journalists always notified, got permission from, and protected the Twitter users whose tweets were being used, or if mainstream news outlets and journalists were inclusive of all the different types of Black voices that exist on Black Twitter. Unfortunately, this usually doesn't happen. Twitter's terms of service (when writing this chapter) are currently written in such a way that tweets posted from a public account can be used in any way desired by the person using it. Hashtags work in a way where a journalist can see the top trending topics and tweets related to an issue, take them, and write about them without truly understanding the written topic of choice. These two things have helped create a system where Black Twitter can be used for stories and to make headlines while not getting proper credit, nor its topics understood enough, as evident through some of the articles that have been written in the past.

It's not all bad, though; with the growing use of Black Twitter-generated content by mainstream news outlets, Black Twitter's influence will only continue to grow. Through this, the consolidation of information by users continues to increase, and the accuracy and diversity of reported news will ideally continue to get better. While it is unfortunate that our diversity of thoughts, identities, histories, and so forth continues to get ignored and left out when used by the mainstream media, Black Twitter is helping make sure it is being documented somewhere. History works in such a way that what's not written down is often eventually forgotten. Twitter is working in such a way that the Black community is able to use the existence of Black Twitter to document our history the way it is authentically happening.

An amazing thing is starting to happen. There are instances where Black Twitter users have begun coming together to create syllabi on the stories being written by mainstream media outlets and journalists to provide the context that's often missing, unknown, or intentionally left out. Sometimes, these syllabi are completed even before the news outlets have finished putting their stories together. These syllabi don't always focus on stories being written by news outlets and journalists and are sometimes made to provide more context on highlighted events within the Black community. Here's a fun example, when Beyonce released Lemonade in 2016, Black feminists tweeted reading suggestions that would help people understand the historical context and references for the visual album through the hashtag #lemonadesyllabus. There are many such syllabi that have been created and exist on Black Twitter. See what you can find, and if one doesn't exist, then it's likely only a matter of time before it is created.

As always, Black Twitter continues to educate wherever possible.

Final Thoughts on Black Twitter

Jonathan Pitts-Wiley said, "For people who aren't on the inside, it's [Black Twitter] sort of an inside look at a slice of Black American modes of thought."

Facts.

Black Twitter is just a slice, a piece, a small fractional representation of Black people and the diversity of thoughts and experiences that exist within the Black community as a whole. We come together to talk, share, motivate, support, and even argue with one another the same way any family would. So, if you're going to try to start interacting with Black Twitter after reading this chapter, like you would when you go to your friend's house, be genuine, engaged, and, most important of all, respectful. Oh! Almost forgot - for those whose homes this applies to, take off your shoes. Thanks!

If you'd like to explore more of what's happening within the Black community on Black Twitter, try exploring:

#BlackBoyJoy

#BlackBoysRock

#BlackCulture

#BlackExcellence

#BlackGirlMagic

#BlackGirlsRock

#BlackHistory

#BlackLivesMatter

#BlackTwitter

#BlackVoices

#ForTheCulture

Twerking

"Not everyone knows how to twerk, and not everyone knows how to handle getting one."

- Tunde

Storytime: My first experience with twerking in the way most people recognize it today that didn't have to do with a TV or a music video was during my senior year of high school homecoming dance. I went to a predominantly Black high school, so twerking wasn't an out-of-place thing for us to do at a dance or party. It was normal to do and was even expected. I even remember moments where the Black girls in my high school would try, cause Lord knows some of them didn't know what they were doing, to teach each other how to twerk during lunch.

Being the good African child that I was, I was not partaking in any of the twerk-related activities that were going on at my homecoming dance. One, I was paranoid and afraid that my parents would randomly pop up and catch me in the act of getting twerked on, and two, I did not know what one was supposed to do when getting twerked on. High school was already embarrassing enough for me, and with it being senior year, I did not want to add "embarrassing myself for not knowing how to handle a twerk" to the list of the 1000 and 1 cringe-worthy memories I had already accumulated for myself. If anything, I was in awe of what was going on, and more than anything, I was intrigued. The rhythmic speed at which the girls at the party were able to move their butts, to the types of dance moves they were able to pull off while twerking, coupled with their male and female dance partners who somehow knew exactly when to drop low with them, is something I'll never forget.

When people think about twerking, they imagine a person bent over, or slightly bent over, shaking their butt, sometimes with a partner unto the crotch area, in an amazingly fast and sometimes intense gyrating motion. If that was your assumption, then you wouldn't be wrong, but that's not all that twerking is. It's deeper than just the act you sometimes see and has a much richer history than one might expect.

So, What Exactly IS Twerking?

Before we go into what twerking is, first, we need to agree on what twerking is not. Just to be clear, I'm not going to be talking about **whining**: "the dance where a woman grinds with or without another male or female to dancehall/Caribbean music," but twerking, the dance that many people want to know how to do, but don't. Lol :D

Simply shaking or wiggling your butt to the beat of a song is not twerking. Shaking your hips really, really fast to a song is not twerking. Jumping up and down while you try to shake your butt is not twerking. Putting your hands on your knees and moving your back up and down is not twerking (lol, Tina from Bob's Burger). These can all be considered variations of trying to twerk, but they don't truly capture the essence of what twerking really is. If you are a man or woman who did one of these actions and considered it twerking, then I don't mean to offend, but if you're going to try and do something, then you might as well know how to do it right, right? It's a lot more involved than just shaking your butt. Twerking isn't easy, and that's why not everyone knows how to do it.

Webster's dictionary defines **twerking** as "sexually suggestive dancing characterized by rapid, repeated hip thrusts and the shaking of the buttocks especially while squatting"

Oxford Dictionary defines **twerking** as "to dance to popular music in a sexually provocative manner, using thrusting movements of the bottom and hips while in a low, squatting stance"

Now here is my definition of **twerking**: "Twerking is a type of dance performed primarily but not exclusively by women, which involves the moving of the butt, rhythmically, in a sometimes squatting-like position, either individually, with a group, or with a partner."

My definition of twerking moves away from Oxford and Webster's definition of the dance having to be in a 'sexual' manner because, since when does dancing have to be sexually provocative? It's a dance that can be and should just be enjoyed as that. Don't believe me? Well, here's a list of dances from around the world where the argument can be made that they can be perceived as being 'sexually provocative' due to the outfits or body movements required, yet we only appreciate them for what they are, a dance.

- **Angola**: The Kizomba
- **Brazil**: The Samba
- **Cuba**: The Cha Dance (not to be confused with The Cha Slide)
- **Cuba**: The Mambo
- **Cuba**: The Rumba
- **Cuba**: The Salsa
- **Dominican Republic**: The Bachata
- **Dominican Republic**: The Merengue
- **Egypt & Saudi Arabia**: Belly Dance / Oriental Dance / Raqs Sharqi Dance
- **France & Italy**: Ballet
- **Guadeloupe**: The Zouk Dance (not to be confused with the Brazilian Lambada)

- **New Zealand**: The Haka Dance
- **Tahiti**: Tahitian Dance (also known as the Ote'a)

See my point? These dances and many others that exist can technically be considered 'sexually provocative', but they are not. So why is twerking considered 'sexually provocative'? Well, because it's primarily done by Black women, but we'll talk about this point in a bit more detail later in this chapter.

The Evolution of Twerking and Where It Comes From

Focusing on twerking as a dance, and not just the modern-day iteration and definitions of what it is today, is important because of its roots and where it comes from. 'Twerking' has actually been happening for centuries and originated in West Africa's Côte D'Ivoire or the Ivory Coast. Locally known as the Mapouka, the dance involved the moving of one's buttocks in a rhythmic manner. The Mapouka, meaning 'the dance of the behind,' is a ritualistic dance that has been used in celebrations such as weddings, festivals, feasts, and even to worship. Many other West African countries have similar dances, with such examples being the Ndombolo dance by the Congolese, the Sabar from Senegal, Niiko from Somalia, and the Soukous from the Congo. These dances were not sexual provocations and were primarily used to celebrate and express joy. Growing up as a Nigerian, I've witnessed the varying types of these dances being performed by older women in a celebratory act and sometimes even in church! It was never considered sexual, and that was never the lens that I and people from other African cultures have used to look at these women when they did these dances, especially because they often did/do these dances to celebrate something and/or express joy for blessings they recently received. I think back to my childhood memories and even remember a whole group of women 'twerking' as part of a traditional dance during my parents' wedding celebration.

I'm sure the question many of you may be asking now is, "Well, with roots in such rich African heritage, how did we then go from the cultural dances to the twerking we see today?" Well, taking it all the way back to slavery, enslaved people were brought over to different parts of America from different parts of West Africa and Africa in general. What is now known as New Orleans was one such place that enslaved people were brought to. As history will prove, many of the African traditions that enslaved people brought over, such as dance, music, hairstyles, and so forth, have been passed down from one generation to another, continuing up until present-day times. So, let's fast forward from slavery and stop in the early 1990's. During this time, 'bounce' music, a form of hip hop that was very call-and-response based, was becoming more popular in New Orleans. Then, in 1993, DJ Jubilee recorded a song called 'Jubilee All' that had the lyrics, "Twerk baby, twerk baby, twerk, twerk, twerk," and the rest has been history ever since. No, seriously, look:

➢ In 1995, New Orleans female MC Cheeky Bank dropped the song 'Twerk Something'

➢ In 2000, The Atlanta rap duo Yin Yang Twins dropped their debut single 'Whistle While You Twurk'

➢ In 2001, Bubba Sparxxx's debut album had a collaboration with Timberland called 'Twerk A Little'

➢ In 2005, Beyonce's #1 hit "Check on It" featured the lyrics "Dip it, pop it, twerk it, stop it, check on me tonight" in the chorus

➢ In 2009, The twerk team – three teenage girls from Atlanta uploaded a video of themselves twerking to Soulja Boy's 'Donk.' It received over a million views in a week. They also got suspended for it. (Crazy lol).

➤ Then, between 2011 and 2012, songs such as 'Round of Applause' by Waka Flocka ft. Drake, 'Express Yourself' by Diplo ft. Nicky Da B, 'Pop that' by French Montana ft. Drake, Lil Wayne & Rick Ross, and 'Bandz A Make Her Dance' by Juicy J ft. Lil Wayne & 2 Chainz were all released

The domino effect of these events eventually led to the night in 2013 when twerking went viral outside of the Black community. **I'm talking about the 2013 VMA's where Miley Cyrus famously, or infamously, twerked on Robin Thicke.**

Social media lost its mind, and some major news outlets even talked about it in their recap of the VMAs the next day. People were either curious, appalled, upset, excited, and so forth, but no matter the reaction, twerking had captured national attention. After going viral, twerking, twerk music, twerk classes, and everything else that has stemmed from it have been growing in popularity. "What is twerking" was even the #1 Google search term in Australia back in 2013. Now, even suburban moms with minivans twerk. I've seen it; I lived across the street from a park and have witnessed the 5/6 am stroller mom workout classes twerking as part of their workout while I'm on the way to my own workouts; for those of you who are wondering, I primarily workout at Gold's Gym.

Black Women, Black Women, Black Women

I've often gotten the question, "Why do Black people like to twerk?" and the answer is simple: why do people like to dance? It's because they like it; there really is no deeper reason for it other than that. Earlier in this chapter, I mentioned that twerking, by the official definitions that exist today, needs to be sexually provocative. I also promised that we'd get into why I said twerking is considered sexually provocative due to it being primarily performed by Black women, so let's get into that.

Freelance writer Meagan Jordan writes that even though twerking is often described as "shameful," "uncouth," and "sets Black women back," it is not that at all. She writes that twerking is about "empowerment, self-expression, and most of all, community." When we think back to the true origins of twerking, the Mapouka dance was about all these things and more. To take a dance with a rich heritage and history and degrade it to this sexually provocative thing because it was originally and is mainly performed by Black female bodies is wrong. Jordan also writes that "Black femme bodies twerking, especially on video, have been perverted into a solely sexual lens, which opposes its historic[al] purpose – a way for feminine energy to bond and celebrate." The point being made here about the over-sexualization of Black women is an important one, but not a new one. Going back to slavery within the United States, Black women were often referred to as Jezebels. Merriam-Webster defines a Jezebel as an impudent, shameless, or morally unrestrained woman. The term Jezebel being applied to Black women was used to insinuate that Black women were not only promiscuous but were sexual predators as well. This warped perception of Black women and Black female bodies has unfortunately managed to persist to present day and continues to affect how Black women are viewed. To help better explain the point that I just made, a 2017 Georgetown Law study found that Black girls are collectively viewed as being more adult than White girls. The data collected during this study discovered that "Black girls were more likely to be viewed as behaving and seeming older than their stated age; more knowledgeable about adult topics, including sex; and more likely to take on adult roles and responsibilities than what would have been expected for their age." Pretty messed up, isn't it? The over-sexualization of Black women doesn't begin when Black women are, well, women, but according to this study, it starts as early as when they are five years old. As you guys must have noticed by now, I'm never going to make a statement and not back it up with some data, so here are a couple more stats for you relating to the over-sexualization of Black women:

- A 2015 report by the African American Policy Forum and the Center for Intersectionality and Social Policy Studies found that Black women and girls are often portrayed in popular culture as overly sexualized and hypermasculine, contributing to negative stereotypes about their bodies and behavior

- A 2018 study by the American Psychological Association found that Black girls are more likely to experience body shame and negative body image compared to girls of other races, which can contribute to their over-sexualization and objectification. Black girls are often viewed as older and more sexually mature than they actually are, leading to increased sexualization and objectification

- A study of media images of Black women found that 77% of the time, Black women were portrayed as sexualized, in contrast to 49% of the time for White women

- A study by the American Sociological Association found that Black women are less likely to receive assistance when they report sexual assault due to harmful stereotypes about their sexuality and perceived promiscuity

- A study by the American Journal of Public Health found that Black women who are incarcerated are at a higher risk for sexual victimization due to the over-sexualization of Black women in society

- A study of music videos found that Black women were more likely to be shown in sexually suggestive clothing and positions compared to White women

- Black women are more likely to be targeted with sexually explicit language and requests on social media than women of other races

- Black female characters on prime-time television are more likely to be sexualized than White female characters

I could throw statistics like this all day at you and still have stats for days. The facts are Black women are sexualized and fetishized more than any other ethnic identity. As Black women continue to fight for equality and respect, it is important to recognize the ways in which they are objectified and sexualized. The hyper-sexualization of Black women has deep roots in colonialism and slavery, and it continues to affect the way society views and treats Black women. This is especially evident in the way that Black women are judged and stigmatized for something as innocent as dancing. The clear double standard that exists when it comes to twerking perpetuates harmful stereotypes about Black women and reinforces the idea that their bodies are not their own. This also isn't to say that non-Black women can't be sexually stigmatized when they twerk as well, but the likelihood of that happening is just substantially lower.

As we can see from these stats, Black women are often hypersexualized and objectified in media and popular culture, which perpetuates harmful stereotypes and reinforces the notion that Black women are merely sexual objects. This can lead to negative health outcomes, such as higher rates of sexually transmitted infections and unplanned pregnancies. It can also impact the mental health and self-esteem of Black women, as they may feel pressure to conform to unrealistic beauty standards and struggle with the perception that their worth is tied to their sexuality. Additionally, over-sexualization can limit the professional opportunities of Black women, as they may be viewed as lacking competence or intelligence due to their appearance. Overall, the over-sexualization of Black women is a complex issue that impacts their physical, mental, and professional well-being and requires systemic change to address.

Twerking Today

Now, as I write this book, twerking has become normalized and is more readily accepted. While I'm happy to see twerking take on the life that it has, I want to reiterate my point that twerking, when it was originally primarily performed by Black bodies, was not only looked down upon but was also oversexualized. Black women were called "freaks," "sluts" and "uneducated" when they twerked. It's crazy to think about, but the over-sexualization of Black women in popular culture often leads to their exploitation and under-compensation, while non-Black women may, and often, receive higher financial rewards for similar performances. So, is it exciting to now see non-Black bodies twerking and receiving none of that backlash or hate? Not exactly. It's even less thrilling to know there are non-Black women profiting from teaching twerk classes, a dance that was originally looked down upon when Black women did it, without knowing, understanding, or giving credit to its rich cultural heritage. Though I say this, thank you to the few of you who teach these classes, but always give credit where credit is due. Though the discussion of whether you should even be teaching these classes if you're not Black is a completely different discussion with nuances that go beyond the scope of this book (the short answer is: it depends).

Twerking has evolved, and the spaces and ways we'll see it being used will likely continue to change with it. While present-day twerking may have deviated from the original intents behind the Mapouka dance, it's not necessarily a bad thing. Jordan writes, "Although many have been intellectually separated from the reasons this dance [twerking] continues to persist, the historic[al] memory continues to live on within Black bodies."

How To Twerk

Now that we've had the serious conversation we needed to have let's talk about how to twerk. I bet you never thought that you'd learn how to twerk from a book, huh? Learning how to twerk has been a challenge for some and comes more naturally to others. There are twerk classes where people can learn how to twerk and twerk fitness classes where twerking is the primary workout of choice. Twerking isn't easy, and when looking at the benefits of a twerk workout class, we see that it tones your legs and butt, improves your core strength, strengthens your arms, it improves your confidence, it's really fun, and, best of all, you learn how to actually twerk. Let me clear up a misconception about twerking – you don't have to have a big butt to be able to twerk. It helps because the extra muscles in your glutes can provide you with more control, but you don't need it. As long as you have rhythm, mediocre control of your butt, hips, lower leg muscles (glutes, hamstrings, etc.), and most of all, confidence, then that's all you really need. Pretty much the same things you need to have to do any other type of dance. Twerking is also about attitude, doing it, embracing it, and loving it. It's your body, so express yourself however you choose to do so. Lastly, to the question of where and when to twerk, as with all dances, you can do it almost anywhere and at any time where it's appropriate to do so. Look at your environment and use your best judgment before you bust those moves out. I would not Dougie to the Cha Cha Slide the same way you wouldn't do The Twist to the Macarena.

How exactly do you twerk, then? Well, given that this is a book, it'll be hard to really learn how to twerk by reading about it. Instead, I've included some really good twerk tutorial video links below. Before you look at any of these videos, I recommend looking up 'Mapouka dance' and see what you find:

Video Title	Video Link
(How To) Dance Combo for Parties or The Club	https://www.youtube.com/watch?v=RbDCGRmt7fM
How To Twerk | Club Dance Moves	https://www.youtube.com/watch?v=NgoyVRO0A0E
How To Twerk |	https://www.youtube.com/watch?v=bNnCldG5Ug0
How To Twerk for Beginners Step By Step | Twerk Tutorial	https://www.youtube.com/watch?v=3g5S2pouzKE
How to Twerk One Cheek at a Time! Part 2	https://www.youtube.com/watch?v=eVFDJXOci88
How to Twerk the Jamaican Way	https://www.youtube.com/watch?v=mOVN6Hk39gg&t=263s
How To Twerk Tutorial and Leg/Booty Workout	https://www.youtube.com/watch?v=64i2Y-VygVE

Learn How to Twerk Step by Step	https://www.youtube.com/watch?v=dxh--9hVuYk
Learn Step by Step Beginner Twerk from Kelsey	https://www.youtube.com/watch?v=VKsAWkeWgko

MEN, this note is for you. If you are a guy who wants to get a twerk (aka, get twerked on or catch a twerk), do not just go up to a woman who is twerking and start rubbing your crotch all over her butt like you are entitled to do so. Twerking is not an invitation for creepy and sexually exploitative behavior, so please do better. Make sure you somehow ask for permission, either verbally, with your eyes, or with your body language, before you try to start dancing with the person who is twerking. Also, if you're going to try and catch a twerk, know your limits, and make sure your legs are strong enough to handle dancing with whoever it is you're trying to dance with. As with any dance, there will be people with different skill levels when it comes to twerking. Take a page from my book and smartly sit some out the same way I did during my senior year high school homecoming dance. Trust me, you're not going to want to embarrass yourself for no reason.

With that being said, I know at the beginning of this chapter I said all the things that twerking is not, but at the end of the day, regardless of anyone's personal feelings towards it, twerking is just a type of dance, and with all dances, there likely exist hundreds of variations in the world. So, while there may be an official 'correct' way to do it, have fun with it and make it yours; it's your body, after all. Whenever you decide to twerk, remember its rich origins and all the things the original Mapouka dance is meant to represent.

There are honestly hundreds, if not thousands, of songs one can twerk to. I do not know all of them, but I wanted to include some of the objectively best-known twerk songs that twerking can be practiced with. I hope you enjoy!

Author Suggested Twerk Songs		
Ayy Ladies Travis Porter	**Back That Thang Up** Juvenile Ft. Mannie Fresh & Lil Wayne	**Bring It Back** Travis Porter
Clappers Wale Ft. Nicki Minaj & Juicy J	**Dance (A$$)** Big Sean Ft. Nicki Minaj	**Donk** Soulja Boy Tell 'Em
I Wanna Rock "Doo Doo Brown" Luke	**No Hands** Waka Flocka Flame Ft. Roscose Dash & Wale	**Pop That** French Montana Ft. Drake, Rick Ross & Lil Wayne
Round of Applause Waka Flocka Flame Ft. Drake	**Scarred** Uncle Luke	**Twerk** City Girls Ft. Cardi B

Disclaimer – The lyrics in all of these songs are pretty explicit, so I suggest not playing them around people until after you've had a chance to listen to them by yourself first.*

The "Black-Guys" Handshake

**"The 'Black-Guys' handshake is called the DAP.
DAP stands for 'Dignity and Pride'"**

- Tunde

You have likely seen it happen more times than you can count. Whether walking down the street, at the grocery store, at the hospital, at a park, at a restaurant, at a sports game, in movies, TV shows, music videos, or any other possible place you can think of. Perhaps you've seen your favorite Black athlete do it, perhaps you've seen your Black friends do it, or maybe you saw the Key & Peele 'Obama Meet & Greet' skit. It looks fun and enticing, and the different variations you've likely seen of it were probably pretty cool. You probably called it the "Black guys" handshake once or twice and maybe even wanted to learn how to do it. Perhaps you've even been taught how to do it and or do it all the time. The DAP is just a cool handshake that all Black guys do, right? Wrong. For one, literally everyone does the DAP now, not just "Black guys" and two, the DAP is much more than just a handshake. Much like twerking, the DAP has a really rich history that one wouldn't expect.

The Origins of the DAP

The DAP, which was created by Black soldiers during the Vietnam War, stands for 'Dignity and Pride', and its origins are something that even I didn't know about before writing this chapter. It's crazy when I think about it because I've been DAPing people up for as long as I can remember! Anyway, back to the origins of the DAP.

During the Vietnam War, Black war troops made up a little over a third of the troops who were stationed and going into action. The Vietnam War, which lasted between 1955 and 1975, occurred during an era in American history that was even less favorable towards Black people than it is today. You have to understand just how mind-blowing it is that Black war troops made up a little over a third of the troops stationed and going into action during the Civil War. Segregation in the United States hadn't legally ended until President Lyndon B. Johnson signed the Civil Rights Act in **1964**, which was *during* the Vietnam War. It's really some shit that one out of every three Army soldiers was Black during a time when 'separate but equal' laws were in place. Coincidentally, this was also at a time in U.S. history when we started to see the rise of the Black Power movement. Due to this, Black war troops were coming from cities that were protesting against oppression, systemic racism, over-policing, police brutality, lack of employment, and just blatant racism (sound familiar?). So, when these Black troops were in Vietnam, there was this space of hyper-solidarity they created for themselves.

The DAP was created within this space of hyper-solidarity. The DAP was not just a handshake but a gesture of solidarity that sent the message, "You and me, brother, **against the world**." The DAP showed fraternity, brotherhood, and togetherness; it was a confirmation of survival. It brought the Black soldiers together, gave them pride and courage, and united them. This togetherness was critical to the survival of many Black troops during the war. Then, when these Black soldiers returned home and were faced with the harsh treatment Vietnam veterans received, the bond they had created during the war continued. As these soldiers returned home to the different cities they came from, they showed their friends and family the DAP they had learned while they were stationed overseas. Much like the way slang and language change based on geographic locations, so too did the DAP. The different variations of the 'Black guy's handshake' that we see today are a result of different geographic regions and groups taking the DAP and making it their own.

Although performed differently now, when originally performed, the order of hand movements of the DAP represented "I'm not above you, you're not above me, we're side by side, together" – then the embrace hug, when you see two Black guys pull each other in close for a hug represents, "I got your back, and you got my back," and that is the original DAP.

The DAP Today

It is not a stretch to say that Black culture heavily influences pop culture. So, it comes as no surprise that the DAP has found its way into mainstream media and sports. In fact, sports are a big reason why the DAP has become so popular. There were so many different variations of it being performed across different sports. There was the rise of the two-hand slap DAP between players in the NBA in the 70's and 80's. We see NFL and NBA players use it to support each other and to celebrate. Athletes everywhere, from Pop Warner to professionals, use it. School teachers use it to bond with their students. Now the DAP has evolved and transformed; it is common to see it all over the place. Still rooted in its origins of "Dignity and Pride," the DAP today is a silent way of saying, "How are you? I love you; we are brothers." (Pretty cool, huh?). While writing this chapter, I read an article about how Steve Kerr, head coach of the Golden State Warriors, was confused about the DAP, what it means, why players and some staff do it, and even when to do it. Well, Steve, if you ever read this chapter, I hope it'll help (by the way, I would also love some tickets to a Warrior's game. Thank you!).

Unspoken Rules About the DAP

If you want a good laugh, Google 'Obama Handshake – Vine', I promise you it's worth it. Better yet, here's a link → youtube.com/watch?v=LmnqihRlcaI

Now, let's get into some DAP etiquette. Usually, these set of rules we're about to go over are unspoken, but for the sake of the purpose of this book, I'm going to lay out some of the most important ones:

1. **Keep your nails short if you're going to DAP people up – nobody wants to get cut by your nails - It hurts, it's gross, and it's simply unhygienic**

2. **Don't ask for a DAP; if it's meant to happen, it'll happen naturally. You either get DAP-ed up, or you don't**

3. **If you do get DAP-ed up or decide to DAP someone up, unless you're cool with them, don't do all that extra stuff; keep it simple**

4. **Don't just DAP anybody up; only DAP up actual friends or people you're really cool with; everybody else gets a fist bump or a head nod**

5. **You generally don't DAP up girls/women – I never really understood this one before, but looking at the origins of the DAP during the Vietnam War, it makes sense why it never translated over to them**

6. **Never DAP with sweaty hands – that's gross, and again, it's unhygienic**

7. **If you're not that close with someone, don't go in for the DAP that leads into the bro hug; respect people's personal space**

8. If you're sick and someone is going in for the DAP, let them know and go with the fist bump or, preferably, a head nod instead

9. If you're going to go for the DAP, fully commit; no one likes weird DAPs

10. *This one is optional* - Always snap after the completion of a DAP

While these sets of rules are the most common and important ones, be aware that everyone is different, and different places may have slightly different rules concerning DAP etiquette. If all else fails, use your best judgment.

How To DAP

Before we end this chapter, I figured it would help if I gave you some resources on where to actually learn how to DAP. If you have the time, I recommend checking some of these out. I thought they were pretty interesting and wanted to share them with all of you.

Recommended DAP Resources	
The Movie: "Black Vietnam: Into the Light"	**Tunde's Comments:** This one is more of an honorary mention. It's not really focused on the DAP, but it will provide some additional insights into what Black soldiers went through during the Vietnam War and will help provide additional context on the origins of the DAP
The Movie: "Da 5 Bloods"	**Official Description:** "Four African American vets battle the forces of man and nature when they return to Vietnam, seeking the remains of their fallen squad leader and the gold fortune he helped them hide." **Tunde's Comments:** It's currently available on Netflix (at the time I'm currently writing this book)
Your Black Guy Friend	**Tunde's Comments:** Just ask, you'll likely get a positive answer

Final Thoughts on the DAP

You do not have to be Black to do the DAP. It has grown well beyond just the Black community and is now part of everyday interactions. If you do the DAP with your friends and you guys have this crazy elaborate handshake that goes along with it, that's fine; just don't expect other people to somehow know the routine as well. Also, Black guys do not just come up with some of the variations of the DAP that you'll see us do on the spot. If you see us do a bunch of extra stuff with it, it's because we are close friends and have practiced it enough times behind closed doors to feel comfortable executing it in public without mistake. We also do not have a special handshake reserved for everyone, so don't expect one. Also, not all Black guys DAP or even know how to DAP; it's not a thing we all do.

Lastly, just be who you are and keep the DAP simple when you do it - it should never be forced. If you feel like the DAP is going to be forced, a simple head nod will suffice. So, if you are going to do the DAP, I hope you now have a better understanding of its depths and roots and do it with sincerity and love.

A little secret - if a Black guy starts DAPing you up when he wasn't before, it means he now sees you as more of a friend than just an acquaintance. Don't make a big deal out of it; do the DAP correctly, and be cool about it. To those of you who aren't yet there with your Black guy friends to get the customary DAP, maybe your Black friend doesn't Dap, and if they do, don't worry, you'll get there with them eventually, and if you don't, that's cool too, just keep on being yourself.

Black Fashion

"Fashion is an expression of identity and individualism"

- Tunde

Storytime: I have always been fascinated by fashion and the endless possibilities of it all. From the colors, fabrics, and styles that proudly proclaim my Nigerian culture and heritage to the tracksuits, sneakers, and bucket hats my Black neighbors would wear to all the different styles I would see on TV as a child. Growing up in the Bronx during the late 1990s and early 2000s (yes, I am a millennial), I lived 15 minutes from Fordham and 30 minutes from Manhattan. This unique living situation allowed me to live in an area where I was able to witness and experience fashion from people from all different walks of life. Whether that be the traditional Nigerian clothing that my Nigerian friends and family wore, what Black Americans wore, what non-Black Americans wore, and everyone in between. I've always enjoyed fashion for both aesthetic (I like how colors and styles can come together) and selfish reasons (I wanted the social clout that comes with having a really good style). When I was in elementary school, because I wanted to be cool and fit in (but let's be honest, who didn't), I remember asking my parents for the same types of clothes the 'cool' kids wore and begging them for the expensive sneakers that would be my ticket to being able to sit in the back of the school bus with all the other cool kids (I never did get those sneakers). Though I never ended up being one of the cool kids, my passion and interest in fashion never lessened; if anything, it grew. This interest would later be my motivation to participate in the various fashion shows I was in while in college.

Fashion is ever-evolving and changing all the time. I'm not just talking about high fashion and what color is in this year. No, I'm also talking about clothes that anybody can pick up at the mall today. Much like the DAP and Twerking, Black fashion is mainstream. People from all over the world constantly emulate elements of fashion/style that are born within the Black community. Now, not only do people adopt aspects of Black fashion in their everyday style, but Black fashion is now also reflected and used in high fashion. **While tensions currently exist between Black designers and the fashion industry because of a lack of credit and recognition for their works and contributions to fashion**, Black designers and the Black community have continued to shape the way we think about style and what is considered 'cool.' To further prove this point, we are going to spend this chapter exploring trends in fashion today that became popular due to influences from Black culture and the Black community.

18, Actually 17, Fashion Trends Made Popular by The Black Community

1. Dashikis (African Print Clothing)

Dashikis have gained more popularity in recent years. More and more Black and non-Black Americans are wearing them now more than ever. While there are many conversations about the cultural appropriation vs. cultural appreciation of this type of clothing; no one can deny dashikis are now widely appreciated more than ever before. As a Nigerian, it is both ironic and pleasing to me that the same clothes I was made fun of for wearing as a kid are now the same clothing that everyone is trying to get their hands on. As a good friend of mine likes to say, "Oh, how the turn tables have turned."

Providing context, the word dashiki comes from the word 'danshiki' or 'dan ciki', meaning shirt in Yoruba and Hausa languages spoken primarily by people in Nigeria. The word 'dashiki' was later created in 1967 by Jason Benning. The materials this clothing is made of allow it to be free-flowing, and it is the perfect clothing to wear during hot summer days. The dashiki is unisex clothing and is worn most often by men and women during Black History Month, Kwanza, and other related African and African American cultural events. Besides the shirt, the dashiki comes in many different variations, such as suits and dresses, and the patterns can act as add-ons to other pieces of clothing. Since there are informal and formal versions of the dashiki, it can be worn to just about any event. Recently, the dashiki has become part of streetwear thanks to an increasing number of celebrities being photographed rocking the prints. It is even often worn by non-Black people when they are trying to show solidarity towards the Black community during protests and, sometimes, cringy apologies. Today, Black people and non-Black people can be seen wearing dashikis on nights out, graduation, prom, weddings, birthdays, and other notable events.

2. Sneaker Culture

Sneakers have been around for decades, but sneakers being considered part of fashion, especially street fashion, started in the 80s and '90s due to the influences of Black athletes. In 1984, Michael Jordan, one of the greatest basketball players of all time, collaborated with Nike to create Air Jordan. This collaboration was the beginning of sneaker culture as we know it today. Black youths started wearing these sneakers in creative, inventive, and stylish ways as part of their outfits. Black rappers such as Run-DMC and Grandmaster Flash also started wearing sneakers as fashion, which helped increase the perception that sneakers were cool to wear and more than just functional wear. This trend continued, and now, years later, the Black community has changed the idea of the sneaker and how it can be worn, transforming it from a shoe just worn for sports-related reasons to a coveted piece of fashion by many.

Today, sneakers are a key piece of clothing in pop culture. With the rise of sneaker culture, we now see more luxury brands such as Christian Dior, Supreme, Commes Des Garcon, Gucci, Louis Vuitton, Yeezy, and others collaborating with sneaker designers and brands to create their own vintage sneakers. The people who collect these shoes in mass amounts due to either shoe preference or the value of the sneaker or are just collectors of sneakers due to their love for sneakers are known as 'sneakerheads.' Sneaker culture now has a global reach, with sneakers being worn as fashion by people from all walks of life.

Below are the socially agreed upon best places to get new, vintage, and exclusive sneakers (this list doesn't include places like Nike, Adidas, New Balance, JD Sports, Sneakersnstuff (SNS), Kith, Ssense, Feature, A Ma Maniere, Social Status, and Tradeblock):

Recommended Sneaker Shops	
Hypebeast.com	**Tunde's Comment:** This site is unique. Not only do they have vintage and exclusive sneakers and outfits to match, but they also have the latest news and updates on fashion and the latest streetwear
Goat.com	**Tunde's Comment:** A great site to buy vintage and exclusive shoes and clothes to match

Stockx.com	**Tunde's Comment:** One of the biggest, if not the biggest, resale sneaker platforms currently available. As this is a resale platform, be careful not to get ripped off here and spend $$$ getting fakes. They're also currently being sued by Nike for selling fakes, so be careful here
Flightclub.com	**Tunde's Comment:** This was one of my favorites growing up, and I still rely on them to find vintage shoes
Sneakercon.com	**Tunde's Comment:** Not only can you buy sneakers from here, but they usually host events where sneaker lovers from all over come together to network, show off, and buy/sell sneakers
Stadiumgoods.com	**Tunde's Comment:** Another favorite site of mine; you can buy sneakers and outfits to match

3. Logomania (Monogram Print)

When referenced in streetwear fashion, logomania is described as taking the logo of a luxury brand and printing it all over the clothing. So, a shirt, or pants, or both, usually in the form of a tracksuit with the Gucci, Versace, Louis Vuitton, Fendi, or Dior logo printed all over it. Originally notorious, now-famous fashion designer Dapper Dan made this trend a coveted piece of streetwear back in the 80s. Dapper Dan, a Black boutique shop owner based in Harlem, used different fabrics covered in knockoff designer logos to style hip-hop artists and anyone else who could afford them. It didn't stop at just clothes either; Dapper Dan could customize almost anything you wanted him to in whatever logo you wanted. Dapper Dan received support from the entire Hip-Hop,

Rap, and R&B community but was eventually put out of business in 1989 due to legal copyright issues by the very brands whose logos he was using. This created a gap in the market between the demand for these clothes and the supply, which, not surprisingly, began being filled by the same brands that put him out of business. Though recently, Dapper Dan has been making a comeback due to a partnership that began with Gucci in 2018. Hopefully, we'll see more of Dapper Dan's designs in years to come.

4. Tracksuits / Velour Suits

As someone who loves working out, I love tracksuits, velour suits, and athleisure in general. You know, the Nike, Adidas, and PUMA ones that have a matching top and bottom with some comfortable sneakers to match. My favorite color combo is blue and white, and I think Pennsylvania State University (Penn State) probably has the coolest-looking blue and white combo tracksuit for their football team. Not just them; I've seen some really cool versions from other college teams and professional teams alike. Originally made in velour or silk, tracksuits can now be bought in almost any material and are a fantastic addition to any closet. Tracksuits became popular due in part to logomania and the different styles created from it. Celebrities love them, the mean girls in the movie 'Mean Girls' loved them, the world of rap loves them, and today, tracksuits are accepted as a notable piece of streetwear.

5. Bucket Hats & Kangol Hats

These used to be widely known as fisherman hats, they still are in most places, and were designed for functionality over fashion. Farmers and fishermen used these hats for protection from the rain and sun. Then, in the 80s, Black rapper Big Bank Hank of Sugar Hill Gang wore a bucket hat on the TV show 'Soap Factory.' This was just the beginning, as other rappers like LL Cool J, Jay Z, members of Run-DMC, and EPMD also rocked this hat. LL Cool J, in particular, made the red Kangol Hat part of his statement look, and it was an iconic part of his public image. He helped increase the popularity of bucket hats and helped cement them as a cool and trendy fashion accessory to wear. I own about three bucket hats and plan to get more in the summer.

6. Oversized Clothing / Baggy Jeans

While currently a popular trend, its origins are a tad bit sad. In the 80s and 90s, the Black community was even more disenfranchised than it is today. This led to a situation where younger Black family members would wear the handed-down clothing of older family members so the family could save money by not having to buy new clothes. So, to better connect with their fanbases and acknowledge where they may have come from, Black rappers wore oversized and baggy clothes whenever they performed. Years later, baggy clothing is now accepted and worn as part of mainstream streetwear. Some brands will even create styles and looks where the clothes are intentionally meant to be baggy. It's crazy how poverty became mainstream and turned into high fashion (yes, that was shade).

7. (Gold) Hoop Earrings

Hoop earrings have been worn since 2500 B.C. and date all the way back to Sumerian women. In fact, 4th-century Nubian women also wore them. Fast forward to the 1920s, and hoop earrings were a notable fashion accessory worn by Civil Rights activist Josephine Baker, an icon of her time who represented the beauty and vibrance of Black women and Black culture. Four decades later (in the 1960s), hoop earrings became a prominent statement piece associated with Black beauty in the Black Power movement and were soon after adopted by the Latinx community. Hoop earrings have since been popularized by artists such as Nina Simone, Angela Davis, Diana Ross, Janet Jackson, Tina Turner, Madonna, Cher, Missy Elliot, Lil Kim, Aaliyah, Lauryn Hill, Eve and Erykah Badu. Though Black women and women in the Latinx community have often been called "ghetto," "ratchet," and "unprofessional" for wearing them, hoop earrings have now become a major fashion accessory.

8. Acrylic Nails & Nail Art

Women love getting their nails done, and it seems like every year, there is a new service women can receive to make their nails longer, stronger, more glamorous, and more aesthetically creative. Acrylic nails were actually created in the U.S. in 1950, but they didn't become popular until the 70s when they became associated with disco stars. It was during this time that acrylic nails started being more widely offered as a service performed by salons. Then, during the 1980s, Florence Griffith-Joyner, a Black U.S. Olympian athlete and one of the greatest to ever run track, broke the 100-meter record three times and graced the cover of Sports Illustrated in 1988 with her vibrant and colorful acrylic nails. Not long after, acrylic nails became popular in the 90s with the rise of hip hop and R&B. Though today, Black women who wear acrylic nails are still looked at as 'tacky' and 'uneducated.' Acrylic nails and nail art are now enjoyed by people of different ethnic backgrounds all around the world.

9. Name / Scripted Necklaces for Women

The most well-known non-Black person to have owned a scripted necklace is Carrie Bradshaw (Sarah Jessica Parker's character) from the show 'Sex and the City.' It's pretty ironic that a fictional White TV character made this fashion trend popular and accepted when you think about the history of where these necklaces actually come from. During the 80s, women in the Black and Latinx community wore name/scripted necklaces as a way to show off their pride and dignity in their names. As we know, Black and Latinx names are often looked down upon as being 'made-up,' lacking meaning, or being hard to pronounce. On one hand, it allowed women from these communities to show off their 'hard to pronounce' names, and on the other, it was a rite of passage that showed a young woman was mature enough to own jewelry. Unfortunately, like some of the other fashion trends we've discussed, Black women and women in the Latinx community were, and are, often looked at as 'unprofessional' and 'ghetto' for wearing these types of necklaces, only for these same necklaces to now be accepted and worn by non-Black and non-Latinx women of all communities.

10. Matching Denim Jackets & Jeans

The Black community did not explicitly make denim jeans a popular fashion trend. Denim is a fashion staple today because of the various groups that adopted it, such as punk rock, the flower power movement, and everyday factory and construction workers. By the 80s, denim was no longer considered workwear but a fashionable look. By the 90s, labels like Guess Jeans, Versace, Calvin Klein, and Moschino were the top brands to get when it came to the more luxurious fashion-focused denim. Black-owned labels like FUBU (For Us, By Us) and Phat Farm further added to the popularity of denim as part of the 90s hip-hop fashion wardrobe. The Black community made denim more popular when Black artists such as Tupac and Eazy-E of N.W.A and others took denim a step further and were some of the first to rock the oversized denim jackets with matching jeans. This helped create a street style that was very quickly adopted by their fans and others within and outside the Black community.

11. Timberland Boots

I'll admit that being from New York, owning a pair of Timbs (Timberland boots) might be a New York specific fashion trend, but knowing how NYC is, you weren't cool unless you owned a pair of Timbs. Going back to the 90s, hip-hop, Biggie, Tupac, Nas, Aaliyah, Jay-Z, Alicia Keys, and just about every hip-hop and R&B artist have worn them and still do. Not even trying to promote or market Timbs, but Timbs are great. The only other boot you might see worn often by Black people

(Black men specifically) in NY is the Men's UGG boot, the Butte version. I've also had a pair of these, and wow, but yeah, Timbs are cool.

12. Overalls / Dungarees

Only farmers, little kids, and industrial workers wear overalls, right? Wrong again. A style that's stuck since the 90s, overalls have become a staple of street fashion. Worn by both men and women, completely strapped up or with one strap undone, overalls became mainstream because they were popularized by Black artists such as TLC, Tupac, Biggie, The Fugees, Will Smith, and others. Rocked with either a white tee, colored tee, or no tee, in addition to white sneakers or Timberland boots (Timbs), overalls are here to stay.

13. Lettuce Hem

Lettuce hem is a really popular trend used by different high fashion and street brands. Ironically, this trend was accidentally created by African-American designer Stephen Burrows in the 90s. The story goes like this: while working at Vogue, Stephen received a request from Diana Vreeland, who wanted a dress made in 'lettuce green.' Stephen misunderstood the request and made the ripple design – for those of you who know how to sew; it's a zig-zag overlock stitching pattern on knit material. This design is now widely worn and loved by women everywhere and styled with a variety of outfits. It's common to see it being used in lingerie and bridal wear.

14. Camouflage Pants / Military Colors

Camo print pants / military color attire have been worn in the Black community since the 1980s due to the influences of rap and hip-hop artists. The history behind it is as follows: rap group Public Enemy often wrote raps about the struggles of the life of a Black person in America. The military attire symbolized their status as soldiers of America's urban warzone, pretty much the inner cities like NY and

Chicago. Additionally, military gear was readily available from army surplus stores, so it made it easy for people in urban cities to get their hands on them when they had little to no money for clothes. Since then, rappers like Biggie, Tupac, Das EFX, Jay Z, Nas, Kendrick, Missy Elliot, Kanye, and countless others have donned the colors with their outfits and have made it part of their style.

15. Grillz / Tooth Bling

The act of putting silver/gold in your teeth as decoration has been around for centuries. It has been done as a way to show off wealth and class in society. Fast forward to the 1980s, and Jamaican dancehall musicians Shabba Ranks, Flava Flav of Public Enemy, Big Daddy Kane, and other artists made grillz slowly start becoming more popular within and outside the Black community. Since the 2000s, other artists/celebrities such as Raheem the Dream, Kilo Ali, Chris Brown, Kanye, Rihanna, Lil Wayne, Nelly, ASAP Rocky, Ludacris, Jay Z, DaBaby, T-Pain, Wiz Khalifa, Nicki Minaj, Travis Scott, Kelis, Lana Del Rey, Kesha, Cara Delevingne, Jessica Simpson, Ryan Lochte, Madonna, Katy Perry, Rita Ora, Miley Cyrus, Kim, Khloe, and Kylie Kardashian, Justin and Hailey Bieber, and even Beyonce have or have had grillz at least once at one point in time.

16. Sports Jerseys as Street Wear

Baseball Jerseys, Basketball Jerseys, Football Jerseys, and now even Hockey Jerseys are worn outside of tailgating events and are part of everyday streetwear. While not limited only to these sports, these are the most common to see people wearing on a day-to-day basis. Being part of hip-hop culture, wearing sports jerseys is part of the throwback look/style. This look was often rocked by Will Smith's character on the Fresh Prince of Bel-Air. This style has now grown outside the Black community and is often creatively worn and styled by non-Black people.

17. Puffer Jackets / Bubble Coats

Puffer Jackets are a trend that started in inner cities like New York and Chicago. Both places are known for having cold winters, so brands like The North Face, Moncler, and Helly Hansen naturally became a must-have for anyone who lived in these cities. Much like Timberland boots, Butte Ugg boots, and beanies, these wintertime clothing were worn stylishly. Black artists who grew up in these cities took these styles, made them more popular, and spread the look to their fans who were both in and outside the Black community. While puffer jackets were never made to look stylish but more for practical reasons, they have nevertheless become a staple winter-time wear.

18. Black Hairstyles

While I have this here (no pun intended), it's not really a trend, nor should it be considered as one. Black hairstyles can be a touchy (lol, no pun intended again) subject because when they're worn by people who are not part of the Black community, they usually fall heavily under the umbrella of cultural appropriation and not cultural appreciation. We will talk about Black hair, Black hairstyles, and many of the questions surrounding it in the next chapter due to how controversial and complex the topic is. But for now, this is a perfect transition to talk about cultural appropriation vs cultural appreciation.

Cultural Appropriation vs. Cultural Appreciation

Before we move on, I want to address the elephant in the room: **will it be considered cultural appropriation if you decide to wear some of the trends we just explored?** Before I answer that question, lets first look at a definition of **culture**:

"Culture is anything associated with a group of people based on their ethnicity, religion, geography, or social environment. This includes beliefs, traditions, language, objects, ideas, behaviors, customs, values,

or institutions. Culture is thought of as anything that belongs to particular ethnic groups."

Now that we have defined culture let's look at a definition of **cultural appropriation**. *"Cultural appropriation is the unacknowledged or inappropriate use of objects, elements, practices, customs, or aesthetics of a non-dominant culture in a way that doesn't respect their original meaning, give credit to their source, reinforces stereotypes or contributes to oppression."*

Essentially, cultural appropriation is when someone takes aspects of a culture that's not their own for their own personal use without understanding the history of what they are taking or giving credit to the group that they are taking it from. To further explain, let us look at some examples of things that can be and have been known to be culturally appropriated:

- Clothing and fashion
- Dance
- Decorations
- Hairstyles
- Language
- Music
- Symbols
- Tattoos

So, going by this definition of culture and cultural appropriation, my answer to the question, "Will it be considered cultural appropriation if you decide to wear some of the trends we just explored?" **depends**. Some of you may not like that answer, but I say it depends because the answer is not that black and white; in fact, it's a huge grey area. Even in the definition of cultural appropriation, there are caveats where it is not considered as such. In the definition, it says, "...*in a way that doesn't* *respect their original meaning, give credit to their source, reinforces* *stereotypes* or *contributes to oppression*." This is where cultural appreciation comes in. There are ways to engage with and interact with another person's culture as long as it **respects** the original meaning, **gives credit** to their source, **doesn't** reinforce stereotypes, or **contributes to oppression**.

Cultural appreciation can be defined as such:

"*The respectful borrowing of elements from another culture while giving credit to the original creators; seeking to understand and learn about another culture in an effort to broaden perspectives and connect with others cross-culturally.*"

This is probably a bit confusing. It probably creates the question, "So, under cultural appropriation, it is not okay to rock fashion trends that come from the Black community, but under cultural appropriation, it is okay?" Let me clear up the confusion. The key here is that when you decide to 'borrow' fashion trends/elements that come from the Black community, or anything else that comes from the Black community and other cultures for that matter, depending on how and when you do it, it can be either cultural appropriation or cultural appreciation. As an example, it would not be cool if a non-Black person wore a dashiki to a sporting event, but it would be if they were going to an African-related cultural event and were invited to do so. Another example is it would not be cool if I decided to wear a Native American head wrap to a costume party, but it would be if I were on a Native American reserve and was invited to do so as part of a cultural or ritualistic event. It's a grey area **because the line between appreciation and appropriation is circumstantial**. It really is dependent on the environment you're in, who you're around, the relationship you have with them, the timing of when you do it, and so on and so on. My best advice is to use your best judgment and ask the people you're around for their thoughts on you wearing, saying, or doing certain things. It's important also to note that what may be frowned upon and seen as appropriation in America can be considered integration and celebrated in other countries in the world. So again, just use your best judgment.

Give Me My Credit Or Give Me Back My Shit

For decades, the Black community has been ostracized, mocked, and even villainized for wearing many of the fashion trends we spoke about in this chapter. So, for people of the Black community to now see people not of the Black community wearing and being praised for putting on the same clothing items, people in the Black community have been looked down upon for decades for wearing leaves a sense of befuddlement that can't be explained. Much like twerking, the DAP, slang, and even dances, elements that are representative of the Black community and Black culture are often taken, rebranded, and introduced as this 'new' thing in pop culture. Content and experiences related to the Black community are often taken with credit rarely being given to the original creators until the people who take these aspects of the Black experience are called out for it. This happens all the time and, as a real example, is part of why the app TikTok has faced tensions with the Black creators on the app. Cultural appropriation was so bad on the app that Black creators literally went on strike and refused to create new content due to a lack of credit, recognition, and exposure. (TikTok has since made efforts to address this, but still, it's not enough). Think about it: people are out here thinking that Carrie, a fictional White character from 'Sex and The City' started the scripted/name necklaces trend, when not only do these necklaces have a deeper history than the show portrayed, but the Black community had already been doing it for decades prior to the show being written. So, if Carrie is managing to get away with it, what else do I need to say about modern-day content theft from Black creators? It's absolutely ludicrous.

The final answer I will give to the question, "Will it be considered cultural appropriation if you decide to wear some of the trends we just explored?" will stay the same; it **depends.** After looking at the differences between cultural appropriation vs. cultural appreciation, it's like this: if you're mindful of the circumstantial situation you're in, respectful in how you go about 'borrowing' fashion trends that were started by the Black community (aka you wear things when appropriate), and give credit to the Black community when asked about the particular, Black-related trend that is being borrowed, most people in the Black community will not mind. I say most because, again, since things are circumstantial, you can do everything right and still offend someone. It's only fair and respectful to give credit where credit is due. How would you feel if you or people from your culture created something, and not only is everybody now using what you or people from your culture created, but nobody ever gives you or people from your culture credit? Then, these same people also look down on you and people from your culture for using the very thing you guys created!

Lastly, I'll reiterate this point: all people are different; even if you do all the right things, give credit where credit is deserved, and wear some of these trends under the right circumstances that would fit under the umbrella of cultural appreciation, there may still be some people who may take offense. I said most earlier because you cannot please everyone. As long as you're doing things the right way, it's fine, just do you.

Final Thoughts

My final thoughts on cultural appropriation vs. appreciation are this: if you're ever in doubt about whether something is okay to wear and when you can wear it, just ask someone from that culture, and if you can't, just use your best judgment or google it. I hope you enjoyed this chapter and that you learned about the history of some of the most popular fashion trends and their connection to the Black community and Black history. I personally learned a bit more about some of my favorite styles and where they came from as I wrote this chapter. Some things were surprising, and others not so much. The more I learned, the more pride I took in the continued realization that Black culture truly is wide-reaching. Some of you may agree, and some of you may not. I just hope that as you continue to read this book, you begin/continue to appreciate Black culture for all the things it continues to bring into our everyday lives.

19. Bonus! – Eyewear

While glasses are not a trend made popular by the Black community, they are still accessories that the Black community has helped make trendy. Below are some of the most popular Black-owned brands of glasses. These glasses are all amazing in style and creation, and I hope to own a few pairs in the future.

Recommended Black-Owned Eyewear Brands	
Coco and Breezy	**Website: Cocoandbreezy.com** **Official Description:** "Coco and Breezy Eyewear, founded in 2009, is an eyewear brand based in New York City by twin designers Corianna and Brianna Dotson. They have been featured in Vogue and Harper's Bazaar, and their line has been embraced by celebrities such as Prince, Nicky Minaj, and many others."

Bôhten Eyeglasses	Website: Bohten.com **Official Description:** "Bôhten Eyeglasses is an African American owned global company that produces beautiful prescription and sunglass frames from sustainable materials sourced from Africa."
Nroda	Website: Nroda.com **Official Description:** "Nroda is an eyewear brand that believes if you look like a boss, you'll feel like a boss! Nroda strives to provide a luxury eyewear brand that embraces lavish trends such as crystals, fine metals, and other unique components"
SWAV Eyewear	Website: Swaveyewear.com **Official Description:** "SWAV Eyewear was created by Isiah Fowler, and was founded on a mission to motivate, inspire, and empower goal-oriented visionaries to achieve greatness"
LEX: MARQ OPTIQUE	Website: Lexmarqoptique.net **Official Description:** "LEX: MARQ OPTIQUE is a network of Opticians, Frame Stylists, and Fashion Enthusiasts. This network has collaborated to merge fashionable and functional eyewear at affordable prices, delivered straight to your front door." **Tunde Comments**: They also offer mobile sales and custom repair services in many cities to better serve their customers.
Krewe	Website: Krewe.com **Official Description:** "Krewe creates hand-crafted frames you won't find anywhere else. This brand is 'Inspired by the endless diversity of life,' which is what they bring to every pair of eyewear they design"

Vontélle	Website: Vontelle.com **Official Description:** "Vontélle was founded to satisfy the demand for vibrant, fashion-forward eyewear. Each of their products and accessories are designed to pay homage to African ancestry with traditional colors and patterns that channel African, Caribbean, and Latino heritage."
AOX	Website: Aoxeyewear.com **Official Description:** "MADE BY A HUMAN, FOR A HUMAN Each pair is handcrafted in their shop in Sorrento, Italy. They mount lenses of the highest quality with scratch-resistant and anti-reflective coating treatments, at no additional cost."
3rd Eye View	Website: shop3rdeyeview.com **Official Description:** "3rdeyeview's brand offers affordability & inclusivity for the people. The brand's specialty is based off a combination of color, comfort and cost."

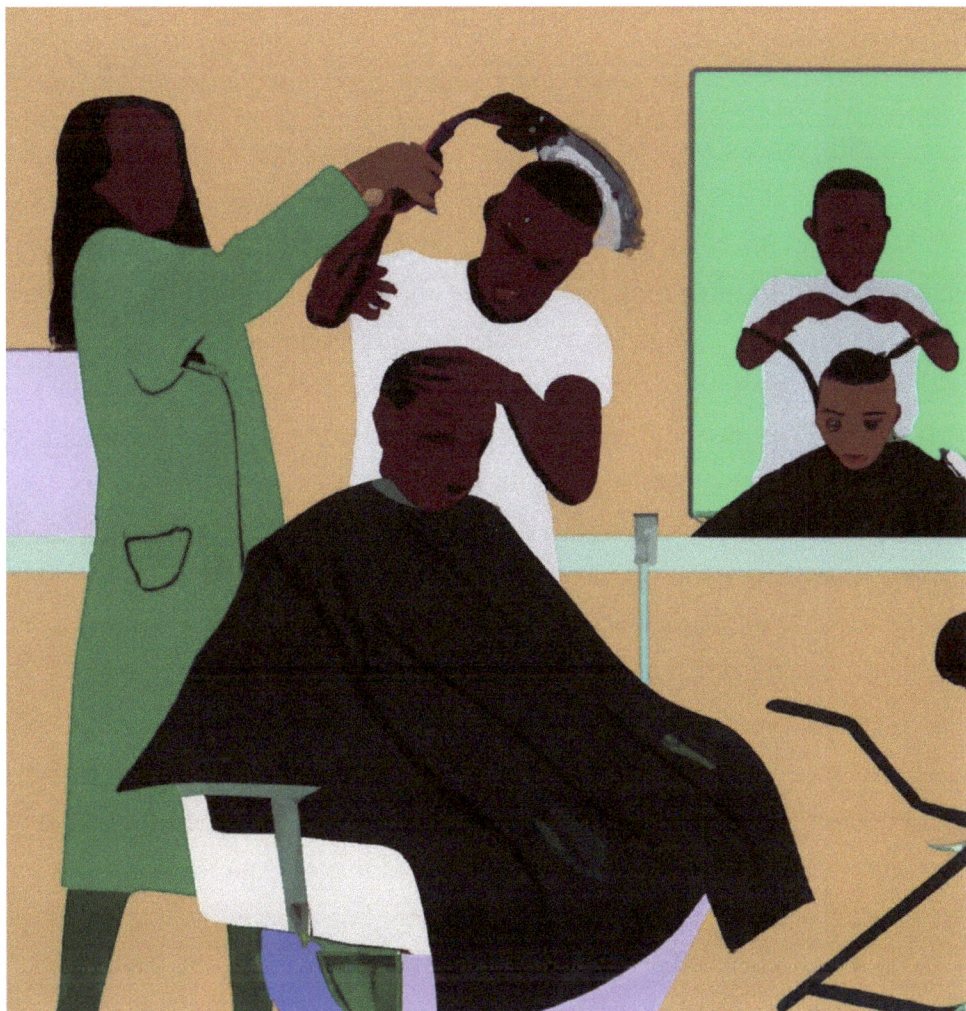

Black Hair

"Black hair is different and quite often misunderstood. Black Hair is also magic."

- Tunde

Storytime: My earliest memory of being aware that my hair was 'Black' came about after my family and I had moved away from the city and into the suburbs. Prior to moving, my mom was the one who always cut my hair, but after moving, I was around the age where I realized the haircuts my mom was giving me were not good (I love you, Mom, but they weren't). I didn't have the type of hairline or haircut that my Black friends from school who went to an actual barber had, and I was made fun of because of it. This realization led me on a quest to find a place where I could cut my hair in the suburb my family and I had moved to. Being young and an immigrant, I had the bliss of youthful ignorance in believing that any barbershop I went to could cut my type of hair. Boy, was I terribly, terribly wrong. I still remember it: the first barbershop I went to was run by this Italian family. This isn't to say that non-Black people can't cut black hair, but the barbers in this particular shop could not. I walked into the barbershop, and the barbers all turned to look at me and were pleasantly surprised that I was there. Their looks of surprise probably should have been the sign I needed to walk right back out, but hey, youthful ignorance. When I sat in the chair, my barber admitted that he had never cut my type of hair before, and me believing it was fine, put the fate of how my haircut would come out in his hands. Well, needless to say, things did not go as planned or as hoped. My haircut came out terrible and when I got back to school the following Monday, I got made fun of even more. One of my friends was curious and asked me what happened, and after I finished explaining, he promised to take me to the Black barbershop he frequently went to, and of course, that was after laughing at me for getting my hair cut by someone who had never cut Black hair before! Three weeks later, thank God for hair growth, I was in a chair in the Black barbershop, and the barber proceeded to ask me how I wanted my hair cut, how I wanted it styled, and what type of hairline finish I wanted. I was admittedly confused by some of his questions, as it was my first time in a Black barbershop, but after he explained and allowed me to respond, I knew things would turn out okay. About 30 minutes later, I walked out with a huge grin on my face because the haircut was perfect. I could not wait to go to school the following Monday and proudly show off my new haircut.

My experiences with figuring out my hair, what to do with it, what I could do with it, where to go, and all the other things associated with it are not unique to just me. Across America, Black people of all ages are still figuring out their hair, what to do with it, and most importantly, how to love it. Black hair has always been misunderstood in America, which is why we're going to spend this chapter talking about Black hair, its history, debunking myths, and the different types of hairstyles that exist for both men and women.

A Brief History of Black Hair in America

The history of Black hair in America began in Africa way before the slave trade began. Hair was used as a way to identify someone's tribe, social status, whether they were part of the royal family, a warrior or a peasant, occupation, age, religion, and even their mood. Then, the transatlantic slave trade began, and African traditions, language, and even grooming methods began to disappear. During this time, the hair of Black people was compared to animal wool by slavers and was used as one of the justifications to dehumanize the Black people who were being turned into slaves. This is partially when the roots of colorism (we talked about this in the 'Dating A Black Person When You're Not Black

Chapter), the differences in treatment and opportunities due to skin tone, first began. For slaves who would be domestic workers, slaves with more European features and looser textured hair were treated a bit better and were sold for higher prices than those who did not. Without any access to the natural herbs and oils in Africa, slaves were forced to use bacon grease, butter, and kerosene as conditioner for their hair. This historical aspect is tied to the stereotype that Black people use butter and bacon grease as hair conditioners.

Fast forward about a little bit more than two centuries, and as slavery begins to end, you have pockets of places in America where Black women and men were able to wear their hair with pride. New Orleans was one such example where free Creole women of color would wear elaborate hairstyles that displayed their kinks, coils, and curls with pride. Then, the city imposed the Tignon Laws, which required these women to wear a tignon, which is a scarf or handkerchief over their hair, to show they belonged to the slave class, even if they were free. During my research for this chapter, I found insinuations that White women were the ones who forced these laws to be passed because White men were attracted to these elaborate hairstyles. In response to these laws, Black women started styling these tigons in even more fashionable and elaborate manners. Fast forward to 1865, and slavery is over with the passing of the 13th amendment, but discrimination against Black hair is still ongoing. 'Good' hair, looser, more textured hair, becomes a requirement for Black people to be able to enter certain schools, churches, social groups, and business networks. Black Americans started looking for hair care routines and products that would help them straighten their hair, and eventually, the hot comb, a heated metal comb that was designed to straighten and smooth kinky afro hair textures, was invented and became a widely used product.

Enter the 1900's. Madam C.J Walker, who was Black, became one of America's first self-made millionaires with her line of hair products made specifically for Black hair. Garret A. Morgan, who was also black, created the relaxer, a hair treatment that permanently straightened Black hair. Then, in 1956, George E. Johnson took it a step further by creating a version for men before creating a version for women. Now, it is the 1960s - 1970s, and America is experiencing the rise of the Civil Rights Movement and the Black Power movement. This is when elements of the natural hair movement began. We will touch more on this later in this chapter. The afro became popular as a symbol against oppression, a turning away from the European standard of beauty, and a celebration of Black heritage. During this time, the Jheri curl, a hairstyle that allowed Black people to have straighter hair but still retain their curls, also became popular. Eddie Murphy rocked this style in his 1988 comedy, 'Coming to America,' and this was the same iconic style that Michael Jackson had throughout the latter half of his career. From the late 1970s to the present day, Black hairstyles have become more popular and embraced. Shows like The Fresh Prince of Bel Air, Moesha, Martin, Sister Sister, Family Matters, The Wayans Bros., and A Different World were shows, among many others, that helped increase the representation of Black people and Black hair in mainstream media. These shows celebrated and explored Black intellect, beauty, and excellence and helped make Black hair 'cool' and normalized. Black people no longer had to be ashamed of and even, in some cases, hate their hair.

Black Hair Today

Black hair has gone through many evolutions in American history, and while It has come a long way from how it is viewed, taken care of, and loved, there is still a lot more work that needs to be done. Even as I write this book, Black hair in America is still discriminated against. Black people have been kicked out of school because of their hair, claiming it is a "distraction," violates school dress code policies, and have even been fired from jobs, turned down from interviews, passed up on promotions, prevented from participating in athletic events, and even looked at as unprofessional simply for wearing their hair naturally or using a hairstyle that is specific to Black hair. It's one thing to get treated differently because of the color of your skin, but imagine getting treated differently simply because your hair grows differently and, therefore, must be styled differently.

Hair discrimination has been long rooted in American history since the 1700s when the hair of Black people was compared to animal wool. In fact, the discrimination has been so bad in some places that legislation has had to be passed recently to ban race-based hair discrimination. The "Creating a Respectful and Open Word for Natural Hair Act," also known as the CROWN Act, was introduced by California and was finally passed in 2019, with Colorado, New York, Maryland, Virginia, New Jersey and Washington, Connecticut, Delaware, Illinois, Nebraska, Oregon, and others passing this law soon after. It doesn't just stop with these states; there are efforts currently underway to get all the states to pass this law. Even the Army had to make changes to their grooming policies in 2017 to remove the ban on dreadlocks, also known as 'locs' for female soldiers with textured hair, and then made additional amendments to their policy in 2021 to be even more inclusive of Black hair and Black hairstyles. Who would have thought that hair could be so political?

eventually leading to the worldwide #naturalhair movement by Black women across the globe (check this hashtag out on Twitter). This movement has been great because it's been cool to see Black women all over the world start to embrace and begin sharing their journeys of wearing and (re)discovering their natural hair on social media. The movement became so big that in 2017, Michelle De Leon would create World Afro Day – an annual celebration and education of Black hair. The natural hair movement is still growing, with more and more women joining the movement every year. The natural hair movement is also more than just about hair for Black women and men, it is a lifestyle, it is an exploration, a journey of self-love and self-care.

Myths About Black Hair

The issue around Black hair is so much more expansive than what the scope of this book is intended for, but I hope the issues we were able to touch on provided some much-needed clarity on any possible confusion around Black hair. In order to further address any possible confusion, I wanted to spend this section of the chapter debunking all the different myths about Black hair I have heard, been told myself, or have witnessed other Black people having to explain.

1. Black Hair Is Dirty / Smelly

This is not true. There is this misconception, a stereotype even, that Black people must use all these butters and oils and even grease to style our hair. Black people go to great lengths to care for and maintain our hair. While not exclusive to just men and women who are part of the natural hair movement, Black people, usually women, have a wash day where we spend most, if not all, of the chosen wash day, going through a step-by-step process to ensure the cleanliness and health of our hair. It's called wash day because it can take almost the whole day, if not the whole entire day, simply because of how long some of the different steps required during this day can take. Much like Black people, Black hair is different; wash days look completely different from person to person and take up different amounts of time.

2. Black Hair Is Not Combed or Styled

This is also not true. Black hair is different and, therefore, can and, in some cases, must be styled differently. Because of this, Black people have different hair products that most non-Black people do not have. It is also very expensive to maintain our hair, especially for Black women. Some of these styles are different and may even look exotic or out of place to non-Black people. Always remember that different does not mean unkept. Black hair may only look uncombed or unstyled to someone who may not understand our hair, and that's okay.

3. Black Hair Is a Distraction

This can actually come off as an insult if not an outright microaggression (literally a micro insult). Just because something is different does not mean it is a distraction. Black people often face this criticism at work and in educational settings. What's actually a distraction is the conversations that have to be had about Black hair being a distraction. Different is not a distraction, and if a person feels distracted by Black hair, it speaks to their lack of exposure to different cultures and hairstyles. That's a personal problem the person thinking Black hair is a distraction must deal with on their own because how can something that grows differently truly be a distraction? It's just such an ignorant comment to make, so please don't make the mistake of calling our hair a distraction. That would be like me saying that blonde or red hair is a distraction simply because most Black people can't grow blonde or red hair... come on now.

4. Black Hair Is Rebellious / A Political Statement

No, again, natural Black hair is simply different. While the afro hairstyle has been used and is sometimes identified as part of the Black Power Movement, hair is not and should not be political. It's hair. It's only become political because so many people don't understand it simply because it doesn't conform to the Eurocentric standard of beauty. Things that are different do not always have to warrant a political discussion. It only becomes political when unfair and discriminatory policies around Black hair are in place in different sectors of our society. Don't get me wrong, there's nothing wrong with businesses having standards in place for how 'neat' they want their employees to appear, but to claim Black hair is rebellious or that someone is using their hair to make a political statement simply because their hair literally can't fit the so called 'neat' standard due to how it grows is crazy, don't you think?

5. Black Hair Does Not Grow

This one is funny to me – **story time**: there was a time in college when I relaxed my hair on a random Tuesday. Don't worry; I will explain what relaxing my hair means later in this chapter! I relaxed my hair because, for my Halloween costume that year, I was going to be a Chippendale. Plus, I had always been curious as to how my hair would look relaxed, so I said, "Why not now?" After all, we all do and try new and crazy things in college. Due to having some of my classes every other day, the people who saw me on Monday were surprised and shocked on Wednesday at how quickly my hair 'grew' seemingly overnight. When I tried to explain I had relaxed my hair which is why it was so much longer, they had no idea what I was talking about, and it led to even more questions. (This was also a defining moment for me on the difference between Black and non-Black culture because most of my Black friends would have understood what I meant). Due to how curly or kinky Black hair can be, our hair is always much longer than it appears. Shrinkage is why our hair always looks shorter than it actually is and creates the illusion that Black hair does not grow. In fact, when Black hair is dry, it can experience shrinkage of anywhere between 20-30% and, in some cases, up to 75%! Remember, looks can be deceiving.

6. Black Hair Does Not Move

The same shrinkage causing Black hair to be densely packed, making it look like it does not grow, is the same shrinkage that can make it coarse. This is what gives the illusion that Black hair does not move, but once our hair gets longer or wet, or if we decide to perm it or relax it, it blows in the wind just like everyone else's.

7. Black Women Do Not Wear Their Real Hair

This is a rude assumption to be implied for all Black women. In the same way, people are different, so, too, is hair. I learned at an incredibly young age to never question what women do with their hair. When Black women do decide to put extensions in their hair or wear a wig, aka, not their real hair, it's usually because it's being used as a form of a protective hairstyle for their real natural hair. Additionally, women, regardless of whether they are Black or non-Black, may at times not wear their real hair. Hair extensions and wigs are not only limited to Black women or men.

8. Black Hair Has Bugs in It

This is just a personal hygiene thing for anybody, whether Black or non-Black. If someone has bugs in their hair, they likely need professional intervention in some way, shape, or form. Additionally, due to how curly or dense Black hair is, Black people are very unlikely to have bugs in their hair. In fact, our hair is very resistant to them. Not only is our hair difficult for bugs to navigate through, but the products we use to keep our hair neat and styled are disliked by bugs.

On the other hand, Lice, a bug that many non-Black children can get, is not common in Black people. So no, Black hair does not have bugs in it.

9. Black Hair Is Unprofessional

Different does not mean unprofessional. Saying Black hair is unprofessional is a microaggression. A person saying this is implying that because Black hair does not resemble the Eurocentric standard of hair, it, therefore, does not belong in a working environment. Black natural hair has no correlation or impact on a Black person's ability, effectiveness, and productivity when it comes to doing their job. So no, Black hair is not unprofessional; black hair is professional as fuck.

10. You Are Allowed to Touch a Black Person's Hair

No. The question, "Can I touch your hair?" is probably one of the most uncomfortable questions Black people get asked all the time. Most Black people may go along with it and let people do it because they do not want to cause a scene or make the person who asked to feel uncomfortable. Others may not and will cause a scene. Imagine if Black people started going up to non-Black people and started asking, "Can I touch your hair?" and then touched it even before the person had a chance to respond. That's what happens to many Black people. If you are really close with a Black person and decide to ask if you can touch it, then that is up to you, but to ask someone you don't even know that question because you're intrigued is rude and a little bit demeaning. Additionally, we don't know where your hands have been, so no, don't ask to touch our hair. Our hair is not this exotic or different thing that you need to be fascinated about. Again, it's just hair.

Lastly, I know I focused on Black people overall for this section, but all the things I've talked about for #10 apply even more to Black women. I, as a Black man, do not touch nor even attempt to touch a Black woman's hair, especially without the verbal permission to do so.

Black Hairstyles!

As Black hair is very versatile, there are dozens of different types of hairstyles for Black men and women, with dozens of variations of each hairstyle that exist. To help everyone out, I'm going to be providing an expansive list of some of the most common hairstyles for Black women and men. This may require some googling from you, but this way, when you spot a Black hairstyle out in public, you will know exactly what it is. If you remember enough of them, it can even be used as a conversation starter.

Lastly, I wore a du-rag often in college, and many of my non-Black friends were often confused by what it was, what it did, and why I was wearing it. To answer that question here, the silky 'scarf' like thing that you see Black men (and sometimes men from other ethnic backgrounds when they're trying to be 'cool' or appropriate Black culture) wear on our heads is called a du-rag. It comes in different colors and designs and is a key hair product used by Black men to help us develop a particular curl pattern. This du-rag enforced curl pattern, as well as a bunch of other different types of steps, ultimately helps us create the hairstyle 'waves.' I figure some people may have no idea what I'm talking about, so please google 'Black hairstyle waves.' I've also included an example below in the 'Popular Black Hairstyles for Black Men section.'

Popular Black Hairstyles for Black Women

**Bantu Knots**	**Cornrows**	**Jumbo Twists**
**Faux Locs**	**Box Braids**	**Afro**
**Dreadlocks**	**Twist-Outs**	**Curly Pixie**
**High Bun**	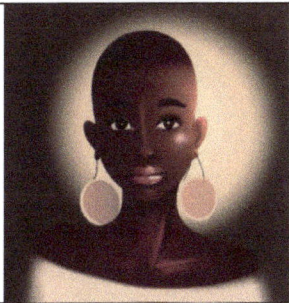**Short Cut**	**Fulani Braids**

Popular Black Hairstyles for Black Men

Waves	**Caesar**	**Caesar Fade**
Faux Locs	**Box Braids**	**Afro**
Dreadlocks	**Short Dreadlocks**	**Faded Dreads**
Taper Fade	**Cornrows**	**Line With Up A Design**

Glossary On Important Black Hair Terms

Words You May Hear & What They Mean	
Perm (Also known as Relaxing)	When non-Black women (and sometimes men) say that they're getting a perm, they may be talking about the process of adding a permanent curl to their hair through a chemical process. Within the context of the Black community, we are usually talking about the chemical process of permanently straightening our hair, so a bit of the opposite
Weave	This is a type of hairstyle extension. First, a woman's real hair is braided into cornrows or any other type of scalp braid. Then, extra hair is woven/sewn into those braids with a needle and string made specifically for hair weaving. It's not as painful as it sounds, but it can definitely hurt if not done properly
Hair Extensions	Extensions are a little bit like weaves in the sense that extra hair is added to a woman's real hair. Unlike weaves, extensions don't require cornrows as a base. Depending on the type of extensions, hair can be added by braiding it with the real hair, through a special type of glue, or through the use of clip-ons'
Natural Hair	This refers to Black hair that has not had its natural hair texture altered by any chemicals. Depending on the person or hair type, the person may opt not to use any chemicals at all or anything that does not naturally occur in nature
Wash Day	This refers to a day (it can be any day of the week) that a Black person has dedicated to washing and styling their hair. It is considered a "day" because it depends on their hair care routine and the number of steps that might be involved in maintaining that particular person's hair

Lace Wig / Lace Front	A type of wig that is tied into a nearly invisible lace or lace-like material at the front of the hairline. It's different from a regular wig because it gives the illusion that the wig is not actually a wig. Basically, it's a more natural-looking wig

Recommended Movies on Black Hair	
Good Hair	**Official Description:** "Prompted by a question from his young daughter, comic Chris Rock sets out to explore the importance of hair in Black culture. Rock interviews celebrities such as Ice-T and Raven Symone and visits hair salons, stylist competitions, and even an Indian temple to learn about [Black] hair culture" **Tunde's comments:** I loved this movie; I laughed a lot and learned a lot. It's only about an hour and a half and is definitely worth the watch.
Hair Love	**Official Description:** "Hair Love, an Oscar®-winning animated short film from Matthew A. Cherry, tells the heartfelt story of an African American father learning to do his daughter's hair for the first time" **Here is a YouTube link for it:** **https://www.youtube.com/watch?v=kNw8V_Fkw28** **Tunde's comments:** This was a really cute and heartwarming short film. I absolutely loved it.
The Big Chop	**Official Description:** "Part of Issa Rae's #ShortFilmSundays: The Big Chop follows 10-year-old Kris on her natural hair journey of self-love and acceptance. Once a diehard lover of her big afro, negative hints from her mom and teasing on the playground causes Kris to get a perm. She continues to perm her hair as an adult until one day, she has had enough. She stands in the mirror and does the "big chop." **Here is a YouTube link for it:** **https://www.youtube.com/watch?v=CFiDQdpll2w** **Tunde's comments:** If you've ever been curious about what the "Big Chop" that Black woman do is

	like, then look no further than this. While short, this film touches upon many of the different deeply rooted psychological reasons behind why some women can be hesitant against going natural.

Recommended Documentaries on Black Hair	
Celebrating Black Hair: Crown and Glory	**Official Description:** "A short clip by the HuffPost: Black people have been suspended from school and have been barred from employment due to their hair texture. However, Black hairstyles and salons continue to connect Black people across the African diaspora" **Here is the YouTube link for it –** **https://www.youtube.com/watch?v=p9eep4H31wo** **Tunde's comments:** I was surprised by how few views this video has received, especially given the topic of the video and how well-made it is.
My Nappy Roots: A Journey Through Black Hair-itage	**Official Description:** "My Nappy Root" explores the politics, culture, and history of African American hair. This documentary explores questions like: "Is there such a thing as 'Good and Bad' hair?" and "How has the Eurocentric ideal of beauty influenced Black hair through modern history?" **Here is a YouTube link for it:** **https://www.youtube.com/watch?v=lvw_PUbt1Fc** **Tunde's comments:** For those who love documentaries, this one will definitely be up your alley. This documentary explores many of the things this chapter explored and goes into more detail about other related topics that go beyond the scope of this book.
Watch This Documentary on Braids and Appropriation in America	**Official Description:** "Lupita Nyong'o, Young M.A, Ayana Bird, Lacy Redway, Vernon François, and more talk about braids and Black hair culture in America" **Here is a YouTube link for it:** **https://www.youtube.com/watch?v=yFGwmUCH9aI** **Tunde's comments:** If you're still curious about why

	copying Black hairstyles is considered cultural appropriation, then this is a good documentary to watch.

Recommended Ted Talk on Black Hair	
No. You Cannot Touch My Hair!	**Official Description:** "Part of the TEDxBristol: Through her own personal story and the hair-raising experiences of other women and girls, Mena Fombo's TEDxBristol talk is a witty yet compelling and sometimes dark exploration of the objectification of black women. It's an issue she has spent a lifetime experiencing and exploring, with both a political and creative lens." **Here is the YouTube link for it –** **https://www.youtube.com/watch?v=OLQzz75yE5A** **Tunde's comments:** If you wanted more context on why you shouldn't touch or ask to touch a black person's hair, then this is definitely a good watch.

Hari Story by Ayana Bryd and Lori Tharps	**Official Description:** *"Hair Story* is a historical and anecdotal exploration of Black Americans' tangled hair roots. A chronological look at the culture and politics behind the ever-changing state of Black hair from fifteenth-century Africa to the present-day United States, it ties the personal to the political and the popular." **Tunde's comments:** You can get this book from Amazon and any other major book-selling platform. I read parts of this book in research for this chapter, and I was blown away by how well-written and informative this book was.
Twisted: The Tangled History of Black Hair Culture by Emma Dabiri	**Official Description:** "Despite increasingly liberal world views, Black hair continues to be erased, appropriated, and stigmatized to the point of taboo. Through her personal and historical journey, Dabiri gleans insights into the way racism is coded in society's perception of Black hair—and how it is often used as an avenue for discrimination." **Tunde's comments:** I love this author and all of her other content and not just because she's part Nigerian. One of her other books, "Don't Touch My Hair," is also a really informative read.

215

Bonus Part Two Chapter - Black Inventions

"You can't say you don't like Black People and then use the stuff we made"

- Tunde

I have a really interesting question for you: how is it possible that there can be people who hate or strongly dislike Black people but yet continue using/enjoying the things that we Black people create or add to guilt-free? Seems kind of hypocritical, doesn't it? It's even a little bit ironic. It's a bit like, "You suck, and I don't like you or your people, but can I still enjoy some of the food, fashion, products, music, art, etc., that you make?" Like, how can you hate or dislike us but still have sex with us, sing along to our songs, do our dances, eat our foods, watch our TV shows and our movies, steal our content, and still be fans of our athletes, musicians, artists, and so forth? It's like, wooooooooooooooow, you hate us so much but will still use our stuff.

I've also always thought to myself that it's a bit ironic that a non-Black person will pick some Black people to like because that Black person has a particular skill that the person enjoys watching or benefitting from, bypassing the fact that this individual is Black, but then hate the rest of us simply because we're Black. Please, make it make sense. It may seem a bit controversial, but my thoughts on the matter are as follows: unless a Black person did something specifically to a non-Black person to make them dislike, if not hate, said Black person, then the non-Black person should, in general, either respect or at least have a neutral attitude towards all Black people. I'm not asking for much here, just basic respect for all Black people as human beings. What I'm getting to with this idea is that unless a person gives you a reason NOT to, your default towards all people, regardless of the color of their skin or how they identify, should be one of respect. If basic human respect is difficult for whatever reason, then the default should at least be one of neutrality. It seems, however, that there are some people whose default towards Black people is negative UNLESS a Black person is somehow 'different,' and that shouldn't be the case. It's a bit sad and quite a limited way of looking at people and, by extension, the world.

I always hear this sentiment from racist individuals on how Black People are "useless" and "nothing but thugs and murders" and "are lazy and do nothing but abuse the system" and all these other ludicrous and concerning things. I'm sure some of you have heard these sentiments as well, and it's always so interesting to hear, mainly because these are blanket statements that are all untrue. Remember how we talked about the dangers of overgeneralization in the first chapter and all the things it comes with? A person who carries these sentiments really almost should be pitied because they're so wrong; one almost has to question what type of reality they are living in. While I want to pity them, I don't because they're grown and should know/do better, and I opt to educate them instead. Sometimes, people really do need a good verbal whooping to do better; there's nothing wrong with reprimanding someone who does something worth reprimanding them for.

So now, whenever I hear one of these sentiments from a non-Black person who is antagonistic towards Black people, I casually pull out my list of things I'm assuming they enjoy or take for granted that was either co-created or exclusively created by a Black person. I first ask said individual, "If you don't like Black people and believe that we're all stupid and useless, and blah blah blah, would you use the things that we made or watch things that we made or are involved in?" Outside of sports, the answer is usually no, and then I casually tell them, "Okay, then please stop watching or listening to anything that has to do with entertainment whatsoever (sports, movies, TV shows, etc.) that Black people are involved in." I emphasize sports because they usually exclude it, but you're not about to not care about our lives and think all these terrible things about us, and yet you're happily cheering us on because we're on your favorite sports team. Get the fuck outta here... That usually leads to a whole bunch of deflecting and comments around how "non-Black people are involved in those things as well and all these other comments." My response back is always "fair," and then I pull out my list of all the everyday conveniences they have due to an invention made exclusively by a Black person and kindly ask them never to use these things again since, as they previously stated when I asked them if they would ever use a Black-made invention, their response was no. The look of befuddlement is always priceless and usually leads to silence thereafter.

If you would ever like to do the same, below is a list of inventions made exclusively by Black people. It also helps put into perspective all the contributions Black people have had on the world and our society, beyond all the other things we talked about earlier in this book, and all the other things we didn't even touch on.

29 Modern Day Inventions Created by Black People

Automatic Elevator Doors Alexander Miles 1887	**Automatic Gear Shift** Richard Spikes 1932	**Bathroom Tissue Holder** Mary Beatrice Davidson Kenner 1982
Blood Banks Charles Richard Drew 1941	**Blood Plasma Bag** Charles Richard Drew 1941	**Bloodmobiles** Charles Richard Drew 1944
Caller ID & Call Waiting Shirley Ann Jackson 1970s	**Central Heating Furnace** Alice H. Parker 1919	**Clothes Dryer** George T. Sampson 1892
Color Computer Monitors Mark Dean 1999	**Dry Cleaning Method** Thomas Jennings 1812	**Euphonica Guitar** Robert F. Flemming, JR 1886

Folding Cabinet Bed Sarah Goode 1884	**Folding Chair** John Purdy (& James R Sadgwar) 1888	**Gas Masks** Garrett Morgan 1914
Golf Tee (Improved Version) George Grant 1899	**Home Security System** Marie Van Brittan Brown 1966	**Ice Cream Scoop** Alfred L. Cralle 1897
Imaging X-Ray George E. Alcorn 1984	**Improved Dustpan** Lloyd Ray 1862	**Improved Ironing Board** Sarah Boone 1892
Lawn Mower John Albert Burr 1899	**Lawn Sprinkler** Joseph A. Smith 1897	**Modern Toilet** Thomas Elkins 1872

Potato Chips George Crum 1853	**Protective Mailbox** Philip B. Downing 1891	**Refrigerated Trucks** Frederick McKinley 1940
Reversible Baby Stroller William Richardson 1889	**Three-Way Traffic Signal** Garret Morgan 1923	

Part 2.5 - Commonly Asked Questions

"Even if you're nervous or afraid, ask lots of questions. It's the only way you'll ever learn more about things you don't know about before. I promise you that the more you seek to learn and understand, the more you will definitely learn about things you didn't even know that you didn't know."

- Tunde

This section is going to be filled with the other questions I have either been asked or felt were important to talk about. Unfortunately, because of how I decided to structure this book, they didn't really have a 'home,' so to speak. So, I decided to put them all together and give them their own part in this book.

Following the same pattern as the rest of the book, though I do throw the occasional reference to another chapter in subsequent chapters, each chapter can be read on its own. Take your time with each chapter, and I hope you take in something new.

Happy Reading!

What Is Systemic Racism All About?

"Don't get it twisted; systemic racism is still a very real problem"

- Tunde

Whew, what systemic racism is all about is quite a loaded question. So loaded, in fact, that many books, articles, blogs, movies, clips, TV shows, research papers, documentaries, etc., I mean, the list goes on and on the different types of content that have already been created to address this very topic. Though this is the case, I still wanted to provide an overview that touches on many of the core things to know about systemic racism. There are many different definitions of systemic racism, as well as a large, non-exhaustive list of the different ways that systemic racism affects Black people, but before I can even explain or talk about what these things are, we must first begin with discussing and defining racism.

Racism: Oxford Languages defines racism as "prejudice, discrimination, or antagonism directed against a person or people on the basis of their membership in a particular racial or ethnic group, typically one that is a minority or marginalized." If that definition didn't help, Oxford Languages also defines racism as "the belief that different races possess distinct characteristics, abilities, or qualities, especially so as to distinguish them as inferior or superior to one another." In simpler terms, racism is basically an act of saying that groups of people are better than or worse than other groups of people due to how they identify/are identified by society and, therefore, deserve different levels of treatment based on this identification. These differences in treatment then manifest through acts of prejudice, discrimination, or antagonism against whatever group is receiving the racism. Racism can also come in any shape or size. For Black people, the range of racism can go anywhere from being 'tiny' with things like microaggressions to being massive with things like being 'accidentally' killed by the police. And yes, it's quite wild that the range is that wide. It really is just another reality of being Black in America, but I digress.

Racism can then be further broken down into four different types: Internalized Racism, Interpersonal Racism, Institutional Racism, and Systemic Racism:

- **Internalized Racism (Belief)** is "our thoughts, feelings, beliefs, and actions, conscious or unconscious, as an individual." These are the things we may have been taught as children that are then reinforced through social influences such as media narratives, entertainment, friends and family, and so forth. These are the ideas and or beliefs we have normalized as facts about other groups or individuals, examples being: Black people are dangerous, Asians eat exotic animals and family pets, and most members of the Latinx community entered America illegally. This is the type of racism where **prejudice**, **implicit bias**, **stereotypes**, and **racial profiling** primarily exist.

  - **Prejudice**: "An assumption or an opinion about someone simply based on that person's membership or connection to a particular group." You can be prejudiced against someone because they come from a different ethnic background, gender, or religion. Besides racism (yes, I know it's a bit confusing, but racism is also a type of prejudice), other types of prejudice that exist are ageism, classism, homophobia, religious prejudice, and sexism.

  - **Implicit (Unconscious) Bias**: "Unconscious thoughts, feelings, beliefs and attitudes towards any social group of people." This is where you unconsciously associate and act in accordance with stereotypes about a particular group of people. A common example of this type of unconscious association is when a non-Black person is by themselves late at night and sees a Black person walking towards them, and they feel like they are potentially in danger.

- **Stereotypes**: "Mistaken or overgeneralized ideas, beliefs or characteristics about a particular group or class of people based on their race, nationality, sexual orientation or religion." Common stereotypes about Black people are that we are all dangerous, we all like to eat watermelon and fried chicken, we're lazy, or we don't have our fathers in our lives.

- **Racial Profiling**: "The discriminatory practice of using race, ethnicity, skin tone, place of origin, religion, or any combination of these to suspect someone of having committed a crime or an offense but using these very same characteristics to omit certain groups from being suspected of having committed a crime or offense." An example of this is the police stopping only Black pedestrians for information about recent illegal activity in a neighborhood, but not stopping any other non-Black pedestrians that are present for questioning.
  - Racial profiling is similar to but different from criminal profiling, with the key difference being that criminal profiling is usually only performed by the police/law enforcement/someone in a position of authority going after a suspect simply because they may 'fit a description.' Anybody, regardless of what they may do for a living, can act out racial profiling towards another group of people, or in this case, Black people.
    - **Important Food for Thought**: There is evidence that supports the notion that the combined use of racial profiling and criminal profiling by law enforcement toward the Black community is one of the many

reasons for the tensions that exist today between the Black community and the police.

Here are two quick stats for you:

- A 2017 study report by the Stanford Open Policing Project found that police officers were more likely to search Black drivers during traffic stops than White drivers, even when they had no evidence of wrongdoing. The Report analyzed data from more than 60 million traffic stops conducted by 31 state patrol agencies and police departments in the United States

- In a 2019 survey conducted by the Pew Research Center, 84% of Black adults reported that in dealing with police, Black people are generally treated less fairly than White people. In contrast, only 63% of White people reported the same perception. Additionally, 87% of Black people and 61% of White people stated that the U.S. criminal justice system treats Black people less fairly
  - What's crazy about this stat is that most White people would agree that Black people get the short end of the stick when it comes to the criminal justice system, yet still, no massive reform. But anyway, I've digressed again, back to the topic at hand.

Whew, I know that was a lot, but we're almost done with the baseline needed. Take your time to read over the definitions and make sure you really understand them and the examples I used. They will be necessary to help define what systemic racism is and how it affects Black people and other marginalized minority groups. Now that we have a baseline on internalized racism let's move on to the other three. I promise that they're not as long as Internalized Racism was.

- **Interpersonal Racism (Belief in Action)**: "acts of racism between one individual and another individual or group. It's when misinformation, prejudice, implicit bias, and stereotypes, or any combination of these are used as the basis to perform an act of discrimination, harassment, hate, exclusion, or violence towards an individual or group." This is the type of racism where microaggression (micro insults, micro assaults, micro invalidations) primarily exists. Examples of this include being a 'racist Karen' or telling someone to go back to their country. To help connect the dots, Interpersonal Racism is Internalized Racism in action. This is because the discriminatory acts performed during Interpersonal Racism are based on the beliefs that exist in Internalized Racism. Interpersonal Racism is Internalized Racism made real; this is because Internalized Racism, when it's internal, is still an idea. Unfortunately, the moment those ideas are used as the rationale to take a particular course of action or say certain things, those ideas become real. If they weren't real, certain things would not have been said or done. A white woman isn't going to clutch her purse in an elevator if she doesn't truly believe there is a real possibility the big Black man standing next to her could try and snatch her purse. It's the same way she likely wouldn't clutch her purse if it was a big White man or an Asian man. The Big Latinx man is 50/50 on getting the same treatment (lol).

- **Institutional Racism (Belief in Power)**: "the unfair policies and discriminatory practices that overtly or subtly reinforce racist or discriminatory standards within institutions such as schools, workplaces, and organizations." The source of institutional racism can be linked to the racial attitudes of one ethnic group's beliefs, opinions, thoughts, and traditions towards another ethnic group. This is the type of racism that is often confused with systemic racism, but there is a big difference that we'll talk about shortly. Examples of this type of racism are policies in the workplace against natural Black hair in the workplace or academic institution, discriminatory hiring practices within an organization, or redlining performed by banks and discriminatory practices performed by other financial institutions that aim to limit Black people's access to homeownership. This is where Internalized Racism meets lawmakers and other people in positions of power and authority. Much like Interpersonal Racism, Institutional Racism is also largely dependent on Internalized Racism. Think about it: the only way unfair policies and discriminatory practices can be accepted with minimal to no consequences is because the people who wrote and are in charge of the policies and the people who are in charge of handling the cases that have to do with discriminatory practices don't see a problem with it. If they truly saw a problem with it, then it wouldn't take continuous prompting from the people who are affected by these unfair policies to occur before these unfair policies are changed. The policymakers themselves either just wouldn't write unfair policies, or, if they didn't write them, they would just take the initiative to change themselves. Obviously, one needs to know that something is unfair before one can change it, and that's exactly why having a diverse team and social circle is so important. It would limit the influence of Internalized Racism and minimize the reach and impact of Institutional Racism

- **Systemic Racism (Everything is Fucked)**: "Racism that is embedded in our institutions, policies, and practices. It is racism that is embedded in the structures of our society." This is the racism that Black people are generally referring to whenever we say racism still exists in America. Another way to think about systemic racism is that it is the cumulation of all the various aspects of internalized racism, interpersonal racism, and institutional racism working together in a way that perpetuates oppression towards Black people and other marginalized minority groups. It is not as simple as 1+1+1+1 = 4. Because of how complex and intricately connected internalized racism, interpersonal racism, and institutionalized racism is, it is more like 1+1+1+1 = 1,000,000,000. What makes systemic racism so harmful to Black people and other marginalized minority groups is that it exists across many of the institutions that exist within our society, collectively working together in a way that upholds racist policies, practices, and standards, which then negatively impact the quality of life of Black people and other marginalized minority groups. The institutions that contribute to systemic racism in America include but are not limited to banking, the criminal justice system, education, government, housing, health care, and law enforcement, to name a few.

To help visualize how the four domains of racism relate to one another, I've included a graphic on the following page.

The Four Domains of Racism

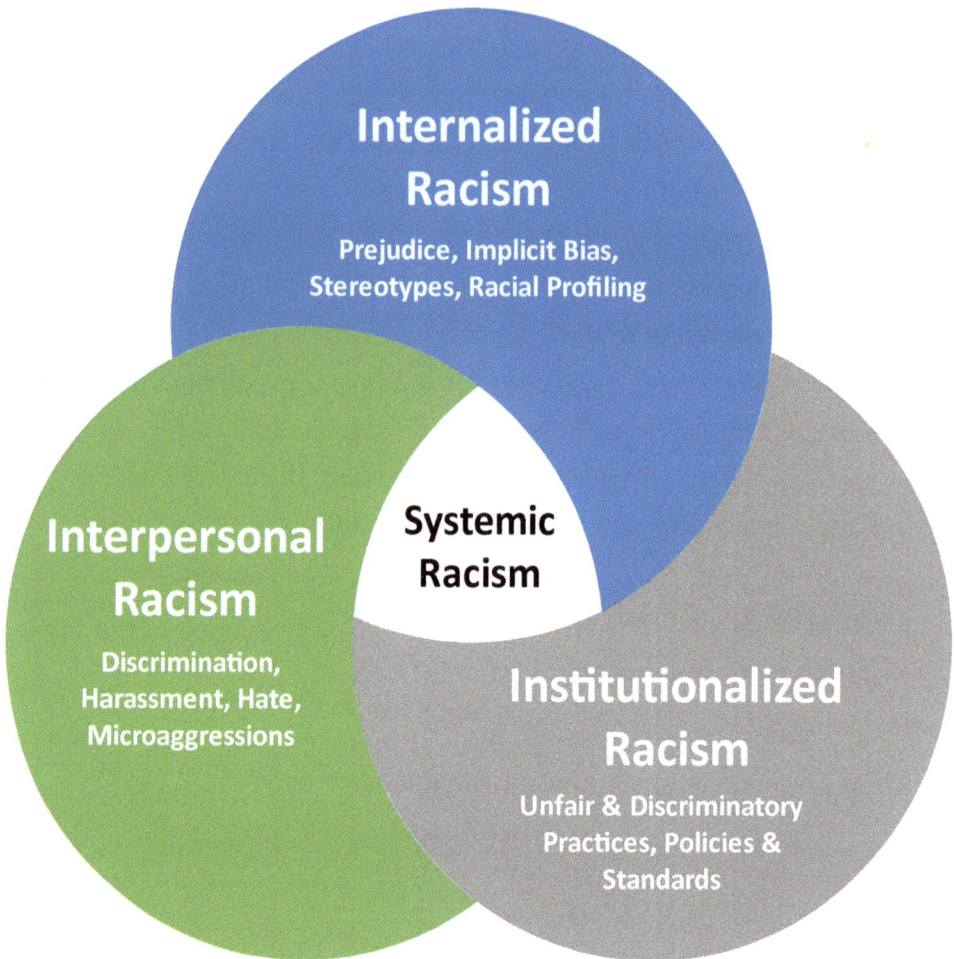

Internalized Racism
Prejudice, Implicit Bias, Stereotypes, Racial Profiling

Interpersonal Racism
Discrimination, Harassment, Hate, Microaggressions

Systemic Racism

Institutionalized Racism
Unfair & Discriminatory Practices, Policies & Standards

The Domino Effect

By this point, I'm sure many of you will be asking, "Well if systemic racism is caused by racist or discriminatory laws, policies, standards, or practices, which ones are they so we can fight against them to have them changed?" Good question; unfortunately, the answer is not that simple. Before I go any further, I want to first state

232

that as of today, in the year 2023, overt systemic racism no longer receives support from the U.S. federal or state government. This means the U.S. Federal government will not **actively** support the efforts of any state government, organization, or individual who attempts to enforce or create rules or laws that would create or maintain a racist or discriminatory social structure between different ethnic groups.

The problem that needs to be addressed is not just any particular set of laws or policies that are racist or discriminatory in nature that need to be changed, but the **legacy of overt systemic racism that still exists in our laws, policies, and practices today**. Although many of the discriminatory laws and policies used to govern our society have been changed, there are still loopholes, exemptions, and exclusions that can still be found in many of our laws and policies. A point that I hope we can all agree on is that in society, it often takes years, if not decades, for amended laws and policies to be fully rewritten and then reflected in how our society operates. Though systemic racism affects Black people and other marginalized minority groups across economic prosperity and advancement opportunities, housing and wealth generation, law enforcement, healthcare, and other functions of our society, for the focus of the scope of this book, I'm only going to focus on how it's affected the economic prosperity and advancement opportunities of Black people. I strongly encourage reading some, if not all, of the brilliant works (I recommend some in the next part of the book) that go into much more detail about how systemic racism affects Black people across all functions of our society.

As I mentioned earlier, to explain how the legacy of systemic racism negatively impacts Black people today, I'm only going to speak to the area of economic opportunity and advancement, but at the end of this chapter, I'm also going to provide some facts and statistics on how systemic racism affects Black people across the functions of housing & wealth generation, law enforcement, as well as healthcare.

Economic Prosperity and Advancement Opportunities

First, let's wind the clock back about 300 years ago to a period during an era of slavery in American history. One thing to remember is that slavery was legal. White people weren't just out there owning Black people for shits and giggles. Slavery was a business, with the number one asset being Black people. Black people were given numbers, traded, and sold like you would any other asset in business because we were seen as 'property.' The laws were fucked, too. If enslaved Black people tried to run away, then **FEDERAL** laws such as the 1793 and 1850 Fugitive Slave Acts helped make sure they were recaptured. Under this law, if enslaved Black people were recaptured, they could be beaten, tortured, mutilated, or killed. Anyone who was found helping slaves escape could also go to jail, not to mention the social criticism they would receive for helping Black people escape. Then, we fast forward a bit to 1863, when slavery was abolished, but this didn't mean that Black people were suddenly free to get any job they wanted or had the ability to live anywhere they wanted. In fact, Federal officials encouraged Black people who were still in the South to enter into labor contracts and do the very same slavery-type work for the very same families who enslaved them! Please go back and reread that sentence. To ensure that this happened, 'Black Codes' were used to force Black people to remain as laborers **by fining them for having any other occupation outside of farming or domestic servitude**. The Jim Crow laws, which were later introduced near the end of the 19th Century, also further limited the types of economic opportunities available to Black people (the whole separate but equal nonsense).

Fast forward to the 1930s or early 20th Century, and the Great Depression has ravaged the American economy. Because of this, the U.S.

introduced the New Deal, which was a Federal law that introduced a number of policies to help struggling families get by and expand access to economic mobility for more people. These policies included but were not limited to providing work for the unemployed, strengthening labor standards for wages and working conditions, and increasing protections for collective bargaining (aka, unions). Though these policies helped many people, their benefits were mainly reserved for White people. Well, to be honest, specifically for White men, while restricting if not completely excluding people of color, and Black people in particular, through exclusions and exemptions written into this law. Now it's 1938, and the New Deal's Fair Labor Standards Act (FSLA) was introduced. It brought us the 40-hour work week (I wish it was a 20-hour work week), helped ban child labor, and established Federal minimum wage and overtime requirements. While the FSLA improved the working conditions of White Workers, people of color, specifically Black people, were once again excluded from having access to these benefits. This is because the FSLA didn't include many domestic, agricultural, and service occupations as beneficiaries of these benefits, the very same occupations Black people were forced into a generation prior to under the 'Black Codes.' By this point, Black people didn't only have to worry about the 'Black Codes,' but they were also dealing with the effects of Jim Crow laws, which caused them to have even fewer if any, real opportunities for upward economic movement. Imagine living in a world where everyone has access to benefits to help them get by, if not ahead, but you. The FSLA would later be amended a few decades later to include the domestic, agricultural, and service occupations originally excluded, but people in these occupations still today remain as some of the least protected employees in the U.S.

That's not all; the National Labor Relations Act (NLRA) of 1935, also commonly known as the Wagner Act, was another law that negatively affected Black people with effects that can still be seen today.

The Wagner Act was a win for the everyday worker because it expanded collective bargaining rights nationwide and gave power to unions. Benefits that union workers were able to enjoy were higher wages, improved benefits, job security, and better working conditions, many of the key things necessary for upward economic mobility. Unfortunately, like the FSLA, the Wagner Act also excluded domestic and agricultural occupations (occupations primarily held by Black people) from its protection. The Wagner Act also didn't prevent union workers from discriminating against workers of color, specifically Black people. Lawmakers eventually banned unions from engaging in racial discrimination, but many domestic and agricultural workers continue to remain excluded from many legal protections until today. It's not just the Wagner Act either; the 1947 Taft-Hartley Act, which was meant to amend some of the restrictions of the 1935 Wagner Act, had clauses that ended up including independent contractors and supervisors to the list of workers excluded from labor law protections. Due to language used in the creation of these Federal laws, language that has still not been changed, most employees today won't be covered by labor law protections if they try and form a union. This means that, in 2023, an employer can legally fire an employee for trying to form a union, go on strike, or protest unfair working conditions. Employers also have the right to completely ignore employees who try to bargain collectively. If you're thinking it is only 'low-level' jobs that are affected by this, then you're wrong. Please read the below.

Based on the language used in the final version of the Wagner Act and the amendments made by the 1947 Taft-Hartley Act, employees who have been excluded from labor law protections include, but not limited to farmworkers, college professors, engineers, babysitters, nannies, housecleaners, home aids, security guards, delivery truck drivers, doctors, nurses, Uber Eats delivery workers, Amazon delivery drivers, Lyft drivers, and Wag dog walkers. The list goes on and on.

Before you assume I'm wrong, think about it: which one of these workers can't be classified as domestic or agricultural workers, independent contractors, or supervisors? If you still think I'm wrong, look it up yourself; though it directly goes against the 1948 Universal Declaration of Human Rights, these exclusions still exist today. It is why so many of the jobs I listed above continue to have problems with low wages, poor healthcare, workplace hazards, unfair treatment, and lots of other pretty messed up working conditions on a massive scale. These were exclusions that primarily affected people of color, specifically Black people when first introduced, but have now expanded to affect a variety of workers across a diversity of ethnicities across multiple industries. The ironic thing about the passing of these laws with the exclusions that were included in them is that it is almost like laying a trap for someone else, only for you to end up falling into the trap yourself, with the only way out of the trap is to admit you actually made the trap and then completely remove the trap.

Play Stupid Games, Win Stupid Prizes

The restrictions on the upward economic advancement opportunities for Black workers and other marginalized minority groups didn't just stop with discriminatory practices, policies, and laws; systems were introduced that enforced them as well. Tipping is a practice I'm sure many of us hate to do, but we've accepted it as a practice we must do if we go to a restaurant, barber, salon, or any other similar type of service provider. When first introduced in America in the mid-1800s, tipping wasn't popular back then either, but what it did enable was a system that allowed restaurants and railway companies to maximize profits by not paying Black employees and other employees of color adequate wages. It wasn't just these two industries either. Many of the jobs Black people were able to have were subject to tipping. Do you see the game being played here? Under the 'Black Codes,' Black people were essentially forced into only being able to have certain types of jobs, and under the FSLA, the jobs that Black people could have weren't protected by minimum wage laws, and their working conditions didn't improve. Under the Wagner Act, Black workers were excluded from many labor law protections and many union benefits, and then, to top it all off, employers of the remaining unprotected jobs that Black people could have could also get out of paying Black employees anything at all by adopting the tipping system. Today, tipping is a common practice across a variety of industries and has its own laundry list of issues (an example of friendly fire) that go outside the intended scope of this book.

Unfortunately, and perhaps intentionally, the Wagner Act and FSLA, which were laws designed to help Americans during times of national financial hardship, ultimately kept poor Black people poor and prevented slightly more stable Black people from the equal opportunity to benefit from the upward economic mobility that non-Black workers were able to experience. These laws caused a wage and benefit disparity based on race, a disparity that has continued until today. Though many of these laws have been amended, the effects of the legacy of these once-discriminatory laws continue to contribute to systemic racism. Today, millions of Black people and other marginalized ethnic groups are still stuck in many of these low-paying jobs that have very little to no benefits, limited job security, and limited upward mobility opportunities.

The Equal Employment Opportunity Commission Comes to The Rescue?

It wasn't all bad, though; efforts were made to try and make things better, but it was a bit like a glass half-full (or empty) situation. In the 1960s, new Federal agencies were created with the mission of holding people and institutions accountable for engaging in discrimination. Federal laws, which were supported by state statutes, were implemented to protect people of color, specifically Black people, from discrimination in the workplace. Unfortunately, not only did lawmakers never fully fund these agencies like the Equal Employment Opportunity Commission (EEOC), but they also provided exemptions that allowed some employers to continue to have discriminatory practices – such as having fewer than 15 employees (sigh, so many loopholes in all the different laws and agencies being created). Though not fully funded, in 1965, the U.S. Equal Employment Opportunity Commission (EEOC) was one such agency created with the mission to enforce Federal laws that make it illegal to discriminate against job applicants or employees based on their race, color, religion, sex, age (40 or older), national origin, or genetic makeup. Protections have since been extended to pregnancy status, transgender status, and sexual orientation. This law applies to all types of work situations like hiring, firing, promotions, harassment, training wages, and benefits. Sadly, even though agencies like the EEOC were created to stop workplace discrimination and promote equal opportunity, exemptions still exist today. Look it up yourself if you don't believe me; the exclusions are stated on the EEOC website. Since its creation in 1965, the EEOC still only applies to most employers with 15 or more employees and 20 employees in age discrimination cases. This means that in 2023, if an employer has less than 15 employees, they are legally able to use discriminatory practices to run their business, though many likely won't because if word gets out, that business will likely very quickly go out of business. To those who wanted an example of racist or discriminatory laws, policies, standards, or practices, here's a blatantly obvious exclusion right here for you. It's not just the EEOC either; most states still have minimum employee requirements for employment discrimination laws to take effect.

The EEOC does what it can to prevent discriminatory practices by employers, but since it doesn't have all the resources it needs, its reach and impact are limited. Research shows while the U.S. population increased from 225 million people to 325 million people between 1980 and 2018, the EEOC budget actually decreased from $412 million to $379 million, while the number of EEOC employees also decreased from 3,390 people to 1,968 people within the same time frame. If you think the budget loss isn't that bad, let's not forget that a lack of adjustment for inflation rates makes this budget loss so much worse. The loss of employees didn't do anything to make the budget bigger, not to mention that fewer people will mean less work can get done. It's not all on the Federal government either; states need to do their part as well to protect workers of color, and some actually have their own anti-discriminatory agencies. Unfortunately, very few states provide their own anti-discriminatory agencies with enough resources to address workplace discrimination, and some states don't even have agencies at all. Though discriminatory hiring practices are now slowly starting to change with the rise of DEI-focused initiatives across industries and businesses of all sizes, studies show that hiring discrimination against Black people has not declined in years.

There is a plethora of topics that can be discussed and other examples that can be pointed to when looking at systemic racism. The fact that loopholes, exclusions, and exemptions are still subtly included in so many of our laws and policies is ridiculous, and that's not even including the harm caused by interpersonal or internalized racism! Let's not forget that systemic racism doesn't only affect Black people and other marginalized minority groups' economic prosperity and advancement opportunities; it affects us across housing and wealth generation, law enforcement, healthcare, and all other functions of our society. If you would like to learn more, **I recommend looking into redlining and all the aftereffects of it as a starting point;** then, as I mentioned at the onset of this section, there are plenty of books and detailed articles that go into so much more detail than I did due to the intended scope of this book.

Some Stats to Help Put Things in Perspective

I'm going to end this chapter on systemic racism and how its legacy continues to affect Black people today with a few statistics across different functions of our society. When reading these statistics, keep in mind that Black people only make up about 13% of the U.S. population. Research shows that:

Housing & Wealth Generation Stats

- Between 1934 and 1962, the Federal Housing Authority (FHA) underwrote $120 billion dollars of home mortgages, and 98% of them went to White families

- In the U.S., White families hold 90% of the national wealth, Latinx families own 2.3% and Black families own 2.6%

- Black people are more likely to be shown fewer houses for sale than White people

- In 2020, the average White worker made 30% more than the average Black worker

- A study from 2015 found that Black people are charged roughly $700 more than White people when buying a car

- Black households have also experienced 25% to 45% lower median incomes than their white counterparts, and these disparities continue regardless of their educational attainment and household structure

- In 2017 alone, the median income for Black and Latinx households was $40,258 compared with $68,145 for White households

    o In 2018, the average household income for Black Americans was $41,361, while it was $70,642 for White Americans

Healthcare Related Stats

- In 2018, only 8.7% of Black people received mental health services compared to 18.6% of non-Latinx White People

- In 2017, 10.6% of Black people had no insurance, compared to 5.9% of non-Latinx White people

- A 2007 – 2016 study by the CDC found that African American women are 3x more likely to die of pregnancy-related issues than White women

- A 2020 report by the CDC based on a study conducted from 1995 – 2018 found that
  - Black Americans have 2.3x the infant mortality rate compared to non-Latinx Whites
  - Black infants are 4x more likely to die from complications related to low birthrate as compared to non-Latinx Whites
  - In 2018, Black mothers were twice as likely to receive late or no prenatal care as compared to non-Latinx mothers

- Black people are more likely to die from cancer and heart disease than White Americans

- Across many chronic illnesses, Black people are more likely to die compared to any other racial and ethnic groups

- Due to residential segregation, due in part to redlining, majority Black and Latinx neighborhoods are more likely to lack hospitals and other health care providers

- A 2016 study found that many White medical students wrongly believe Black people have a higher pain tolerance than White people. Of all the participants who were in this study, 73% held at least one untrue belief about the biological differences between races

- Black people died at 3x the rate of White people from Covid. This is because the Black community has a higher rate of underlying health conditions, higher density in poor neighborhoods, more employed as frontline workers, and poorer access to testing and healthcare

Incarceration Related Stats
- In 2015, although Black and Latinx people only make up about 32% of the US population, they made up 56% of all incarcerated people

- On average, Black people get 20% longer sentences in Federal Prison for committing the same crime than White people

- Black people are incarcerated at more than 5x the rate of White People

- Black women are incarcerated at 3x the rate of White women

- Black youth are committed to juvenile facilities at 4x the rate of White youth

- Black men are wrongfully convicted of murder at 7x the rate of White men

- Black people are wrongfully convicted of sexual assault at 3.5X the rate of White people

- Even though Black people and White people use drugs at the same rate, Black people are still incarcerated at 12x the rate of White people for drug crimes and are 6x more likely to go to jail than White people for drug possession

- A study from 2013 shows that though Marijuana use is equal between Black people and White people, Black people are 4x more likely to be arrested for Marijuana usage

Interaction With Law Enforcement Stats

- A Stanford University study analyzed more than 100,000,000 traffic stops across America and found Black drivers are 20% more likely to be pulled over and searched

- In NYC, 88% of police stops in 2018 involved Black and Latinx drivers, and only 10% were White drivers. Of the 88% of Black & Latinx drivers who were stopped, 70% were completely innocent

- Multiple studies show that Black drivers are 2x more likely to get pulled over than White drivers

- Black people experience the use of force, including tasers, dogs, pepper spray, and physical force, during arrest at 3x the rate of White people

Job Opportunity Stats

- White applicants are far more likely to be offered interviews than Black and Latinx applicants, regardless of educational attainment, gender, or labor conditions.

- One U.S. study found that White applicants with traditionally White-sounding names received 50% more callbacks than Black applicants with traditionally Black-sounding names

- Surveys show that more than half of African Americans, 1 in 3 Native Americans, 1 in 4 Asian Americans, and more than 1 in 5 Latinx members report experiencing racial discrimination in hiring, compensation, and promotion considerations

Is Reverse Racism Really a Myth?

"I love potentially debunking myths, but this is one myth that can't ever be debunked"

- Tunde

Author's Note: If you haven't read the chapter on Systemic Racism, please go back and do so. If you don't, many of the points I'm going to talk about in this chapter may either be missed or misunderstood.

"Why isn't there a White History Month?"

"Affirmative Action is reverse racism"

"Why aren't there White-only scholarships?"

"White Lives Matter Too"

"Why can every BIPOC create a group for themselves, but we can't?"

These are some of the questions and comments I have heard being used to support the argument that reverse racism is real. It's an interesting thought, and looking at it from the perspective of the people using these arguments, I kind of get it. When you're living in a world where different groups of people are being given benefits that you don't qualify for because of your ethnic identity or, more explicitly stated, because you're not Black, it can feel like discrimination.

Here's a fun fact for you: a 2016 Public Religion Research Institute poll indicates that half of all Americans, 57% of all White people, and 66% of the White working-class believe that discrimination against White people is as big of a problem in America as discrimination against Black people. These numbers were a bit shocking to me, and while I was trying to make sense of why the numbers were so high, I realized there is probably a large misunderstanding between what racial discrimination, and what racism, in the truest sense of the word as it relates to systemic racism, really is. So, let's set the record straight. As I previously defined in the last chapter, racial discrimination fits under interpersonal racism:

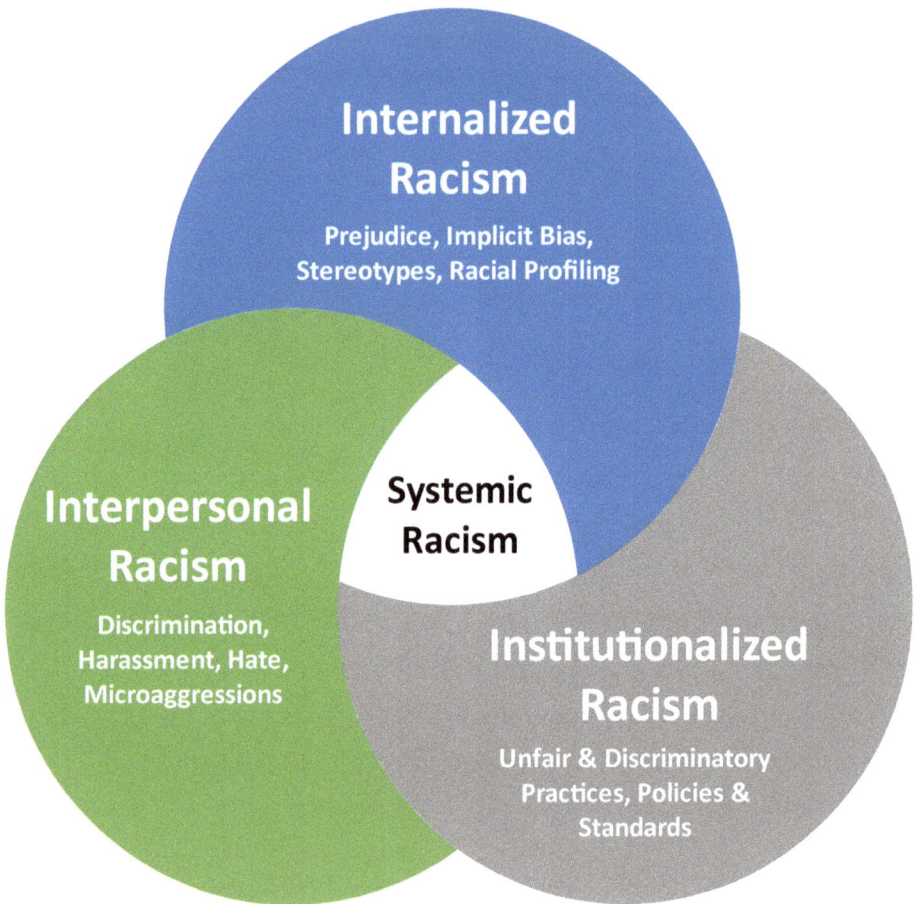

I've realized when people try to use the reverse racism card, it's often because they have felt slighted by a comment or action sent their way (aspects of internalized and interpersonal racism), feel excluded from events, discussions, or spaces (perceived perception of experiencing institutionalized racism), or they believe they lost some type of benefit that should have been theirs (perceived perception of experiencing institutionalized racism if not outright systemic racism).

Prejudice, harassment, stereotypes, and hate are probably some of the few things in the world that everyone, regardless of how much money someone may have, what the color of their skin is, or how educated they are, can and will likely experience at some point in their life. Internalized racism and interpersonal racism play no favorites. So yes, racial prejudice against White people can and does exist. Comments like: "White people don't season their food," "White people have no culture," "Asian women shouldn't be allowed to drive because they can't see well," "Asian people eat family pets and exotic animals," "Latinx people are illegal," and "Latinx people are lazy, uneducated and have lots of babies" are examples of racial Prejudice against non-Black people; but are they examples of systemic racism? No, but it's usually these types of interactions that people who try to use the reverse racism argument are referring to whenever they try and claim that reverse racism is real.

Racism, at its core, is not about a person feeling superiority towards another person and then discriminating against them; that's just racial prejudice. **Racism, at its core, is about a lack of equal access to power, privilege, and opportunities for groups of people who aren't the dominant group**. In America's case, and really most of the world, the dominant group of people is White people. If a White person experiences racial prejudice, yes, it can be hurtful, but it's not going to stop them from getting whatever jobs they are qualified to get, getting a promotion they deserve, having equal pay for equal work, having access to quality health care, having access to affordable housing, being approved for a bank loan, and if they're qualified, being accepted into the university of their choice and every other way in which systemic racism affects people in America who aren't White. **For reverse racism to truly exist, it would mean that the playing field is completely even for everybody. It would mean we have reached a point in society where everybody, irrespective of what racial group they belong to, has equal access to power, privilege, and opportunities.** I don't think it should come as a surprise to anybody when I say that we haven't reached this point in society yet; there is still a lot of healing and forgiveness in the world that needs to occur and work that still needs to happen before we can even hope for this to be our everyday reality not just across America, but across the world.

BuT wHaT aBoUt AfFiRmAtIvE aCtIoN?

Here is another statistic for you: A 2005 Gallup Poll found that if there was a scenario where there were two equally qualified applicants, one Black, one White, White people were more likely to believe the Black candidate would have a higher chance of getting into a given school than a White candidate. A different study by Harvard Business School found that "White people, not Black people, see racism as a zero-sum game that they are now losing." Essentially, White people, according to this study, believe the more often Black people and other marginalized minority groups are able to gain access to power, privilege, and opportunities than White people have always historically had, the less power, privilege, and opportunities White people will have. So, it would make sense why White people would think that an equally qualified Black candidate would have a better chance of getting into a given school than a White candidate.

As an example, it is this perception of racism being a zero-sum game that the argument of affirmative action being reverse racism is often rooted in. Critics of affirmative action try to argue that colleges, universities, and places of employment have these programs to favor one group of people over another simply based on their race and not their intelligence or qualifications. The reality is that affirmative action policies and programs are only trying to repair decades, if not centuries, of institutional racism by providing more opportunities to groups who have been historically underrepresented, oppressed, and excluded from spaces like colleges, universities, and places of employment. They are an attempt to try and provide equal access to these spaces to not just Black people and other marginalized minority groups but women as well! **Ironically enough, if you look at the numbers, White women have historically been the biggest beneficiaries of affirmative action**. It really is unfortunate that some people believe these programs are taking away their potential opportunities or 'spots' and are being given to people who don't truly deserve them simply because they 'check a box.' What's funny is that this very idea that something is being 'taken away' and being given to someone less deserving is not only an example of White privilege acting up, which is a whole separate conversation but proof that White people, at least the ones who try to use the argument of reverse racism, subconsciously know that they have always benefitted from a system created for their success. Nothing 'belongs' to anybody, not a college admission spot, not a scholarship, not a job, not a part in a movie/role/film, not a seat on an airplane, not a seat at a restaurant, nothing. The only thing that 'belongs' to anybody is what they have worked for and the accolades they have accumulated for themselves; after that, nothing is guaranteed, not even your life. After all, even tomorrow isn't promised.

Affirmative Action Myth-Busting

Myth #1: Affirmative action gives positions to undeserving and unqualified Black people and other marginalized minority groups simply because they 'check a box.'

Fact: Affirmative action does not mean that undeserving or unqualified people will be given a position or spot simply because they check a box. By law, this is actually illegal to do. Besides, no one is going to give a position or spot to someone when they are not qualified for that position or spot. If I'm a businessperson, that's setting my business up to fail because it means I am hiring employees who can't do the job they have been hired to do simply because they 'check a box.' If I'm a university, that's setting my admitted students up to fail because they may be academically challenged in ways where they may not be able to keep up with simply because they 'check a box.' No, the best-fit candidate is getting the job, and the most well-rounded students are getting admitted.

Myth #2: Affirmative action forces universities and employers to set quotas for the number of Black people, women, and members of other marginalized minority groups to whom they have to give positions or spots.

Fact: Affirmative action quotas are illegal. Goals are set up to ensure representation for people across all walks of life in places where they have historically been underrepresented. Some universities or employers may time-box goals just to ensure they are meeting the goals they have set for themselves, but actual quotas are illegal.

Myth #3: Affirmative action is no longer needed. Today, anyone can get any job or position they apply for as long as they're qualified (sigh, micro invalidations are everywhere).

Fact: Institutional racism still exists in today's society. A 2015 analysis from FiveThirtyEight found that colleges in states with affirmative-action bans are less representative of the state's demographics that have affirmative-action programs. Research shows that Black people are still unemployed at twice the rate of White people, the average household income for Black families and other marginalized minority groups is still less than that of White families, and women still earn about 70 cents for every $1 a man earns.

Authors 2023 Update: As of June 29, 2023, affirmative action has been repealed.

Food For Thought

Reverse racism is not real, but racial prejudice, irrespective of race, is. When people try to use reverse racism as an argument, it comes off as a very weak and shoddy attempt to minimize the conversations surrounding racism, specifically systemic racism. It's like the person is trying to say, "Black people and other marginalized minority groups don't have it that bad; it's bad for all of us." I agree in the sense that everyone, regardless of their race, is struggling with some type of difficulty, challenge, or unfavorable situation, but it still doesn't mean that systemic racism affects White people the way it does Black people and other marginalized minority groups because it just doesn't.

Last note →: I'm personally not a huge fan of math problems, but I did find this cool formula on a blog written by 'The Anti-Racist Educator' that summarizes this whole chapter in a nice way, and I wanted to share it with you all. I made a few adjustments, but the essence is the same.

Systemic Racism = Power + Prejudice

Racial Prejudice = Prejudice – Power

What's Up with Black Lives Matter (BLM)?

"Say it with me -> Black. Lives. Matter"

- Tunde

Ahh, Black Lives Matter, the simple but true slogan that invokes a variety of emotions and reactions from people depending on who is saying it and who it's being said to. Some people agree and support the movement behind the slogan, while others see the slogan as somehow being racist and exclusionary. Regardless of which side of the argument one may be on, the Black Lives Matter slogan has evolved from a simple three-word slogan to the spark behind much-increased conversations around race in America.

The Origin Story

The 'Black Lives Matter' slogan was created in 2013 after the acquittal of Trayvon Martin's murderer, George Zimmerman. Just to provide some context, Trayvon Martin was an unarmed 17-year-old Black teen who was shot and killed by George Zimmerman, a neighborhood watch volunteer back in 2012. There was much controversy surrounding the court's decision to acquit Zimmerman, especially because the decision followed the pattern of Black people often not receiving due justice in the court of law when it came to unlawful killings. The slogan, which has now grown into a movement, has continued to gain national attention due to the repeated incidents of Black people being unlawfully killed by the police. I gave a very short list of lives unfortunately lost due to police brutality in the 'Black Twitter' chapter. The Black Lives Matter movement eventually reached new heights of national attention and support after the murder of George Floyd in 2020. In case you didn't know why there was so much more outrage than usual, George Floyd died after a police officer knelt on his neck, though he was already restrained for 9 minutes and 23 seconds. Imagine an adult male laying on top of you for even a minute, much less 5 minutes, not to mention a knee to the neck for over 9 minutes. It was also the same day the Central Park Karen (we talked about her in the 'Karen' chapter) called the police on Christian Cooper, a Black birdwatcher who asked her to put a leash on her dog in a designated area where there were signs posted stating that dogs must be leashed at all times. During the incident, not only does the Central Park Karen tell Christian she's going to call the police and tell them there's an African American man threatening her life, but she also actually goes and does it! The threat of the Central Park Karen to use the police against Christian Cooper, coupled with the death of George Floyd by the police on the same day, sparked national outrage. The number of people who participated in the protests that ensued soon after reached historic numbers.

Black Lives Matter: The Movement vs. The Organization

Many people don't know this, but **there is actually a difference between Black Lives Matter, the movement, and Black Lives Matter, the organization**. I bet that surprised some of you, huh? It surprised me, too, when I first found out that the two weren't one and the same.

The Black Lives Matter Movement is more than just a phrase, hashtag, t-shirt, flag, or trend; it's much bigger than that. At its core, the Black Lives Matter movement is a non-violent international social movement, a call to attention, or a rallying cry, if you will, against police brutality and systemic racism. The slogan, which now represents the movement, gained national momentum after the murder of George Floyd. A report from Kivvit shows that #BlackLivesMatter was tweeted or retweeted 39.2 million times but was shared more than 100 million times the month after the murder of George Floyd. Since then, the Black Lives Matter slogan has grown to be representative of all anti-racist, anti-discriminatory, and pro-Black efforts across all organizations across America and, by extension, the world. The movement has been a rallying cry for non-violent protests around the world, has helped influence positive policy changes, and has helped educate people on the racial injustices that Black people face in America and around the world. The Black Lives Matter movement has even been referred to as the largest social movement in U.S. history.

One **VERY IMPORTANT** thing to know about the Black Lives Matter movement is this: **the Black Lives Matter slogan is not saying, nor is it trying to insinuate, that all lives don't matter**; it is not saying that Black lives are more important than the lives of any other ethnic group, it is not even asking society to put Black lives on a pedestal and give us special treatment. It is simply a call to attention to the racial injustices that Black people consistently face in America, especially at the hands of law enforcement and a call to action for change. It is not a demand but a petition (remember, it's a non-violent movement) to treat our lives with the same level of respect as all other ethnic groups. Contrary to what some media outlets have said, the main mission of the Black Lives Matter movement is nothing radical. At its core, the movement simply aims to change the structures in society that perpetuate these racial injustices that stem from systemic racism and make things more equal, equitable, and fair for all, not just specifically Black people.

The ripple effect of the movement has been amazing. Race is now talked about more in places where it wasn't talked about before. People who weren't aware of how bad things were for Black people and other marginalized minority groups due to systemic racism are now becoming aware. Diversity, Equity, and Inclusion (DEI) overall has seen a growth in interest and in the implementation of policies by large organizations across industries. The movement has helped make race and DEI related topics the center of many conversations and more okay to talk about publicly. Thankfully, these conversations have led to actions and changes that have helped move the efforts of 'equality for all' forward.

What causes much confusion and makes people think the Black Lives Matter movement and Black Lives Matter organization are one and the same is because the person who helped create the slogan #BlackLivesMatter, is also one of the co-founders of the Black Lives Matter organization. Though the creation of the Black Lives Matter slogan and the co-founder of the organization has roots in the same individual, the movement, which uses the slogan "Black Lives Matter," is much bigger than and goes beyond the organization itself.

The Black Lives Matter organization, also known as the Black Lives Matter Network, was also started in 2013 (again, separate from the movement). The Black Lives Matter Network, which would later change its name in 2017 to the Black Lives Matter Global Network, is now a multichapter organization that has helped change the way race is now talked about in America. The organization's mission is to "eradicate White supremacy and build local power to intervene in violence inflicted on Black communities." The organization aims to help create a world where "Black lives are no longer systematically targeted for demise." All in all, the organization was built with all the right intentions. Unfortunately, as the organization has grown and changed in how it operates (from a decentralized to a centralized network), it has been plagued with a myriad of controversies and alleged internal challenges and conflicts. From questions about some of the founders' beliefs in Marxism to questions about where donation money to the organization has gone as local frontline grassroots efforts and chapters remain underfunded to questions around the true agenda of campaigns like 'Defund the Police' (which I still think should have been called 'Reform the Police' as that is ultimately what the point is). Unfortunately, the Black Lives Matter organization is currently no longer as popular as it used to be. Though the support and popularity of the Black Lives Matter Global Network will likely continue to fluctuate, the positive impact on communities and changes to discriminatory policies that the collaboration between the movement and organization have caused has been incredible. Hopefully, as things continue to progress, there will be better alignment and reconciliation between the movement and the organization. The good work still needs to continue and scale. It will take everyone working hand in hand in the same direction for the more equitable world that the movement and organization is trying to create to become a reality.

Blue Lives Matter, Thin Blue Line, All Lives Matter, and Everything In-Between

In regard to the Thin Blue Line, I'm empathetic that its original usage has been conflated with the agenda of White supremacists, racists, and their agenda. The original intent behind this slogan and imagery was to stand in solidarity with professionals like police officers and the like, who have dangerous and often difficult professions, and intended to act as a solemn tribute to stand behind and with the friends and family of fallen police officers in the line of duty. That, at least, was the original intended purpose of the Thin Blue Line. I personally also stand in solidarity with people with potentially fatal professions, and my deepest condolences and gratitude to the friends and family members of those who served and were killed in the line of duty. I know that it's not us as Black people against the police; if anything, it's us against systemic racism. Reforms in general to law enforcement just so happen to be one of the many actions that need to happen. Many police officers are kind and do their job with integrity, and that's not even considering that some police officers are Black. Unfortunately, as the age-old saying goes, a few bad apples are ruining the barrel, or is it a batch?

Although the original intent behind this slogan and imagery was well intended, its use in reality and practice has not been. It's unfortunate, but White supremacists and racists have often taken this well-intended slogan and imagery for their own selfish purposes. The 'Blue Lives Matter' slogan and the 'Thin Blue Line' imagery have often been used by White supremacists and some police officers in response to 'Black Lives Matter.' The main argument for this slogan and imagery against 'Black Lives Matter' is because, apparently, there has been an increase in police ambush and killings since the 'Black Lives Matter' movement started picking up. This argument is a false perception created due to isolated incidents that were focused on by the media. A study conducted by Michael White on the ambush killings of police officers from 1970 – 2018 showed that even with recent spikes, **ambush killings of police officers have actually declined more than 90 percent since 1970**. Until there can be a separation of the 'Blue Lives Matter' slogan and the 'Thin Blue Line' imagery from White supremacists, racists, and their agenda, this slogan and imagery will likely continue to be considered equivalents of the Confederate flag and will continue to be elements that represent progress against systemic racism and the whole point of the 'Black Lives Matter' movement. To those who want to argue the points I have made, please feel free to, but once you're done making your points, let's all agree to call a duck a duck. White supremacists and other racist individuals have indeed corrupted the intended use of the 'Blue Lives Matter' and 'Thin Blue Line' imagery and slogan. It's unfortunate but that's were we're currently at with things.

Lastly, I want to address the 'All Lives Matter' slogan that was created as a response to 'Black Lives Matter.' Telling someone "All Lives Matter" in response to them saying "Black Lives Matter" is a microaggression, a micro invalidation to be precise. It shows an obvious lack of understanding of the whole point of the Black Lives Matter movement. To those who may not know, the use of the 'All Lives

Matter' slogan is often used as a way to attack Black people and to blatantly dismiss the racial injustices that the 'Black Lives Matter' slogan is trying to call attention to. As this point always seems to somehow be misconstrued by some media outlets, I want to repeat what I've said earlier. **When we, as Black people, use the slogan "Black Lives Matter," we know that all lives matter; we agree that all lives matter; we're not even trying to argue or insinuate that all lives shouldn't matter; we're just simply asking for our lives not to matter less than others.**

What Is Juneteenth & How Do I Celebrate It?

"Juneteenth was one of the most confusing holidays of 2021"

- Tunde

Juneteenth, short for June 19th, was a seemingly random and 'new' holiday introduced by Congress in 2021, which threw pretty much everyone for a loop.

While Federal holidays are always a welcomed free day off from work, its introduction as the now 11th holiday recognized by the Federal government still left many of us, myself included, scratching our heads as to what Juneteenth really was, what the point of it was, and how to celebrate it. I mean, I had non-Black friends asking me if they should even be going around telling people "Happy Juneteenth," and I thought it was a fair question. To be honest, I didn't have the answers myself and it wasn't until recently I was finally able to make sense of this 'new' holiday.

A Little History Lesson

Allow me to explain. The American Civil War ended on April 9th, 1865, and on June 19th, 1865, Federal troops arrived in Galveston, Texas, and took control of the state to announce and ensure that all the people who were still enslaved were officially free. I will get to why this June date was so significant in just a little bit. The Emancipation Proclamation, which established that people who were slaves in Confederate-controlled states were supposed to be 'forever free,' wasn't being adhered to, so slavery in Texas and most other Confederate-controlled states continued. It's crazy because the Emancipation Proclamation had already been issued by Abraham Lincoln TWO years prior on January 1, 1863. This is why June 19th, 1865, is so significant, as 'slaves' were free by law and didn't even know it! Northern troops had to march into the South just to make sure the Emancipation Proclamation was enforced. It makes sense because the South never really wanted slavery to end in the first place...Imagine all that 'free' labor they were getting. Now, because of how far away Texas is from the North, it had a very low presence of northern (union) troops. Due to this, Texas was able to act as a safe haven for slavery and all Southerners who supported slavery during the Civil War. The Federal troops taking control of Texas on June 19th, 1865, signaled freedom for 250,000+ slaves. Then, in December of 1865, slavery was officially abolished in America with the ratification of the 13th Amendment by Congress, even though Abraham Lincoln had already issued the Emancipation Proclamation back in January of 1863.

Jumping forward a couple of months, it's now June 19th, 1866; the ex-slaves who were now Freeman came together and organized the first of what would become an annual celebration of the end of slavery. As some of these Freemans started to migrate from Texas to other states, the Juneteenth tradition was able to spread. Ironically, in 1979, Texas became the first state to make Juneteenth an official holiday. Several other states, but not all, followed suit and also made it an official holiday. This all eventually led up to Joe Biden signing the holiday into law on June 17th, 2021. In case you were wondering why I kept putting these quotation marks "around the word new when I first started talking about Juneteenth - it's because it's not exactly a new holiday. Juneteenth is new to most of America, but it's old to some.

Why Celebrating Juneteenth is Important

Juneteenth, short for June 19th, commemorates the day in 1865 when Union General Gordon Granger arrived in Galveston, Texas, and announced that all slaves in Texas were free. It's not the official ending of Slavery, though, as that didn't occur until Dec 18th, 1865, when the

13th Amendment was adopted, but Juneteenth was a signal of changing times to come. Anyway, here are some key reasons why celebrating Juneteenth is important:

1. **Emancipation and Freedom:** Juneteenth commemorates the emancipation of enslaved African Americans in America. This marked a crucial moment in American history. It signaled the end of slavery and the beginning of freedom for millions of Americans.

2. **Cultural Celebration:** Juneteenth is a celebration of African American culture and heritage. It provides an opportunity for communities to come together to honor the history, traditions, and contributions to American society.

3. **Educational Awareness:** Celebrating Juneteenth helps raise awareness and educate people about the history of slavery, the struggles faced by African Americans, and the ongoing fight for civil rights. It encourages dialogue about the complex and sometimes painful aspects of American History

4. **Unity and Community Building:** Juneteenth helps foster a sense of unity and community among African Americans, Black people, and allies (please go read the chapter ' Do I Say Black, African American, or POC' if you're confused by why I just did that). It is a time for reflection, remembrance, and a shared commitment to freedom, justice, and equality. Celebrations are often a great way to promote dialogue and understanding between communities

5. **Official Recognition:** The growing recognition of Juneteenth as a significant day in American history has led to increased efforts to make it an official holiday at the state and national levels. Remember, Juneteenth is a Federal holiday. U.S. States have the right not to recognize federal holidays as state holidays. On the

other hand, while Juneteenth is a Federal holiday, it is not a National holiday. Think about it this way: All federal holidays are National holidays, but not all National holidays are Federal holidays. If you're not asking, "Well, what is the difference?" it's recognition.

But What About Black History Month?

I've been told that part of people's confusion with Juneteenth is the existence of the previously existing Black History Month, and honestly, I get it. So, as you have done many times before this, allow me to explain:

Black History Month: Black History Month (BHM) is a period of time (the month of February) dedicated to recognizing and honoring the achievements, contributions, and history of African Americans. It provides an opportunity to educate people about the important roles that African Americans have played in shaping America's history, culture, and society. BHM covers a wide range of historical events, figures, and achievements related to African Americans. It's a time to celebrate African American achievements and accomplishments in various fields such as politics, science, arts, sports, etc.,

Juneteenth: Juneteenth is a celebration of the end of slavery in America. It is even often referred to (within the Black community anyway) as America's second Independence Day. It highlights the emancipation of enslaved African Americans and is focused on the ongoing struggle for freedom and equality

BHM is a celebration and recognition of a broad range of topics, while Juneteenth is a celebration of a major historical turning point in American history. Both are observances that are important for promoting awareness, understanding, and appreciation of African

American history and culture. So, I hope that cleared up the differences between the two. And just so we're clear, Black History Month is celebrated for the whole month of February, while Juneteenth is Celebrated on June 19th. One is a month, while the other is a day. Not that I'm questioning anyone's intelligence; I just want to be as clear as possible.

So, Exactly How Should I Celebrate Juneteenth?

This is a great question! Well, a century and a half later, Juneteenth celebrations can look quite different depending on which part of America you're in. In some places, Juneteenth celebrations are a day long, a weeklong, and in some areas, even a month long. Juneteenth is sometimes referred to as "Emancipation Day," "Freedom Day," or "Juneteenth Independence Day." Aside from the reflecting and planning for the future that is done, Juneteenth celebrations are a time for rejoicing. Celebrations often include music, food, barbecues, picnics, guest speakers, prayer and church services, family gatherings, parades, games, and a whole bunch of other activities. Sounds a lot like the 4th of July, doesn't it?

Celebrating Juneteenth is easy, and here are a few things to note that I've put together for you.

- **What to Say**: Yes, you can go around telling people, "Happy Juneteenth." In fact, depending on where in America you are, you can even say Happy "Emancipation Day," "Freedom Day," or even "Happy Juneteenth Independence Day." It just depends on what part of the country you're in and what is considered appropriate. If you're still confused, look it up or ask someone you feel comfortable asking.

- **How to Celebrate**: Celebrate the same way you would as with any other Federal holiday. Throw a BBQ or a picnic and have red-colored food and drinks, have friends over, go to a church service, go to the museum, or let off fireworks. Celebrate however you would normally celebrate a Federal holiday; it's totally up to you. Choosing to celebrate with Black people or not is totally up to you.

- **How to Reflect**: Don't just spend all day celebrating. Juneteenth is a day where we can look back at how far we have come as a nation and plan for what's next to come. There is still much work to be done before we can honestly say that, as a nation, we have fully stepped out of the shadow of systemic racism and addressed all the damage it's done and continues to do to all communities, not only the Black community. So, don't forget to reflect.

- **How to Join In**: Celebrations will be different city by city. Some will have parades; others will have whole block parties. Go ahead and join in the festivities. Wave the Juneteenth flag around, it too is red, white, and blue. Juneteenth was a win for all Americans, not just African Americans.

What Should I Do If I Get Invited to A "Black" BBQ?

"Ayyyyyyeee, look at you, getting an invite to the cookout"

- Tunde

If you get invited to a Black BBQ, and you don't know what to do or expect, then your best bet will be to ask the Black person who invited you for some clarity. All Black people are different; therefore, all Black BBQs will be different. Some customs and traditions that some families may have may not be the same customs and traditions that other families will have. The worst thing you can do is assume, especially when you have someone you can ask. If you're close enough to a Black person to get invited to a BBQ/Cookout, then you should be comfortable enough to ask what you should do or prepare before you show up to the BBQ and what you should expect while you're at the BBQ/Cookout.

If the above still isn't enough, Michael Harriot wrote a part factual, part humorous piece titled *The Caucasian's Guide to Black Barbecues*. I thought it was funny, and some of the things he outlines were pretty insightful, so, I've included a summary for you below with my own voiceover and additions. Michael's piece is mainly satire, so if you decide to look up and read the original article, please do not take it literally.

How To Prepare & Things to Know When Going to A Black BBQ/Cookout

1. **Bring Something to The BBQ**: This can be optional. Ask your friend who invited you to make sure. Black BBQs are often a group effort. Aside from the venue and all the things the host will have prepared, everyone usually brings something to support the event. The things you can bring might range anywhere from snacks, to food, to desserts, to drinks (preferably adult drinks 😊)

to literally anything else. My next point is partially a joke and partially true: if you're going to bring potato salad to the BBQ, PLEASE make sure you DON'T add raisins to it. Thank you.

2. **Park a Little Bit Down the Street from the BBQ**: Because Black BBQs can be an all-day event, plus you don't want to potentially be blocking someone in who may need to go run and get something for the BBQ (more food, drinks, ice, etc.) and you also don't want to be blocked in by someone else when you decide you want to leave.

3. **You're Going to Primarily Be Outside:** Black BBQs are also known as a cookout, and that's partially because they're usually outside. Cook-OUT, get it? We are outside cooking. Since you will primarily be outside, make sure you have all the things you may need to be outside all day, such as sunscreen, bug spray, etc.

4. **It's Okay If You Show Up a Bit Late:** The event is likely to start up to an hour late. While it is a stereotype that Black people are always late, also known as 'CP' time, aka colored people time, (if you're not Black, you can call it Black people time); it is also host-specific. Personally, if I tell you my BBQ starts at 1 pm, it WILL start at 1 pm. In the same vein, there may be some hosts who will say that their BBQ will start at 1 pm and they will still be setting up at 3 pm. Different folks, different strokes.

5. **Have At Least One 'Black' Dance That You Know How to Do Really Well:** One thing that is definitely going to happen at a Black BBQ will be people dancing, and sometimes, there may even be some sort of dance battle. I'm not kidding; the last BBQ I went to, I somehow ended up in one, and my friend's mom has video proof I was ripping the dance floor up! Believe me, if you get put on the spot, you're going to want a couple of moves that you're really good at that you can pull out.

6. **Try To Make Friends:** The easiest way to make friends at a Black BBQ is to not try too hard, be yourself, and bring adult beverages. Beer is hit or miss, but dark liquor like Hennessy or Crown Royal Apple or light liquor like Casamigos or, preferably, Clase Azul is sure to always be a hit. Trust me, it will instantly win you a couple of brownie points from everyone at the cookout. (I'm personally cool with Truly's and such, but trust me, if you decide you want to bring adult drinks and for sure want to get brownie points, bring a bottle and/or handle of one of the drinks I listed above. Truly's, White Claws, and Wine to a Black BBQ may or may not cut it).

7. **Spades & Dominoes Are Not Just Games:** The two games you're likely going to see being played at a Black BBQ are Spades and Dominoes. While these can be really fun games, I recommend not playing them during a Black BBQ unless you're REALLY good. These games can get extremely competitive and very intense. It's pretty common and honestly expected for there to be some level of trash-talking, yelling, and cursing each other out to happen. Just sit back and watch. I still don't really know how to play either game (I promise I will learn), so I usually sit them out and just enjoy the festivities.

8. **Aluminum Foil Is Your Friend:** It's okay to take food home; in fact, it's encouraged at the end of the BBQ. There is going to be some at the BBQ, so don't worry about bringing any. It will definitely come in handy when you're leaving and need something to cover your to-go plate with.

9. **Respect the Culture:** Show up open-minded, be respectful, ask your friend who invited you any of the questions you may have before you get there, as they may or may not give you a rundown beforehand anyway, and have fun. Like with any social gathering, everyone who is there is there to have fun and have a good time.

In Conclusion

Show up, have fun, and be respectful. Lastly, the things I mentioned in this chapter may or may not apply if you get invited to a dinner. Wine would probably be the safest bet for a dinner, but everyone is different, and everyone's dinners are different. Plus, who's to say one can't take shots during and/or after dinner? :D (If you drink, that is). Anyway, if you have any further questions, don't make such a big deal of things and just ask whoever invited you. It's chill.

How Can I Be an Ally to Black People & Other Marginalized Groups?

"Being an ally is all about actions, not just words"

- Tunde

Ally: Any person who supports, empowers, advocates for, and stands with individuals and groups other than their own.

Allyship: An informed, empathetic, and **consistent** effort to uphold a culture of Diversity, Equity, and Inclusion for all.

Supporting social movements and social causes shouldn't be a trend that someone does when it's 'cool' to do. It shouldn't be something someone does because they were bored at home all day in lockdown because of a global pandemic, and there was nothing else to do. It shouldn't be something that someone does for social media likes, follows, or attention. It should be something that comes from the heart. With the core of any action or commitment made when deciding to be an ally, there are a variety of ways one can be an ally to Black people and other marginalized groups. When you decide to be an ally, you're going to be learning a lot, so it's okay if you're uncomfortable at first; lean into the discomfort and stay with it. Get comfortable being uncomfortable because if you're able to stay committed, the discomfort will eventually go away. Most of all, the best way to be an ally is not to say you're an ally or wear a t-shirt that says you're an ally but to prove it with your actions. Believe me, when someone is an invested ally for a cause or movement, the people associated with that cause or movement will know. Real, recognize real.

What Does It Mean to Be an Ally?

According to "The Guide to Allyship" by Amelie Lamont (of course, with edits from me), when you are an Ally who practices Allyship, you:

1. Take on the struggle of the individual and or group you are supporting as your own

2. Transfer the benefits of whatever privileges you may have to those who lack it

3. Amplify the voices of the oppressed before your own

4. Acknowledge that even though you may feel pain or discomfort, the conversation is not about you

5. Stand up for what's right, even when you feel scared or uncomfortable

6. Own your mistakes and de-center yourself; it's not about you, but the people you are trying to support

7. Understand your education is up to you and no one else

I read Amelie's entire guide on allyship and think she's done an incredible job of nailing the basics.

If you would like to learn more, please visit →
guidetoallyship.com

Guidelines For Being an Ally

- Apply the **Platinum Rule**, which is to help others not as you want to or think you should help them but as **they** want to be helped.

- Anybody can be an Ally. You don't need to be asked to be one; just take the initiative yourself and run with it. There is no 'correct' way to be an Ally; you just are.

- Anyone can be an Ally for anyone else. You just have to pick an individual or group that you want to be an Ally for and do it.

- You're going to make mistakes. Even if you've been a seasoned Ally for years and years, you're still only human. Just learn from your mistakes and keep going.

- Don't just say you're an Ally; prove it with your actions. As I said earlier, real recognize real.

- Being an Ally doesn't mean it is just going to be you doing all the work; the people who you're being an Ally for will not only appreciate you, but also support you.

- Being an Ally is often not fun. There are times when you're going to be stressed, and times when you may even get depressed by some of the realities of the world, you are now able to see. It's okay; thank you for doing what you can and staying committed.

Actions Steps to Take to Be an Ally

It wouldn't be right if I told you what it meant to be an Ally, provided the guidelines for being an Ally, but then didn't tell you the action steps you can take to be an Ally. So, here they are:

1. **Educate Yourself**: Do your best to learn about other cultures and histories. You don't know what you don't know, but the work begins with you. Anyone who is part of a group you would like to be an Ally for can help you learn things along the way, but we're not going to do the work for you. Find books (I recommend a whole bunch related to the Black community in the next part of the book), movies, articles, seminars, classes, and even training you can attend. It's not going to be a walk in the park, but if you really care, you'd be willing to at least start by doing the work yourself. Take your time with learning and educating yourself; Rome wasn't built in a day, and you're not going to suddenly become this super woke, socially conscious person overnight.

2. **Reflect**: Do some honest reflections and try to identify areas where you may have bias. We all have them; I have them, too, so it's nothing to be ashamed of. Be willing to accept any mistakes you may have made in the past and try your best to learn from them. When you know what your starting point is, you will know where you are currently, and it will be so much easier to know how much work you still have to do. Plus, it will be that much easier to identify the path you need to take to move forward.

3. **Own Your Privileges**: This one might be hard for some people to do. It is effectively admitting you have likely benefitted from a system you may not have known existed for your benefit, which can be an uncomfortable thing to do. That's okay; no one is asking for you to feel guilty about it. Now that you know and accept the privileges you

have had, you can use them to support the causes or movements you are trying to be an Ally for.

4. **Be A Friend**: In other words, just be human. Being an Ally doesn't just mean supporting, it means connecting with the people who are directly implicated by the cause or movement you are trying to be an Ally for. Talk to them and have meaningful conversations. It will help you with the learning and self-education you're doing. Plus, it would be hard to try and stay committed to being an Ally for BLM, the feminist movement, or the LGBTQ+ community but you didn't have a single Black friend, female friend, or friend on the spectrum, or perhaps any other group you wanted to support. I'm not saying this is impossible; I'm just saying that it would be hard. Take your time with this step though. Acquaintances are easy to make, but good friends can take a while to find.

5. **Listen**: Remember, it's not about you but the individual or group you are trying to be an Ally for. You're not going to have all the answers, and that's okay; it's expected. But if someone is telling you something or giving you feedback, make sure you really listen to what they have to say. Opinions on things are always going to be different, even for people who support the exact same cause or are affected by the same social constructs. Try to listen to as many different perspectives as possible; it will help you as you continue to educate yourself.

6. **Get Involved**: It's really easy to support a cause or movement from the comfort of your couch. You can like a post, share something, or comment (remember #hashtag activism from the chapter "#BlackTwitter?"), but real Allyship is more than just that. It means showing up to events to listen, learn, and show support. It means doing your part to help in whatever capacity you're able to.

7. Stay Engaged: Join groups that support the cause or movement you want to be an Ally for. Subscribe to email lists and follow and interact with them on social media. Share posts and do what you can to bring awareness to other people. Being an Ally can be hard because things are always going to be happening. It can get depressing at times, but push through it. The people affected by the cause or movement you want to be an Ally for have to show up every single day. Even if you're not actively overt actions to show that you're an ally, there aren't really any days off. Being a good ally is a little bit of a lifestyle, not just a decision.

8. Teach Others: It doesn't just end with you. Do your best to teach your family members, friends, and colleagues about all the things you have learned. Real change for causes and movements only happens when people not directly negatively affected by the cause or movement they are supporting, well, show support. It wasn't just Black people marching during the Civil Rights protests or at Black Lives Matter protests; non-black people from every walk of life showed up. Real change only happens when we all show that we care.

9. Speak Up: If you see or hear something wrong, say something. Right is right, and wrong is wrong. Don't be afraid to call people out for being hateful or ignorant, especially if they're directing that hate or ignorance towards someone else. If possible, don't offer your sympathies after the event has passed, but offer your support at the moment. This can possibly be uncomfortable because the perpetrator could be a friend, family member, colleague, significant other, and so forth. If you say nothing, then the spread of that hate and or ignorance will continue.

10. Donate: Find an organization that supports whatever cause or movement you want to be an Ally for. Many of us may not be aware of it, but often, these organizations are underfunded. You'd be surprised how far even a $10 donation can go in helping to support a cause or movement. You can do a one-time donation or an ongoing donation, it's really up to you, so don't feel pressured either way. Also, if you're going to support an organization, please do your research. Don't just give them money because their mission sounds good; make sure you feel comfortable knowing where the money is going and what the money is being used for. If you can't find this information, that's a red flag. Lastly, if you want to donate to a Black organization, don't just give money to the Black Lives Matter organization because 'that's what everybody does.' Really find a cause you want to support. As an example, when I was in college, I mentored disenfranchised Black youth through an organization called Collegiate 100 (C100 for short), which is supported by the 100 Black Men of America. While I support the Black Lives Matter Movement overall, I focus much of my efforts on mentoring and supporting younger African American/Black males.

Examples of Being an Ally

- A person and their friend attend an event or protest that supports a particular cause or movement

- A person tells their friend or family they no longer want to be part of jokes or conversations that put down a marginalized group of people

- A person tries to teach their friends or family about the struggles of a marginalized group either through informal conversations or respectfully calling them out if they say something insensitive

- A person stands up for the rights of another person when they are being bullied or mistreated

- An organization launches DEI initiatives internally and externally to educate their employees and partners on the different aspects of Diversity, Equity, and Inclusion

- An organization gives employees time off for religious observance

- An organization decides to sponsor workers from marginalized groups

An organization does periodic reviews of its policies to ensure they have taken into account Diversity, Equity, and inclusion

Part 3 – Everything You Wish You Knew

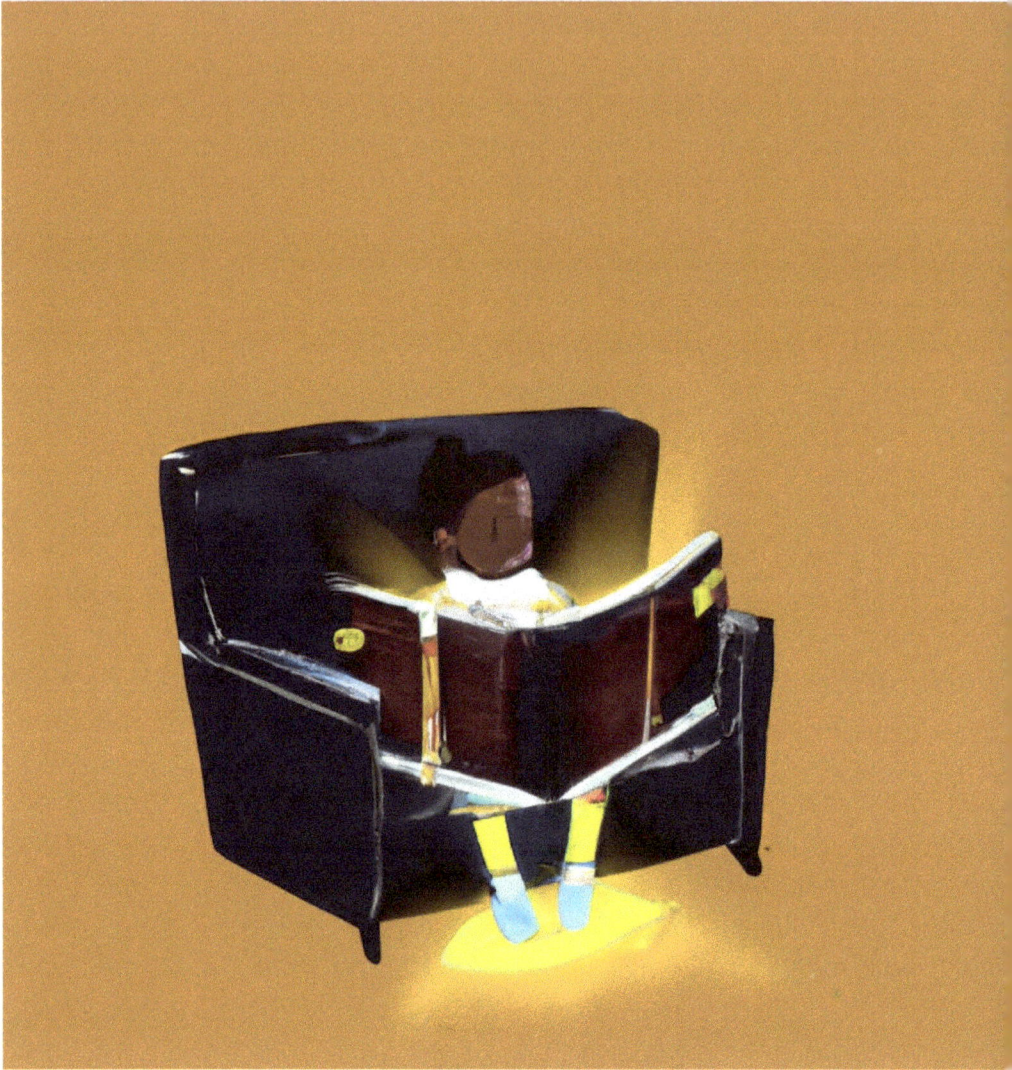

Note About Part Three:

I mentioned this during the preface, but I also wanted to include the reminder here as well. Nothing in this part of the book, or any part of the book for that matter, is sponsored. I did not make any money for picking something over another. Every link and recommendation I have throughout the book, and every recommendation I have in this part of the book is fully self-sourced. I personally spent months searching through all the different options that exist and individually picked everything myself to curate the most diverse lists possible. I was as objective as possible as some of my own personal favorites aren't even on some of these lists. I believe if you're going to recommend a range of things something to someone, then you should be as unbiased as possible.

Lastly, due to the interactive nature of some of the options I recommend in this section, there may be some discrepancies in social media follower count, podcast hosts/owners, link availability, etc., simply due to the time gap between when I published this book and when you read it. Regardless, I did my best to keep things as current as possible and kept updating things right up until print.

With that being said, I hope you enjoy and happy exploring!

Author Recommended Additional Readings

As I mentioned at the beginning of this book, I was not going to do a deep, deep dive into specific topics like systemic racism, oppression, White privilege, race, unconscious bias, and the like. I wanted this book to help support conversations around those topics, but I truly do believe they are topics so broad and complex they deserve their own books. Thankfully, they do.

Below is a list I've compiled of really great books I believe do an amazing job of doing a deeper dive into these complex topics for you, so you don't have to. You don't have to read all the books on this list to be able to have a better understanding or even talk about these topics. Slow and steady wins the race. Just pick one and go from there. The journey of self-education, since no one can do it for you, is yours and yours alone. It will be tough at times to read about some of these topics, and some of the revelations you'll have may cause you to self-reflect. You may realize ways you have perpetuated certain stereotypes. You may learn things about society you didn't know about before. A lot can happen, but one thing I can promise is that while doing what you can to learn more about these topics, your worldview will expand. You will be well on your way to being a global citizen, and that's pretty cool. You don't know what you don't know, so give yourself a chance to learn more about what you don't know. Go out into the world, have real conversations with people and learn about all the different ways in which you can help.

Author: Jennifer L. Eberhardt PhD

Year: 2020

Book: *Biased: Uncovering the Hidden Prejudice That Shapes What We See, Think, and Do*

Official Description: "How do we talk about bias? How do we address racial disparities and inequities? What role do our institutions play in creating, maintaining, and magnifying those inequities? What role do we play? With a perspective that is at once scientific, investigative, and informed by personal experience, Dr. Jennifer Eberhardt offers us the language and courage we need to face one of the biggest and most troubling issues of our time. She exposes racial bias at all levels of society—in our neighborhoods, schools, workplaces, and criminal justice system. Yet she also offers us tools to address it. Eberhardt shows us how we can be vulnerable to bias but not doomed to live under its grip. Racial bias is a problem that we all have a role to play in solving."

Author: Cole Brown

Year: 2021

Book: *Greyboy: Finding Blackness in a White World*

Official Description: "Cole has heard it all before—token, bougie, Oreo, Blackish— the things we call the kids like him. Black kids who grow up in white spaces, living at an intersection of race and class that many doubt exists. He needed to get far away from the preppy site of his upbringing before he could make sense of it all. Through a series of personal anecdotes and interviews with his peers, Cole transports us to his adolescence and explores what it's like to be young and in search of identity. He digs into the places where, in youth, a greyboy's difference is most acutely felt: parenting, police brutality, Trumpism, depression, and dating, to name a few."

Author: Ibram X. Kendi

Year: 2019

Book: *How to Be an Antiracist*

Official Description: "Antiracism is a transformative concept that reorients and reenergizes the conversation about racism—and, even more fundamentally, points us toward liberating new ways of thinking about ourselves and each other. At its core, racism is a powerful system that creates false hierarchies of human value; its warped logic extends beyond race, from the way we regard people of different ethnicities or skin colors to the way we treat people of different sexes, gender identities, and body types. Racism intersects with class and culture and geography and even changes the way we see and value ourselves. In How to Be an Antiracist, Kendi takes readers through a widening circle of antiracist ideas—from the most basic concepts to visionary possibilities—that will help readers see all forms of racism clearly, understand their poisonous consequences, and work to oppose them in our systems and in ourselves."

Author: Crystal Fleming
Year: 2019

Book: *How to Be Less Stupid About Race: On Racism, White Supremacy, and the Racial Divide*

Official Description: "How to Be Less Stupid About Race is your essential guide to breaking through the half-truths and ridiculous misconceptions that have thoroughly corrupted the way race is represented in the classroom, pop culture, media, and politics. Centuries after our nation was founded on genocide, settler colonialism, and slavery, many Americans are kinda-sorta-maybe waking up to the reality that our racial politics are (still) garbage. But in the midst of this reckoning, widespread denial and misunderstandings about race persist, even as white supremacy and racial injustice are more visible than ever before."

Author: Austin Channing Brown
Year: 2018

Book: *I'm Still Here: Black Dignity in a World Made for Whiteness*

Official Description: "Austin Channing Brown's first encounter with a racialized America came at age seven, when she discovered her parents named her Austin to deceive future employers into thinking she was a white man. Growing up in majority-white schools and churches, Austin writes, "I had to learn what it means to love Blackness," a journey that led to a lifetime spent navigating America's racial divide as a writer, speaker, and expert helping organizations practice genuine inclusion."

Author: Ijeoma Oluo
Year: 2019

Book: *So, You Want to Talk About Race*

Official Description: "In So You Want to Talk About Race, Ijeoma Oluo guides readers of all races through subjects ranging from intersectionality and affirmative action to "model minorities" in an attempt to make the seemingly impossible possible: honest conversations about race and racism, and how they infect almost every aspect of American life."

Author: Frederick Joseph
Year: 2020

Book: *The Black Friend: On Being a Better White Person*

Official Description: "Speaking directly to the reader, The Black Friend calls up race-related anecdotes from the author's past, weaving in his thoughts on why they were hurtful and how he might handle things differently now. Each chapter features the voice of at least one artist or activist, including Angie Thomas, author of The Hate U Give; April Reign, creator of #OscarsSoWhite; Jemele Hill, sports journalist and podcast host; and eleven others. Touching on everything from cultural appropriation to power dynamics, "reverse racism" to white privilege, microaggressions to the tragic results of overt racism, this book serves as conversation starter, tool kit, and invaluable window into the life of a former "token Black kid" who now presents himself as the friend many readers need. Backmatter includes an encyclopedia of racism, providing details on relevant historical events, terminology, and more."

Author: Emmanuel Acho
Year: 2020

Book: *Uncomfortable Conversations with a Black Man*

Official Description: "In Uncomfortable Conversations with a Black Man, Acho takes on all the questions, large and small, insensitive and taboo, many white Americans are afraid to ask—yet which all Americans need the answers to, now more than ever. With the same open-hearted generosity that has made his video series a phenomenon, Acho explains the vital core of such fraught concepts as white privilege, cultural appropriation, and "reverse racism." In his own words, he provides a space of compassion and understanding in a discussion that can lack both. He asks only for the reader's curiosity—but along the way, he will galvanize all of us to join the antiracist fight."

Author: Dr. Robin DiAngelo
Year: 2018

Book: *White Fragility: Why It's So Hard for White People to Talk About*

Official Description: "In this "vital, necessary, and beautiful book" (Michael Eric Dyson), antiracist educator Robin DiAngelo deftly illuminates the phenomenon of white fragility and "allows us to understand racism as a practice not restricted to 'bad people' (Claudia Rankine). Referring to the defensive moves that white people make when challenged racially, white fragility is characterized by emotions

287

such as anger, fear, and guilt, and by behaviors including argumentation and silence. These behaviors, in turn, function to reinstate white racial equilibrium and prevent any meaningful cross-racial dialogue. In this in-depth exploration, DiAngelo examines how white fragility develops, how it protects racial inequality, and what we can do to engage more constructively."

Author: Beverly Daniel Tatum
Year: 2017

Book: *Why Are All the Black Kids Sitting Together in the Cafeteria? And Other Conversations About Race*

Official Description: "Walk into any racially mixed high school and you will see Black, White, and Latino youth clustered in their own groups. Is this self-segregation a problem to address or a coping strategy? How can we get past our reluctance to discuss racial issues?

Beverly Daniel Tatum, a renowned authority on the psychology of racism, argues that straight talk about our racial identities is essential if we are serious about communicating across racial and ethnic divides and pursuing antiracism. These topics have only become more urgent as the national conversation about race is increasingly acrimonious. This fully revised edition is essential reading for anyone seeking to understand dynamics of race and racial inequality in America."

Author Recommended Black Hosted Podcasts

I love podcasts because you can literally find a podcast on just about any topic you want to learn more about. They're great for metro rides, long car rides, flights, and just casual listening around the house. When I first started listening to podcasts, I was an addict. I used to curate my podcasts the way a DJ would curate their playlists. You should have seen me scouring the internet until all odd hours of the night trying to find all the coolest podcasts I wanted to listen to. I probably looked like Dobby from *Lord of the Rings* with my podcast list by the time I was done making my list. Well, you're welcome because I definitely looked like Dobby putting this list of recommended Black-hosted podcasts together, so you don't have to. All jokes aside, these podcasts are all great because not only are they Black-hosted (please continue to support Black businesses), and not only do they all consistently put out quality content, but they're podcasts that focus on different aspects of the Black experience. If there was a question about Black culture or the Black experience you still have, that I wasn't able to answer in this book or isn't addressed in any of the books that I recommended, then you will likely be able to find the answers within one of these podcasts. Pick any one of them and give them a listen; I promise you won't be disappointed.

These podcasts are available to be streamed/tuned into on at least one of the major podcast platforms. This is great because if you already listen to podcasts, you likely won't have to create a new account just to give one a listen. Feel free to follow their social media accounts as well. All of these podcasts except for 'The Nod' and 'Still Processing' have at least a Twitter account where they post clips of their podcasts. I'll leave it to you guys to discover an additional IG, Facebook page, or social media page in general.

Code Switch

Hosts: Shereen Marisol Meraji & Gene Demby

Official Description: "What's CODE SWITCH? It's the fearless conversations about race that you've been waiting for. Hosted by journalists of color, our podcast tackles the subject of race with empathy and humor. We explore how race affects every part of society — from politics and pop culture to history, food, and everything in between. This podcast makes all of us part of the conversation — because we're all part of the story. Code Switch was named Apple Podcasts' first-ever Show of the Year in 2020."

I Am Athlete

Hosts: Brandon Marshall, Chad Johnson, Fred Taylor, and Channing Crowder

Official Description: "I Am Athlete podcast is candid, unscripted weekly discussion among former NFL greats: Brandon Marshall, Chad Johnson, Fred Taylor and Channing Crowder. These gridiron giants pull no punches and have no filter while expressing themselves on the importance of the issues and topics they cover. Each week the podcast is growing in popularity and its subscribers due to the panelists frankness in sharing their thoughts and views on relevant topics covered each week. Making a weekly appearance, Chef Nancie not only prepares delicious meals for the guys to try but also serves up some knowledge as the discussions heat up! A new episode premieres every Monday at 12pm Eastern. I AM ATHLETE is a thought provoking and in-depth podcast that offers multiple perspectives on subjects ranging from sports to controversial topics, to fashion to lifestyle, covering all cultural conversations and building a platform to educate but encourage viewers to engage."

Jemele Hill is Unbothered

Hosts: Jemele Hill

Official Description: "Emmy Award-winning journalist and Webby Award winner Jemele Hill shares her unbothered, nuanced opinions on news, pop culture, politics, and sports. She also conducts intimate interviews with some of the biggest names and most thought-provoking contributors to culture, music, and entertainment. New episodes air every Monday."

Louder Than a Riot	**Hosts: Rodney Carmichael and Sidney Madden** Official Description: "Rhyme and punishment go hand in hand in America. Louder Than a Riot reveals the interconnected rise of hip-hop and mass incarceration. From Bobby Shmurda to Nipsey Hussle, each episode explores an artist's story to examine a different aspect of the criminal justice system that disproportionately impacts Black America. Hosted by NPR Music's Rodney Carmichael and Sidney Madden, this podcast is invested in power from all angles — the power the music industry wields over artists, the power of institutional forces that marginalize communities of color, the power of the prison industrial complex and the power dynamics deep-rooted in the rap game."
Still Processing	**Hosts: Wesley Morris and Jenna Wortham** Official Description: "Wesley Morris and Jenna Wortham are working it out in this weekly show about culture in the broadest sense. That means television, film, books, music — but also the culture of work, dating, the internet, and how those all fit together."
The Breakfast Club	**Hosts: DJ Envy, and Charlamagne the God** Official Description: The World's Most Dangerous Morning Show, The Breakfast Club, With DJ Envy, Angela Yee, and Charlamagne Tha God! Author Comment: The Breakfast club is a top tier radio show within the Black community on Hot 97.1 in NY, so I'm really glad they've turned the episodes into a podcast (I also recommend the "Ebro in the morning" radio show, which is also on Hot 97) Author Update 2023: Angela Yee was an original cast member of this show but has since left and started her own show called "Way Up with Angela Yee."
The Joe Budden Podcast	**Hosts: Joe Budden, Ice Ish, Parks Vallely** *Original Hosts: Joe Budden, Jamil "Mal" Clay (who replaced Marisa Mendez in 2016) and Rory Farrell* Official Description: "Tune into Joe Budden and his friends.

	Follow along the crazy adventures of these very random friends"
The Nod	Hosts: **Brittany Luse and Eric Eddings** Official Description: "The Nod tells the stories of Black life that don't get told anywhere else, from an explanation of how purple drink became associated with Black culture, to the story of how an interracial drag troupe traveled the nation in the 1940s. We celebrate the genius, the innovation, and the resilience that is so particular to being Black -- in America, and around the world."
The Read	Hosts: **Kid Fury and Crissle** Official Description: "Join bloggers Kid Fury and Crissle for their weekly podcast covering hip-hop and pop culture's most trying stars. Throwing shade and spilling tea with a flippant and humorous attitude, no star is safe from Fury and Crissle unless their name is Beyoncé. (Or Blue Ivy.) As transplants to New York City (Kid Fury from Miami and Crissle from Oklahoma City), The Read also serves as an on-air therapy session for two friends trying to adjust to life (and rats) in the big city."
The Stoop	Hosts: **Hana Baba and Leila Day** Official Description: "The Stoop podcast explores stories from the Black diaspora that we don't always share out in the open. Hosts Leila Day and Hana Baba start conversations about what it means to be Black, and how we talk about blackness in America, and globally. It's a celebration of Black joy in all its diversity, with a mission to dig deeper into stories that we need to talk about."
Honorable Mentions	**2 Dope Queens** (Phoebe Robinson and Jessica Williams), **85 South Show** (DC Young Fly, Karlous Miller, and Chico Bean), **All the Smoke** (Matt Barnes & Stephen Jackson), **Another Round** (Heben Nigatu and Tracy Clayton), **Bodega Boys** (Desus Nice and The Kid Mero), **Drink Champs** (N.O.R.E and DJ EFN), **Strong Black Lead** (Tracy Clayton), **The Brilliant Idiots** (Charlamagne the God and Andrew Schulz)

Author Recommended Black Movies

Movies have always been a great way for people to get together. Movies can often reflect and influence a community's beliefs, social values, language, and even customs. Movies are also a wonderful way to learn about different elements of other communities' experiences and, to a certain degree, traditions and culture. I have probably spent far too much time watching movies in my life, but you know what? Just like all my late-night snacks... Worth it.

I think Black movies are great because they also help with representation. There are so many amazing films made by and for Black people that non-Black people can also enjoy. If books and podcasts aren't your thing, then hopefully movies are. There is so much you can learn if you can pick up on the subtle references made by the director and writer(s). I wanted to provide this list to give you all a visual look into aspects of the Black experience.

This list does not contain popularly known movies like 12 Years A Slave, Black Panther, Get Out, Coach Carter, Creed, Hidden Figures, Moonlight, Precious, US, or Straight Outta Compton, but other movies that have influenced and are often referenced within Black Culture, but aren't as well known outside of the Black Community. Enjoy!

Top 10 Movie Recommendations		Author Comment
Baby Boy	**Details:** **2001 |Crime, Drama, Romance |Rated R** **Official Description:** "The story of Jody (Tyrese Gibson), a misguided, 20-year-old African American who is really just a baby boy finally forced-kicking and screaming to face the commitments of real life. Streetwise and jobless, he has not only fathered two children by two different women-Yvette (Taraji P. Henson) and Peanut (Tamara LaSeon Bass) but still lives with his own mother. He can't seem to strike a balance or find direction in his chaotic life."	This movie isn't officially listed as also being a comedy, but it should have been because of all the funny moments it had
Boyz 'N The Hood	**Details:** **1991 |Crime, Drama |Rated R** **Official Description:** "Tre (Cuba Gooding Jr.) is sent to live with his father, Furious Styles (Larry Fishburne), in tough South- Central Los Angeles. Although his hard-nosed father instills proper values and respect in him, and his devout girlfriend Brandi (Nia Long) teaches him about faith, Tre's friends Doughboy (Ice Cube) and Ricky (Morris Chestnut) don't have the same kind of support and are drawn into the neighborhood's booming drug and gang culture, with increasingly tragic results"	"Rickkkyyyyyyyyyyy" Honestly, Ricky should have ran left or right. Who runs straight in the situation he was in????

Friday	**Details: 1995 |Comedy, Drama |Rated R** **Official Description:** "It's Friday and Craig Jones (Ice Cube) has just gotten fired for stealing cardboard boxes. To make matters worse, rent is due, he hates his overbearing girlfriend, Joi (Paula Jai Parker), and his best friend, Smokey (Chris Tucker), owes the local drug dealer money -- and that's all before lunch. As the hours drag on, Jones and Smokey experience the gamut of urban life, complete with crackheads, shoot-outs and overly sexual pastors, concentrated into one single, unbelievable Friday"	One of my favorite movies growing up. "Next Friday" and "Friday After Next" were also pretty good sequels
Juice	**Details: 1992 |Action, Crime, Drama |Rated R** **Official Description:** "Four Harlem friends -- Bishop (Tupac Shakur), Q (Omar Epps), Steel (Jermaine Hopkins) and Raheem (Khalil Kain) -- dabble in petty crime, but they decide to go big by knocking off a convenience store. Bishop, the magnetic leader of the group, has the gun. But Q has different aspirations. He wants to be a DJ and happens to have a gig the night of the robbery. Unfortunately for him, Bishop isn't willing to take no for answer in a game where everything's for keeps"	This movie was a bit intense at different points in time but keeps you at the edge of your seat
Love & Basketball	**Details: 2000 |Drama, Romance, Sport |Rated PG-13** **Official Description:** "Monica (Sanaa Lathan) and Quincy (Omar Epps) are two childhood friends who both aspire to be professional basketball players. Quincy, whose father, Zeke (Dennis Haysbert), plays for the Los Angeles	This movie is kind of a chick flick. If you ever need a movie date idea for a girl who plays ball, this is your film

	Clippers, is a natural talent and a born leader. Monica is ferociously competitive but sometimes becomes overly emotional on the court. Over the years, the two begin to fall for each other, but their separate paths to basketball stardom threaten to pull them apart"	
Paid In Full	**Details: 2002 |Action, Crime, Drama |Rated R** **Official Description**: "In the late 1980s, Ace (Wood Harris) is a young man employed by a Harlem dry cleaning shop, working hard to stay out of the drug business. While making deliveries, he meets Lulu (Esai Morales), a drug dealer who convinces Ace to join him. Ace recruits his friends Mitch (Mekhi Phifer) and Rico (Cam'ron), and the trio become major players in the Harlem drug underworld, a violent business that will test the friends' loyalty and wits as the money rolls in and the dangers grow beyond their control."	Watching this movie made me realize how much I didn't want to be in the streets and how much I would rather stay in school. Gangbanging isn't for me
Poetic Justice	**Details: 1993 |Drama, Romance |Rated R** **Official Description**: "Still grieving after the murder of her boyfriend, hairdresser Justice (Janet Jackson) writes poetry to deal with the pain of her loss. Unable to get to Oakland to attend a convention because of her broken-down car, Justice gets a lift with her friend, Iesha (Regina King) and Iesha's postal worker boyfriend, Chicago (Joe Torry). Along for the ride is Chicago's co-worker, Lucky (Tupac Shakur), to whom Justice grows close after some initial problems. But is she	This movie is a classic. That's all that needs to be said

ready to open her heart again?"

Sister Act 2	Details: **1993 |Comedy, Family, Music |Rated PG** Official Description: "In this sequel, Las Vegas performer Deloris Van Cartier (Whoopi Goldberg) is surprised by a visit from her nun friends, including Sister Mary Patrick (Kathy Najimy) and Sister Mary Lazarus (Mary Wickes). It appears Deloris is needed in her nun guise as Sister Mary Clarence to help teach music to teens at a troubled school in hopes of keeping the facility from closing at the hands of Mr. Crisp (James Coburn), a callous administrator. Can Deloris shape the rowdy kids into a real choir?"	While the prequel "Sister Act" was also pretty good, I liked the songs in this one better. To this day I still randomly go "la la la la la la la" in my head
The Wood	Details: **1999 |Comedy, Drama, Romance |Rated R** Official Description: "Three old friends -- Mike (Omar Epps), Roland (Taye Diggs) and Slim (Richard T. Jones) -- recount memories of their shared childhood in Inglewood, Calif., as they prepare for Roland's wedding to his fiancée, Lisa (Lisa Raye). When the groom goes missing without a word, Mike and Slim struggle to find their nervous friend and return him to his impatient bride before the wedding begins. Along the way, they continue to swap stories about lessons learned during their awkward teenage years."	I was wayyyy too young when I first watched this movie, but that second time around? Wow. I became nostalgic for good reason. A really well-made film that I can now really relate with
Training Day	Details: **2001 |Crime, Drama, Thriller |Rated R** Official Description: "Police drama about a veteran officer who escorts a rookie on his first day with the LAPD's	One of the best quotes of the movie: "King Kong ain't got

	tough inner-city narcotics unit. "Training Day" is a blistering action drama that asks the audience to decide what is necessary, what is heroic, and what crosses the line in the harrowing gray zone of fighting urban crime. Does law-abiding law enforcement come at the expense of justice and public safety? If so, do we demand safe streets at any cost?"	shit on me"
Honorable Mentions	**Other Really Good Movies: ATL** (2006), **Coming to America** (1988), **Barbershop** (2002), **Bad Boys 1&2** (1995, 2003), **Don't Be A Menace** (1996), **Drumline** (2002), **Fruitvale Station** (2013), **Girls Trip** (2017), **House Party** (1990), **How High** (2001), **I Am Not Your Negro** (2016), **Love Jones** (1997), **Pariah** (2011), **Soul Food** (1997), **The Best Man** (1999), **The Color Purple** (1985), **The Players Club** (1998), **White Men Can't Jump** (1992)	These movies were all great and have a lot of influences on Black culture today. Many memes referenced in Black culture also come from these movies

Author Recommended Black TV Shows

There have been many great TV shows made for and by the Black community, and if I'm being honest, it was hard narrowing it down to my recommended top 10. This list does not contain popularly known shows like Atlanta, Black-ish, Dear White People, Grown-ish, Insecure, Pose, Power, or even The Fresh Prince of Bel-Air. Don't get me wrong, all of these shows are absolutely incredible and have made their impact on the Black community in some way, shape, or form, but the focus of this list is to recommend shows that are just as good, but you probably haven't heard of before.

For the recommended shows below, I added the streaming services where you can watch full episodes of each show, but streaming rights are constantly changing even as I write this book, so apologies in advance if one of the platforms I recommend no longer has the show on it. I know not everyone may have a subscription service, so I've also indicated the platforms where you can watch each show for free with a (Free) after it. Please remember some of these shows are from a different time, so there may be some scenes that were appropriate 10-20 years ago but may not be as appropriate during our time.

Happy Watching! Try not to binge.

Top 10 TV Show Recommendations		Author Comment
Chappelle's Show	**Details: 3 Seasons |Comedy, Music | 22 Minutes** **Official Description:** Comedian Dave Chappelle hosts this sketch-comedy show that parodies many of the nuances of race and culture **Available On:** Amazon Prime Video, Apple TV, Comedy Central (Free), Google Play Movies & TV, HBO Max, Netflix, Pluto (Free), Vudu, YouTube	Dave left the show due to personal reasons, so season 3 is a bit short. Nevertheless, this show is still a classic
Empire	**Details: 6 Seasons |Drama, Music | 42 Minutes** **Official Description:** A hip-hop mogul must choose a successor among his three sons who are battling for control of his multi-million-dollar company, while his ex-wife schemes to reclaim what is hers **Available On:** Amazon Prime Video, Apple TV, Google Play Movies & TV, Hulu, Vudu, YouTube	Honest confession, I haven't watched this yet, but I've heard nothing but great things
Girlfriends	**Details: 8 Seasons |Comedy |30 Minutes** **Official Description:** A sitcom focusing on a mixed batch of Black women who face life's tests and triumphs together. From dating to divorce & friends to family to relationships, Joan, Maya, Lynn, and Toni support each other despite their differing backgrounds, learning about true friendship in the process **Available On:** Amazon Prime Video, Netflix, Philo	I am not ashamed to admit that not only did I watch this show growing up, I also really enjoyed it

Martin	**Details: 5 Seasons | Comedy, Drama, Romance | 30 Minutes** **Official Description:** A sitcom centered on radio & television personality Martin Payne. The series focuses on his romantic relationship with his girlfriend Gina, her best friend Pam, & escapades with his best friends Tommy & Cole **Available On:** Amazon Prime Video, Apple TV, BET+, Google Play Moves & TV, Sling TV, Vudu, YouTube	My Nigerian parents also watched this watched this show with me and they loved it. So that's how you know it's good
The Arsenio Hall Show	**Details: 6 Seasons | Comedy, Family, Music | 1 Hour** **Official Description:** A late-night talk show hosted by Arsenio Hall. The show features predominately African American celebrities **Available On:** This show is syndicated, so it's unfortunately not on any streaming platforms	I used to stay up late to watch reruns of this show. There's also a renewed version that ran briefly from 2013 – 2014
The Bernie Mac Show	**Details: 5 Seasons | Comedy, Drama, Family | 30 Minutes** **Official Description:** Bernie and his wife, Wanda, reluctantly step into the role of parents when his sister drops off her three kids -- naive Bryanna, nerdy Jordan, and teenager Vanessa -- en route to rehab. His views on child rearing are hardly politically correct, but Bernie tries his best **Available On:** Amazon Prime Video, Hulu, Peacock (Free), Philo	R.I.P Bernie Mac. This was one of my favorite shows growing up. It always put a smile on my face
The Boondocks	**Details: 4 Seasons | Animation, Action, Comedy | 22 Minutes** **Official Description:** The adventures of Rile and Huey Freeman, two boys who undergo a culture clash when they move	If it was Friday night and I had to choose between Family Guy, South Park or The

	from Chicago to the suburbs to live with their grandfather	Boondocks, I'm choosing The Boondocks 7/10 times lol
	Available On: Adult Swim (Free), HBO Max, Hulu, Sling TV	
The Parkers	Details: **5 Seasons |Comedy |20 Minutes**	"Ohhhhh professor"
	Official Description: The adventures of Rile and Huey Freeman, two boys who undergo a culture clash when they move from Chicago to the suburbs to live with their grandfather	If you know, you know lol
	Available On: Adult Swim (Free), HBO Max, Hulu, Sling TV	
The Proud Family	Details: **3 Seasons |Animation, Comedy, Family |30 Minutes**	I also recommend watching the Proud Family movie. It has jokes for dayyyyyssss Also, a renewed version came out in 2022
	Official Description: Fourteen-year-old Penny Proud is growing up! She's trying to gain her independence and faces typical teenage experiences in junior high. With the help of her parents, Trudy and Oscar, and her grandma, Sugar Mama, Penny faces all sorts of comical events	
	Available On: Apple TV, Disney+, Google Play Movies & TV, YouTube	
Wild 'N Out	**Show: Wild 'N Out |16 Seasons |Comedy |30 Minutes**	This show was a genius move by Nick Cannon. It has had so many scenes go viral and continues to deliver to viewers quality content episode after episode. The show's Instagram page is also a great highlights page
	Official Description: Conventional improve comedy games are injected with a hip-hop flavor as host Nick Cannon and celebrity guest stars lead teams of comics in a series of comedy challenges. This show has featured some of TV's most viral moments from celebrity guests and performers Kevin Hart, Iggy Azalea, Shaquille O'Neal, Snoop Dogg, Zendaya, T-Pain, French Montana, Wyclef, Kanye West, Jay Leno, and Ryan Lewis, and others!	

	Available On: Amazon Video Prime, Apple TV, fuboTV, Hulu, Philo, Pluto TV, Sling TV, VH1(Free), YouTube TV	
Other Honorable Mentions	Other Really Good Shows: **Everybody Hates Chris** (4 Seasons), **Kenan & Kel** (4 Seasons), **Love & Hip Hop** (10 Seasons), **Moesha** (6 Seasons), **My Wife & Kids** (5 Seasons), **The Game** (9 Seasons), **The Jamie Fox Show** (5 Seasons), Them (1 Season)	Black TV is great and while these didn't make the list, I'd also recommend if you have the time
Other Honorable Mentions from Before the Year 2000	Other Really Good Older TV Shows: **A Different World** (6 seasons), **Diff'rent Strokes** (8 seasons), **Family Matters** (9 seasons), **Good Times** (6 Seasons), **In Living Color** (5 Seasons), **Living Single** (5 Seasons), **Sanford & Son** (6 Seasons), **Sister Sister** (6 Seasons), **Smart Guy** (3 Seasons), **Soul Train** (35 Seasons), **The Cosby Show** (8 Seasons), **The Jeffersons** (11 Seasons), **The Wayans Bros** (5 Seasons), **What's Happening** (3 Seasons)	Had to show love to the OGs of Black Television

Author Recommended Black Social Media News Outlets

I said at the beginning of this part of the book to "go out into the world and have real conversations." Well, the beauty of today's world is that you can partially do this from your phone. We all have the world at our fingertips (the internet is cool, but still, please go out and experience the real world), which makes it easy for us to find and join spaces we otherwise might not have been able to before. If I want to, I can learn more about what's going on in the Asian or Latinx community or about their cultures in general by following a bunch of social media pages to be exposed to this information. As an example, I started following the Instagram page *NextShark* through the recommendation of a colleague now friend (hi King Yan, a.k.a Lizzy) to learn more about Asian culture and to get a better understanding of the different ways I could help support that community when there was a rise in the number of racially motivated attacks on Asians in America due to Covid-19. Since following this page, I've been exposed to news specific to the Asian community, and I've learned so much about Asian culture because of it. All this has happened without me having to have a single one-on-one conversation… a shout out to all my introverts! It's not always bad news either; they post many successes and wins for the community as well. Recent learnings for me were how important the movie *Shang Chi* was.

In terms of representation for the Asian community. A movie focused on an Asian superhero was big for their community, and it was amazing seeing the reactions of children and elders who went to see it. I have been told by my Asian friends that *Shang Chi* was for them what *Black Panther* was for the Black community.

Social Media Outlets To Follow				
Blavity	**IG**: blavity **Followers:** 491K	**Twitter:** Blavity **Followers:** 222K	**Facebook:** Blavity **Followers:** 880K	**Website:** Blavity.com

Author's Comments: A great page that primarily posts people pulling off different African dance moves from around the world

BOSSIP	**IG:** bossipofficial **Followers:** 593K	**Twitter:** Bossip **Followers:** 357K	**Facebook:** Bossip **Followers:** 614K	**Website:** Bossip.com

Official Description: "Bossip.com is the premier destination for African American popular culture and entertainment, with a voice that's edgy, viciously hilarious, politically aware—and completely unique."

Embracing Black Culture	**IG:** embracingblackculture **Followers:** 1.2M	**Facebook:** EmbracingBlackCulture **Followers:** 8K	**TikTok:** embraceblackculture **Followers:** 4593	**Website:** Embracingblackculture.com

Hot New HipHop	**IG:** hotnewhiphop **Followers:** 936K	**Twitter:** HotNewHipHop **Followers:** 1.5M	**Facebook:** realhotnewhiphop **Followers:** 999K	**Website:** Hotnewhiphop.com

Official Description: "HotNewHipHop.com empowers artists by letting them showcase their music to real hip hop fans. Meanwhile, our members enjoy the latest and hottest in hip hop singles, mixtapes, videos and new"

THE SOURCE	**IG**: thesource **Followers:** 896K	**Twitter:** TheSource **Followers:** 712K	**Facebook:** TheSourceMagazine **Followers:** 1.8M	**Website:** Thesource.com

Official Description: "Music. Culture. News. Sports. Fashion. Lifestyle."

Hollywood Unlocked	IG: hollywoodunlocked **Followers:** 2.7M	Twitter: HollywoodUL **Followers:** 3.6K	Facebook: hwoodunlocked **Followers:** 378K	Website: Hollywood unlocked.com
Official Description: "The Pulse of Pop Culture"				
Baller Alert	IG: balleralert **Followers:** 6.4M	Twitter: balleralert **Followers:** 247K	Facebook: BallerAlertcom **Followers:** 1.7M	Website: Balleralert.com
Official Description: "News, Events, Gossip, Sports and More"				
Complex	IG: complex **Followers:** 9.3M	Twitter: Complex **Followers:**2.5 M	Facebook: complex **Followers:** 5.9M	Website: Complex.com
Official Description: "Making Culture Pop. Complex is a community of creators and curators on a mission to expose the true face of modern America. Armed with the internet, we defy the stale conventions of the past by shifting the world's attention on the movements within convergence culture"				
The Shade Room	IG: theshaderoom **Followers:** 26.6M	Twitter: TheShadeRoom **Followers:** 488K	Facebook: theshaderoom **Followers:** 5.2M	Website: Theshaderoom.com
Official Description: "The Shade Room is the #1 Black-owned independent media company covering entertainment & celebrity news."				

But I digress; the important thing to remember if you decide to follow any of the pages I am recommending is that these are spaces made specifically for and by Black people. It is where we come to talk, laugh, share, and connect, just like Black Twitter, but with actual dedicated pages instead of hashtags. If you're going to enter these spaces, then as I've done with *NextShark*, please be respectful. Feel free to ask questions in the comments, but make sure you do it respectfully. This is a non-exhaustive list and doesn't include OG's (original gangsters) in the space like Media Take Out and BET (Black Entertainment Television), VIBE, The Root, Essence, and Ebony Magazine. I hope you enjoy!

Author Recommended Social Media Pages That Spread A Positive Black Narrative

Narratives are important. Unless we have experienced something for ourselves, what we see, hear, or are told often influences what we believe about people, places, and when looking at the retail side of things or products. Using a real-life example, whenever I want to order food from a place I've never been to before, I go to Google and Yelp for reviews. The reviews available and pictures of the food always influence whether I end up ordering food from the place of interest or not. I like it when a place has at least 300+ reviews because whatever the star rating, the reviews are likely to be accurate. I like having the option of seeing multiple different reviews because, well, everyone's experiences are always going to be different. Some may have had a wonderful experience, and others not so much. Some reviews are objective, and others, well, objectivity doesn't appear to have been the goal. Some reviews will talk about the experience but say nothing about the food. With so many different opinions and experiences that exist, it's usually best practice to look at more than just one review and have more than just one source of reviews to be able to have a really good idea if a place will be good or not. Following these principles, I'm usually able to discover new places to order from and avoid wasting money on others.

The point of this real-life example is to say that reviews are just like narratives; you always need more than just one, and more than just one source to be able to come to an objective opinion about a people or a place. The general media often pushes a negative narrative about Black people and the Black community. Very rarely is positive news about Black people or Black successes reported. So, here are just a few different pages to follow that post about, celebrate, and push a positive Black narrative. It's easy to believe what you can see, so I hope you see more good things.

Social Media Pages That Spread A Positive Black Narrative To Follow

Afro Jump

IG: afrojump
Followers: 646K

Author's Comments: A great page that primarily posts people pulling off different African dance moves from around the world

Afro Tech

IG: afro.tech
Followers: 252K

Twitter: AfroTech
Followers: 33K

Facebook: Afrotech
Followers: 255K

Author's Comments: Follow for news related to Black people doing incredible things in the world of tech

Because of Them

IG: becauseofthem
Followers: 793K

Twitter: Becauseofthem
Followers: 29K

Facebook: becauseofthemwe can
Followers: 1M

Author's Comments: This page celebrates Black history and Black Success

Black Culture News

IG: blackculturenews_
Followers: 341K

Twitter: blackculturenews
Followers: 479

Facebook: blackculturenews
Followers: 346K

Author's Comments: This page does a great job posting about news related to Black culture. There are occasional memes posted as well

Black Love

IG: blacklove
Followers: 961K

Twitter: blacklovedoc
Followers: 19K

Facebook: blacklovedoc
Followers: 698K

Author's Comments: This page shows and celebrates all types of Black love. Check out their douc-series on Oprah.com or on the OWN network

Black Love Bible

IG: blacklovebible
Followers: 420K

Author's Comments: Very similar to the Blacklove page I recommend above, except this page has a lot more memes related to Black love and their all great

The Undefea ted	IG: undefeatedespn Followers: 87K	Twitter: TheUndefeated Followers: 169K	Facebook: theundefeatedsite Followers: 159K

Author's Comments: This is a great page that makes posts related to the intersection of race and sports as it relates to Black people

Travel Noire	IG: travelnoire Followers: 645K	Twitter: Travelnoire Followers:55K	Facebook: travelnoire Followers: 393K

Author's Comments: A page dedicated to Black people traveling the world

Author Recommended Black (Hip Hop) Radio Stations by City

I know pretty much all cars these days allow us to connect our phones and play our own songs. Still, there are times when the radio is preferred, especially if your phone battery is low and you don't have a car charger.

So here are some great radio stations that not only play Hip Hop, R&B, Rap, and the occasional pop but also have great radio shows that speak to and on the Black experience. I tried to get just about every major city, so if you don't see your city here, I apologize in advance. Try tuning into a station for a city near you; it may be the same for you.

Recommended Black (Hip Hop) FM Radio Stations to Tune Into		
Atlanta, GA	• HOT 107.9	• THE BEAT 105.3	• Streetz 94.5
Austin, TX	• HOT 95.9	• THE BEAT 102.3	
Baltimore, MD	• Q JAMS 92.3	• MAGIC 95.9	
Boston, MA	• JAM'N 94.5	• HOT 96.9	
Charleston, NC	• JAMZ 93.3	• THE BOX 99.3	• STAR 99.7
Charlotte, NC	• THE BLOCK 92.7	• POWER 97.9	• Streetz 100.5/103.3
Chicago, IL	• POWER 92.3	• WGCI 107.5	• Streetz 95.1/105.1
Cincinnati, OH	• THE WIZ 101.1	• THE BEAT 102.3	
Cleveland, OH	• WZAK 93.1	• Z107.9	
Columbus, OH	• POWER 107.5	• POWER 106.3	• THE BEAT 106.7
Dallas, TX	• THE BEAT 97.9	• K104.5	• SMOOTH 105.7
Denver, CO	• JAMMIN' 101.5	• FLO 107.1	• KS 107.5
Detroit, MI	• WJLB 97.9	• HOT 105.1	• HOT 107.5
El Paso, TX	• HOT 93.5	• POWER 102.1	

Fort Worth, TX	• THE BEAT 97.9	• K104.5	• SMOOTH 105.7
Greensboro, NC	• QMG 97.1	• JAMZ 102.1	
Honolulu, HI	• THE BEAT 93.9	• DA BOMB 102.7	• POWER 104.3
Houston, TX	• THE BEAT 93.7	• The Box 97.9	• MAJIC 102.1
Indianapolis, IN	• HOT 96.3	• REAL 98.3	• WTLC 106.7
Jacksonville, FL	• THE BEAT 93.3	• V101.5	• POWER 106.1
Kansas City, MO	• JAMZ! 103.3	• KC's 107.3	
Las Vegas, NV	• HOT 97.5	• REAL 103.9	• JAMMIN' 105.7
Los Angeles, CA	• REAL 92.3	• KJLH 102.3	• POWER 105.9
Louisville, KY	• REAL 93.1	• B96.5	• MAJIC 101.3
Memphis, TN	• K97.1	• BUMPIN! 104.1	• HOT 107.1
Miami, FL	• JAMZ 99.1	• THE BEAT 103.5	HOT 105.1
Nashville, TN	• Q92.1	• THE BEAT 101.1	• THE VILLE 102.1
New Orleans, LA	• Q93.3	• THROWBACK 96.3	• KMEZ 102.9

New York, NY	• HOT 97.1	• RADIO 103.9	• POWER 105.1
Norfolk, VA	• HOT 91.1	• THE BEAT 92.1	• JAM 102.9
Oklahoma City, OK	• KRMP 92.1	• V 103.1	• POWER 103.5
Philadelphia, PA	• POWER 98.9	• WRNB 100.3	HIP HOP 103.9
Phoenix, AZ	• POWER 96.1	• POWER 98.3	• THE BEAT 101.1
Pittsburgh, PA	• WAMO 107.3		
Portland, OR	• JAM'N 107.5		
Raleigh, NC	• K97.5	• HOT 97.9	• FOXY 104.3
Richmond, VA	• iPower 92.1	• iPower 104.1	• THE BEAT 106.5
San Antonio, TX	• THE BEAT 98.5	• WE 103.3	
San Diego, CA	• JAM'N 95.7		
San Francisco, CA	• Q102.1	• KBLX 102.9	• KMEL 106.1
Seattle, WA	• KUBE 93.3		
Saint Louis, MO	• WFUN 96.3	THE BEAT 100.3	HOT 104.1

Tampa, FL	• WILD 94.1	• WTMX 94.5	• THE BEAT 95.7
Tucson, AZ	• HOT 98.3	• KTGV 106.3	
Washington, DC	• WKYS 93.9	• WPGC 95.5	WHUR 96.3

Bonus Popular Black Dances

Dance constantly evolves and changes over time. What is 'in' today may not be 'in' tomorrow. Even still, it doesn't stop all of us from trying to learn the new dances as they come and go… at least that's what I do sometimes at 2 am in the morning! This list doesn't contain dances like the Cha Cha Slide (DJ Casper, 2000), Dab (Migos, 2015), or even the Electric Slide (Richard Silver, 1976), but others that are also really fun, that I've personally enjoyed learning myself. One thing to note is the names of many of the most popular dances within the Black Community are also the names of the songs they came from.

It's okay if you have two left feet; not everybody knows how to dance, but please, if you're going to try and pull off one of these dance movies in public, make sure you have practiced at home and really nail it. Can't be caught slipping out here.

The last thing I'll mention is that this list doesn't include any TikTok dances that were created by Black content creators. It's not that they're not influential or viral; they just didn't really work for the list provided here. And I promise this wasn't shade.

Top 10 Recommended Dance Moves to Learn		Author Comment
Cat Daddy	**Creator**: The Rej3ctz Group **Year**: 2011 **Link to Tutorial**: https://www.youtube.com/watch?v=0BZGgf4BtVY	This one might be hard to pull off properly if you don't have good knees
Cupid Shuffle	**Creator**: Cupid **Year**: 2007 **Link to Official Video**: https://www.youtube.com/watch?v=h24_zoqu4_Q	This song will come on at most Black social events. So, listen, follow along, and have fun
Milly Rock	**Creator**: 2 Milly **Year**: 2017 **Link to Tutorial**: https://www.youtube.com/watch?v=uY3uh_pIQ0g	This is a personal favorite because of how smooth and easy it is
Shmoney Dance	**Creator**: Bobby Shmurda **Year**: 2014 **Link to Official Video**: https://www.youtube.com/watch?v=vJwKKKd2ZYE	The official move is from 2:16 – 2:24 and is also a viral moment
Shoot	**Creator**: BlocBoy JB **Year**: 2018 **Link to Official Video**: https://www.youtube.com/watch?v=7t8Gies2Zps Link to Song with Drake: https://www.youtube.com/watch?v=NV-3s2wwC8c	It starts at roughly :28 BlocBoy also does the move in the song he has with Drake called "Look Alive;" it was pretty popular

Swag Surfin'	**Creator:** F.L.Y (Fast Life Yungstaz) **Year:** 2009 **Link to Official Video:** https://www.youtube.com/watch?v=7iTsbnr8e_8 **Link to A Cool Video I Saw of the Swag Surf Being Executed Perfectly:** https://www.youtube.com/watch?v=ywqJ5GItg1k **Link to the Kansas City Chiefs Swag Surfin' on the NY Jets (disrespectfully funny lol):** https://www.youtube.com/watch?v=n4MYkljySxM	I've swag surfed more times than I can count. It can get really rowdy, especially when you do it with your friends. Because it happens a lot at sporting events You've probably done it before and not even known it
(Teach Me How To) Dougie	**Creator:** Cali Swag District **Year:** 2010 **Link to Tutorial:** https://www.youtube.com/watch?v=NJxYiIfr4WM	Not to toot my own horn but, I can do a pretty mean dougie
(You're A) Jerk	**Creator:** New Boyz **Year:** 2009 **Link to Official Video:** https://www.youtube.com/watch?v=qv9VKKXwVxU	I miss having the knees to do this the way I used to. So many good memories from simpler times
Tootsie Roll	**Creator:** 69 Boyz **Year:** 1994 **Link to Official Video:** https://www.youtube.com/watch?v=qs7f3ssuEjA	This is good to know and can come in handy in unexpected places
Wobble	**Creator:** V.I.C **Year:** 2008 **Link to Official Video:** https://www.youtube.com/watch?v=fE_64SdD27w	This one is a line-dance like the Cha Cha Slide and Electric Slide. It's also pretty easy to learn

| Honorable Mentions | Other Really Good Dance Move: **Billy Bounce** (YouFunnyB, 2017), **Chicken Noodle Soup** (Young B, DJ Webster, 2006), **Crank That** (Soulja Boy, 2007), **Lean Back** (Terror Squad, 2004), **Pop Lock & Drop It** (Huey, 2009), **Renegade** (Jalaiah Harmon, 2019), **Shoulder Lean** (Young Dro, 2009), **Single Ladies** (Beyonce, 2009), **Stanky Leg** (GS Boyz, 2009), **The Griddy** (Allen Davis), **The Mop** (TisaKorean, Kblast, Huncho Da Rockstar, 2019), **Walk It Out** (Unk, 2006), **Whip/The NaeNae** (Silento, 2015), **Woah** (KRYPTO9095, 2019) | In about 10 years this list will likely be 5-10 times this size and it's going to be interesting to see what other dances the creative Black Community comes up with |

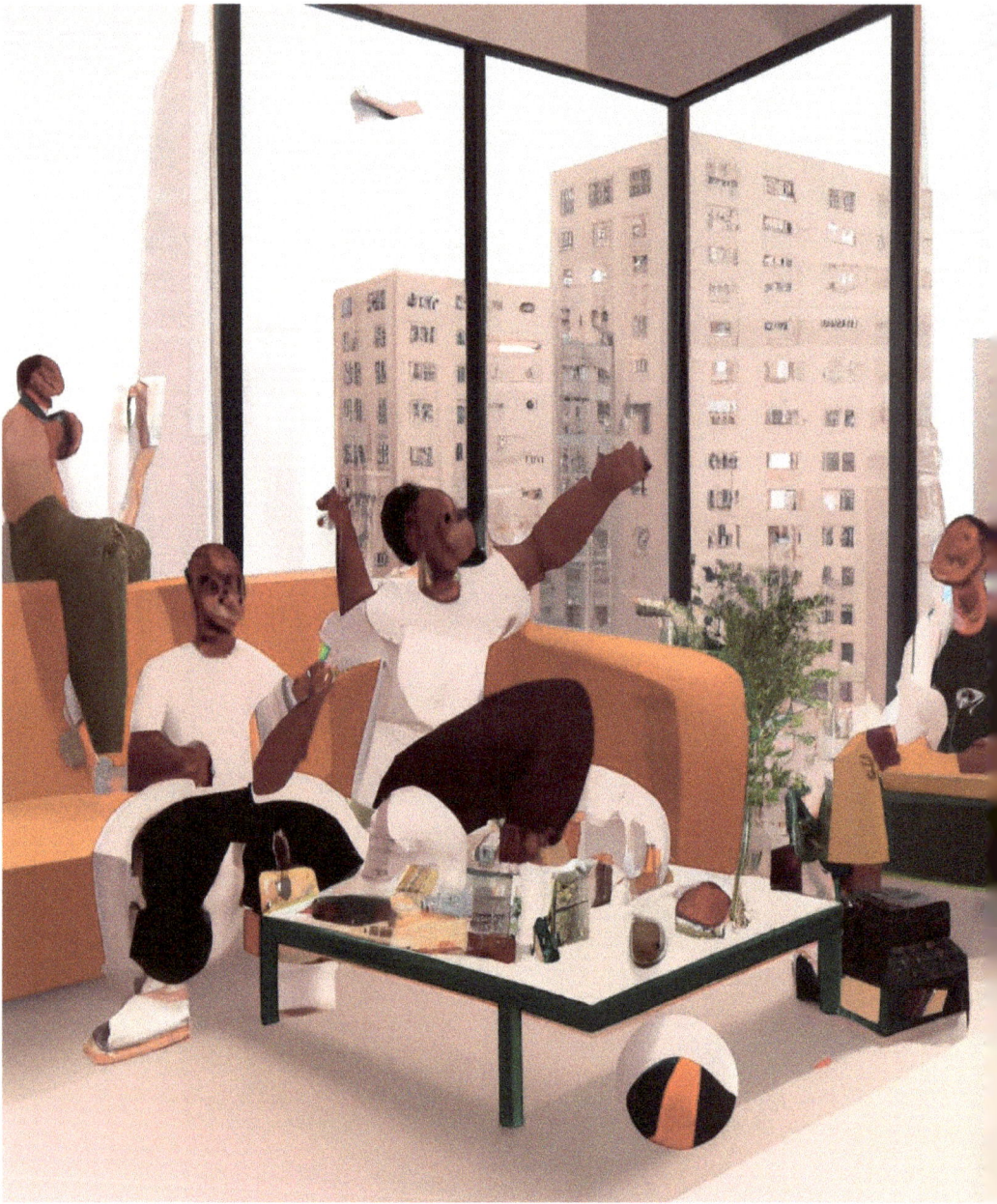

Ebonics

"No, I don't sound White. I'm just well-spoken"

- Tunde

I love Ebonics (said, /ēˈbäniks/). It's such a fun and creative way of speaking, and as someone who already speaks another language, Ebonics gives me even more words and expressions to choose from when I want to express how I'm feeling at any moment in time. What makes Ebonics enjoyable for me is the fact it is always evolving and changing, yet no matter how frequently words or expressions may change, I'm always able to somehow know what things mean intuitively by the context of how words or expressions are used and become proficient with using them within my own everyday speech. Also, with the words or expressions I don't intuitively understand, I can usually ask one of my Black friends, and someone will be in the know, or I just check the comments section when I'm on social media.

Ebonics, at the most basic level, simply means "Black speech," and it was a term created in 1973 by a group of Black scholars who didn't like nor appreciate the negative connotations that came with the term "Nonstandard Negro English." Ebonics is also commonly referred to as African American English (AAE), African American Vernacular English (AAVE), Black Street Speech, and Black English. They're all just different ways of addressing the same thing: the unique speech patterns of African American speech. Ebonics is not just slang but a way of speaking that is rooted in Black history and culture. I will admit that, yes, Ebonics breaks many 'standard' grammar rules. Because of this, Ebonics is often looked down upon as 'ghetto or uneducated speak,' and it's for this reason not all Black people like speaking in this form when we're not with close friends or family. My parents don't use Ebonics when they speak, and I personally don't use Ebonics when I'm at work because it can come off as 'unprofessional.' While there are different views within and outside the Black community on the use of Ebonics, I personally believe that Ebonics truly is another language in and of itself. I'm not saying learning how to speak Ebonics is as difficult as learning how to speak Spanish, French, Italian, Creole, or even Yoruba; it's still English, after all, but there are many unspoken and unwritten rules that it follows where it would be difficult for someone who hasn't been exposed to Ebonics before would find it difficult to understand. Put it this way, I speak Ebonics, and even then, I still find it difficult to understand at times.

Some examples of Ebonics words and statements include, but are not limited to:

- "It's Lit" → Something exciting or to turn up
- "Period" or "Periodt" or "Period Pooh" → That's that, I said what I said
- "It's giving me "___" → It reminds me of
- "It's giving" → the outfit or item being discussed is a great fit for its usage
- "Drip" → A really cool outfit
- "Understood the assignment" → Did an amazing job executing a task
- "YASSSS" or "YASSSS QUEEN" → I'm celebrating with you / I'm uplifting you
- "I be making that money" → I make a lot of money
- "Watchu talmbout" → What are you talking about?
- "Fuck you mean" → What do you mean? Or What are you talking about?

"You Sound White"

Ebonics is not only spoken within the Black community; it's sprinkled into everything we do and create. It's in our music, movies, and TV shows, and it's spoken by celebrities and athletes alike. This alone helps spread Ebonics and terminology within Ebonics outside the Black community. I'm often not surprised when a non-Black friend of mine starts using a word that is rooted in Ebonics because their favorite Black [insert adjective of choice here] used it in something they saw or watched. The uncomfortable juxtaposition for Black people who can speak Ebonics but choose not to in situations where it's not considered "appropriate" is that we're then told we sound "White" or "articulate" simply because we're speaking according to the standard grammar rules that exist (we talked about microaggression earlier in this book in the 'How to Talk to Black People' chapter). Again, speaking according to standard grammar rules isn't "talking White." It's just being well-spoken. It would be great if we could divorce this notion that proper speech is "White speak."

I have been told I sound 'White' plenty of times while growing up, and what's often interesting about being told that I sound 'White' or 'articulate' whenever I speak according to standard grammar rules is that the very same people giving me this 'compliment' are the very same people who use Ebonics slang yet have no idea it's Ebonics. (Who's the articulate one now?) It's not just limited to face-to-face interactions either. Many of the GIFs I've seen going around have words and phrases like 'girl bye,' 'whew, chile,' 'you thought,' and 'and I oop,' written on them, as well a plethora of others often used to express some sort of emotion, are in fact, Ebonics. The facts are, most of the slang that is used today isn't 'internet' or 'social media slang' but is, in fact, Ebonics! I said this statement earlier in this book: "Black culture is pop culture," and I hope that by this point in the book, you also believe this to be at least partially true.

Quick Author Sidenote: There's been a recent rise in the discussion around Digital Blackface and its usage by non-Black people that we will not go into, but I wanted to at least mention it is a conversation that's happening and give a brief overview here. Digital Blackface is "the use of digital images or representations of Black individuals, often in the form of memes, GIFs, emojis, or other online content, by non-Black individuals." It involves the appropriation and, sometimes, stereotypical use of Black people's images or expressions by individuals who are not Black. Digital Blackface is a concern because it can perpetuate racial stereotypes while reducing the very complex identities of Black people to caricatures. Digital Blackface has been gaining attention in discussions about the appropriate use of digital imagery in online communications and social media because some of its usage can be perceived to be offensive. Anyway, as I mentioned earlier, the conversation around Digital Blackface is not one we would get into here.

Non-Black People Using Ebonics Without Knowing It's Ebonics Is Appropriation

A general theme I've spoken about throughout this book is that whenever Black people do something, it's generally looked at as inappropriate, frowned upon, or looked at in a negative light. Yet, as soon as non-Black people do it, it's trendy, new, cool, and hip. As I've subtly hinted at before but will now explicitly say, "That's pretty fucked up." It's unfortunate, but there's something to be said about the social conditioning of our society where you can have one group of people do something, and it's considered bad and frowned upon, yet other groups can do the exact same thing, and it's not only considered cool and good but glorified. How can there be such hate towards us for doing something, but that exact same thing will then be used by non-Black people to try and seem cool or be used to profit from, and sometimes both? There is a long list I will not include here because I don't want to be sued, of non-Black comedians, entertainers, content creators, influencers, and the like who have used and constantly used Ebonics and elements of Black culture to become successful. Many of the followers of these non-Black [insert adjective of choice here] sometimes have no idea that some of the elements they like from their [insert adjective of choice here] are actually elements being pulled from Black culture. I've even seen companies using Ebonics, and often incorrectly, on their social media pages to try and appeal to a younger audience and try to seem "cool." This often happens with little to no credit or appreciation towards the Black community or Black culture.

Appropriation of Ebonics even occasionally occurs within the LGBTQ+ community. Words and expressions that are considered 'gay slang' or 'internet slang' like "Yas," "Yasss Queen," "Shade," "Throwing Shade," "KIKI," and "Slay," are all words that have their origin specifically within the Black queer community. Unfortunately, many people within and outside the LGBTQ+ community are not aware of this fact. These words and expressions went from being used explicitly within the Black queer community to being considered gay slang and then internet slang. These words and expressions became popular because they were adopted by the LGBTQ+ community, with few knowing of their origin, and mainstream media TV shows like Pose (this show was super enlightening), Queer Eye (a personal favorite), and Ru Paul's Drag Race (a national favorite) helping to popularize them. Go figure.

Final Thoughts

Appropriation of Ebonics is important to be aware of, but I also think there is a limit. I'm not the language police, so I'm not going to tell people what words and expressions they can or can't say. As we talked about in the *Black Fashion* chapter, there is a fine line between appropriation and appreciation that exists, and I recognize it can sometimes be difficult to toe the line between the two. Part of what makes language so interesting is how often it can take on a life of its own outside of the people and communities who created it. Whether it be English, Ebonics, Italian, French, Swedish, Spanish, Japanese, or any other language, words and expressions will be used by people who didn't create them, and that's just how language works. There are so many words and expressions I personally love to use that come from other communities and cultures.

A couple of my favorites are:

- Kapeesh → Italian word for "understand"

- Silenzio Bruno → Italian for "Be quiet!" "Shut up!" or "Hush!" I saw Pixar's movie *Luca* and have loved this phrase ever since. It was used in the movie as a way to tell your inner self-doubt to shut up.

- Ce La Vie → French expression for "Such is life" (this is a personal favorite)

- Déjà vu → French expression for "I've experienced this before"

- Jantelagen → Swedish code of conduct that essentially means "Be humble" and "The one is not greater than the sum"

- Claro → Spanish word for "Of course" or "I understand" (another personal favorite)

- Fuego → Spanish word for fire

- Que lo Que → Dominican expression for "What's up" or "What's happening?"
- Salud! → Spanish word for health. Also known as cheers
- Itadakimasu → Japanese expression for "Let's eat" and "Thank you for the food"

You may recognize some of these words and expressions, and you may even use some of them yourself. It's proof of how language constantly transcends the culture and community of those who created it, and that's amazing. What's important is that we understand where these words come from and how to use them properly. Whenever I learn a new word or expression I've never heard before, I always ask many questions about it.

- How do I say it properly?
- When can I use it?
- When can't I use it?
- Where does it come from?
- Are there any other words that are similar that I can use?

The questions above are the questions I usually ask. Is it extra work just to use a word, expression, slang, or otherwise? Yes, but that extra work is the line between appropriation and appreciation. Representation matters, and so does giving credit where credit is due. I would be pretty upset if the world started using a bunch of different Yoruba words or expressions but never gave Nigerians credit for their creation. The golden rule is "do unto others as you want done to you." It is also biblical, and is why I do the extra work. If I can fall in love with a word or expression from a different culture enough to adopt it into my everyday speech, then I should respect it enough to make sure I do it justice when I use it and be able to give credit where credit is due. So, to all the different cultures and communities that I borrow words and expressions from, I thank you. I just ask you all to give Ebonics the same level of energy and respect I give to your cultures and communities. This means giving the Black community credit where credit is due and not masking our words and expressions behind the label of "Internet slang."

Lastly, if my appeal to you had no effect, think about this. It's pretty cringy and embarrassing to use words and expressions when you don't really know what they mean or how to really use them. If you don't want to give us credit for what we've created, at least save yourself from some potential social embarrassment and do your homework. Just something to consider.

To help you with your homework, I've included a non-exhaustive list of Black American slang and expressions that have been relabeled as 'Internet Slang.' Hope this helps!

A quick note about the following chosen words and expressions. Language is influenced by geographic region. What this means is language/slang/words/expressions/ etc., that are used in one region may not be used in another. Due to that, I've tried to only include words and expressions within the following list that are region-agnostic. That being said, I am from New York, so it's very possible there are words and/or expressions that are New York specific. Sorry, not sorry

Commonly Used Ebonics Terminology "Black Slang"	
AYE / **AYEEE**	**What It Means**: A way to celebrate or hype someone up when something good happens **How to Use It:** **Friend 1**: "Yo bro! I just bought a new car. It's the one I've been trying to get for a minute now" **Friend 2**: "AYE, that's what's up, bro!"
A1	**What It Means:** **Definition 1**: Something that is really good or excellent **Definition 2**: A person who is good or genuine. They have been like this since the day you met them **How to Use It:** **Example 1**: "I just had some crazy good Chinese food. It was A1" **Example 2**: "My girlfriend just helped me start a new business. She's been A1 since Day 1"
Bag	**What It Means:** **Definition 1**: Financial prosperity **Definition 2**: To successfully make someone your romantic partner (primarily used by men) **How to Use It:** **Example 1**: "I just got a better-paying job, so you already know I secured the bag." **Example 2**: "I've been trying to bag [insert name] for so long now, but I'm making no progress"
Band	**What It Means**: A way to say $1000 **How to Use It**: "I made a band working over the weekend"
Bae	**What It Means**: Short for baby, the endearment term used on a significant other **How to Use It**: "That's bae, I love her"

Bet	**What It Means:** **Definition 1**: A way to say okay or sure **Definition 2**: A response of affirmation to someone challenging you to do something <div align="center">**How to Use It:**</div> **Example 1**: Friend 1: "Bro, can you meet me at the store at 5?" <div align="center">Friend 2: "Bet, I got you"</div> **Example 2**: Friend 1: "There's no way you're going to ask her out" <div align="center">Friend 2: "Bet, watch me bag"</div>
Bread	**What It Means:** Money **How to Use It:** "Damn, I need to work extra shifts this weekend; I need more bread"
Brick	**What It Means:** A very cold temperature (lol okay, so this one is NY-specific) **How to Use It:** "I need my jacket; it's hella brick outside"
Buggin'	**What It Means:** A person who is being extra or doing the most (this might also be NY-specific) **How to Use It:** "I don't like hanging out with him when he's drunk. He's always buggin'"
Bussin'	**What It Means:** Something that tastes really good **How to Use It:** "Yoooo, every time my mom cooks, it's always bussin'"
Cap	**What It Means:** Another word for lying **How to Use It:** "Nah, that's cap; there's no way you jumped over 10 cars; you capping right now"
Clap Back	**What It Means:** A cleaver comeback to someone trying to insult you or make fun of you

	How to Use It: **Aunt:** "Are you still in college? Why haven't you graduated yet?" **Nephew:** "I don't know, are you still single? Why aren't you married yet?" **Younger Brother**: "Damn, bro, you didn't have to clap back at Auntie so hard"
Cold	**What It Means:** **Definition 1**: Something that's really impressive or cool **Definition 2**: A way to express how bad or disrespectful an insult was How to Use It: **Example 1**: "Did you get a new watch? It looks legit; it's cold man" **Example 2**: "Did you tell your mom to shut up? That was cold, man; you shouldn't have done that"
Cop	**What It Means:** To get or buy something **How to Use It:** "I've always wanted those shoes; I'm definitely going to cop them"
Crib	**What It Means:** A person's house **How to Use It:** "I'm having a party at my crib on Saturday, come through"
Deadass	**What It Means:** Being very very serious (can also be used as a question or confirmation/affirmation) (this might also be just NY) How to Use It: **Friend 1:** "I'm so deadass; I'm tired of my job. I'm going to quit next week" **Friend 2:** "Deadass? You're going to quit? Good Luck, I'll be praying for you"
Down Low	**What It Means:** Something that very people know or is a

	secret
	How to Use It: "This speakeasy is a chill spot, so keep it on the down low, okay?"
Drip	**What It Means:** A really cool outfit / having style
	How to Use It: "Yo bro, I copped the sneakers I was telling you about earlier. They go well with the outfit I've been trying to put together. Look at my drip; what do you think?"
Facts	**What It Means:** An agreement to a statement that you agree with
	How to Use It:
	Friend 1: It's sooooooo hot today"
	Friend 2: "Yo, Facts"
Faded	**What It Means:** To be under the influence of a drug or alcohol
	How to Use It: "I got so faded over the weekend, it's not even funny"
Fam	**What It Means:** Short for "Family" -- A way to address a close friend(s) of yours
	How to Use It: "Fam, when are we hanging out, I haven't seen you in forever"
Finesse	**What It Means:** To trick or convince someone to do something for you that they otherwise may not have done. Basically, getting someone to give up goods and/or services to you
	How to Use It: "I can't believe he let himself get finessed like that. Why did he give that girl he met online but never met in person $1000? Now she's not responding to his calls or messages"
Fire	**What It Means:** Something that's really impressive or cool
	How to Use It: "Yo, that new Drake album was fire"

Fit	**What It Means:** Short for "outfit" **How to Use It:** "My fit to the event is about to be fire"
Flex / **Flexing**	**What It Means:** To show off or to brag **How to Use It:** "Go ahead bro; you've been working super hard; you deserve to flex a little bit"
Gas / **Gassing /** **Gassed Up**	**What It Means:** To hype someone or something up **How to Use It:** **Friend 1:** Ayeeeeee, look who showed up to the party on time with a new car and a fire fit! I want to be like you when I grow up!" **Friend 2:** Factsssssssssss, his fit is on point tonight
G.O.A.T	**What It Means:** Greatest of All Time **How to Use It:** "Muhammad Ali is the G.O.A.T"
Grill	**What It Means:** **Definition 1:** To interrogate or be interrogated by someone **Definition 2:** To stare intensely at someone **How to Use It:** **Example 1:** "Mom, stop asking me so many questions about where I was last night. I hate it when you grill me" **Example 2:** "I was on the bus on the way back home, and this girl just kept grilling me the whole time. It was hella creepy
Guap	**What It Means:** Money **How to Use It:** "As soon as I secure the bag with this new job, I'm going to spend hella guap on brunch every weekend for like a month straight"
Gucci	**What It Means:** To be okay after something bad happens **How to Use It:** "I lost my job, but it's all good; I'm Gucci"

Heated	What It Means: To be very upset/angry How to Use It: "Bro, don't talk to me right now; I'm heated"
High Key	What It Means: The opposite of lowkey. Putting extra emphasis on something obvious How to Use It: "I've been interviewing with that company for over a month now. I high-key want that job"
Hip	What It Means: To be in the know about something How to Use It: "You don't need to tell me how to get to the speakeasy. I'm already hip. I've been going there for a while now"
Hot	What It Means: (Aside from describing how attractive someone is, it's similar to heated) **Definition 1**: To be very upset/angry **Definition 2**: A place that's currently dangerous for someone to go or be at How to Use It: **Example 1**: "Let's give him some space, I think he's hot right now" **Example 2**: "Yo, I wouldn't go over there right now, it's mad hot"
ITIS	What It Means: To be extremely tired and sleepy after a big meal. (I recommend watching "The Boondocks" Season 1 Episode 10 ITIS episode, it's really funny) How to Use It: "I can't believe I ate so much; I need a nap; I have the ITIS"
ight / iight	What It Means: Okay How to Use It: "iight, I'll be there tomorrow at 4"
Jacked	What It Means: Used to describe someone who is incredibly strong (this is probably NY-specific)

	How to Use It: "Aaron Donald on the Los Angeles Rams football team is jacked"
KIKI	What It Means: A gathering of close friends with the purpose of gossiping, talking, or chit-chatting (this is Black Queer slang) How to Use It: "Let's have KIKI on Friday, I have some tea to spill with you. It's low-key, so don't tell anyone else"
L	What It Means: To take a Loss How to Use It: "Go ahead and take this L; you lost the bet"
Low Key	What It Means: The opposite of high key. Something on the down low that not too many people know about How to Use It: "This is the invite to tonight's party. It's super lowkey, so don't tell anybody else"
Mad	What It Means: (Aside from someone being upset) – it means a lot How to Use It: "I wouldn't date him; he's been with mad girls"
Minute	What It Means: A long time – how long "a long time" is, is subjective based on how you want to use it How to Use It: "Dude! I talked to you in a minute! We have to catch up"
Mood	What It Means: A particular feeling or state of mind (often used as a response to a statement or situation) (this is Black Queer slang) How to Use It: Friend 1: "I'm so tired of working, I wish I could just wake up with a million dollars in my bank account" Friend 2: "Mood"
Peeped	What It Means: To notice something How to Use It: "Yeah, I know she likes me; I peeped how

	she was staring at me at the party"
Period / **PeriodT**	**What It Means:** Enough said / that's that / I said what I said (this is Black Queer slang) **How to Use It:** "Stop talking to me; I don't want to hear what you have to say anymore. Period"
Plug	**What It Means:** A person who is connected and can help you get the things that you need that would otherwise be difficult to get without their help **How to Use It:** "I'm not even worried about the sneakers selling out during pre-orders. My plug already got me a pair"
Real Talk	**What It Means:** Honestly **How to Use It:** "Real talk, I'm tired of how we work five days a week to only have two days off"
Receipts	**What It Means:** Proof of something or evidence **How to Use It:** "I know you cheated on me; I have the receipts"
Salty	**What It Means:** To be upset about something happening **How to Use It:** "He's just salty because his team lost, and he ended up losing the bet"
Shade / **Throw** **Shade**	**What It Means:** To send a subliminal jab at someone. Kind of like a lowkey clap back (this is Black Queer slang) **How to Use It:** **Friend 1:** "I can't believe you kissed that many guys over the weekend" **Friend 2:** "Yes, but still fewer guys than you kissed last night. As yes, that was shade!" (this type of response would be the act of throwing shade)
Slaps	**What It Means:** Something that is really good

	How to Use It: **Example 1**: "This song is fire! That beat slaps" **Example 2**: "This chicken slaps! How'd you make it?"
Slay	**What It Means**: To be successful or accomplish something – usually pertaining to an outfit (this is Black Queer slang) **How to Use It**: "Did you see her outfit for the red carpet event last night? She slayed"
Slow	**What It Means**: Something that will not happen, usually meant in a serious, slightly aggressive way (lol, this is NY-specific) **How to Use It**: "I'm not respecting anymore after the way he disrespected me. It's slow for that"
Stack	**What It Means**: A way to say $1000 (this might be NY-specific) **How to Use It**: "If you're going to go on vacation with me, you're going to need at least a stack"
Straight	**What It Means**: Something that's just "okay" **How to Use It**: "The game was straight; we could have done better though"
Sus	**What It Means**: Suspicious **How to Use It**: "I don't like him; he's always being sus"
Tea / Spill Tea	**What It Means**: Gossip (this is Black Queer slang) **How to Use It**: "Spill the tea! What happened on the date last night"
Thirsty	**What It Means**: To have or show a strong desire for someone. Being overly eager and/or desperate for someone's approval or affection **How to Use It**: "He's always liking all of my Instagram posts. He's so thirsty"

Tight	**What It Means:** To be very upset or angry about something **How to Use It:** "I'm tight! I just found out that someone stole my car"
Trash	**What It Means:** Garbage (lol) **How to Use It:** "You can't beat me in any sport, you're trash"
Triflin'	**What It Means:** Someone who is sneaky, despicable or condemnable **How to Use It:** "He isn't a good person. He's always trying to scam people. He's hella triflin"
Trippin'	**What It Means:** Someone who is acting crazy or overreacting **How to Use It:** "I can't come over to your house anymore, every time I do, your mom is always trippin' because she doesn't like me
Turnt	**What It Means:** To be very very drunk **How to Use It:** "Tonight, we are getting turnt, no excuses"
Twerk	**What It Means:** A type of dance. We talked about this in the twerking chapter **How to Use It:** "My girls and I are going to get turnt and twerk all night, girls' night only, sorry"
Violate	**What It Means:** To disrespect someone (this might be NY-specific) **How to Use It:** "My girlfriend's dad doesn't like me. He's always trying to violate"
Whip	**What It Means:** A Car **How to Use It:** "Bro, I'm trying to cop a new whip, come with me to the dealership this weekend?"
Wild	**What It Means:** Something that's crazy

	How to Use It: "Last night's party was wild; I saw some things that I've never seen before"
Woke	What It Means: Being alert/awake to injustice in society such as racism, systematic oppression and such
	How to Use It: "Stay woke my friends"

Black Expressions (Ebonics Pt.2)

Remember what we talked about a couple of pages ago... Appropriation is not appreciation; make sure to do your homework and give credit where credit is due. Next to the definitions of the expressions, you may see a "(BW + LGBTQ+)." This is meant to identify expressions primarily used by Black women and members of the LGBTQ+ community.

Commonly Used Ebonics Terminology "Black Expressions"	
Ate It Up	**What It Means**: To do a really good job at something (BW + LGBTQ+) **How to Use It**: "Did you see their performance last night? They ate it up".
Bye Felicia	**What It Means**: A way to dismiss someone who gives you a request that's outrageous or ludicrous (BW + LGBTQ+) **How to Use It**: "You want me to drive you to the airport that's 2 hours away at 5 in the morning and you're not going to give me gas money? Psht! Bye Felicia"
Come Find Out	**What It Means**: Plot twist **How to Use It**: "He's been making secret phone calls for the last two weeks, so I thought he was cheating on me. Come find out, he's been planning a surprise birthday party for me"
Do You	**What It Means**: Do whatever you want to do, I don't care **How to Use It**: "Since you don't want to be with me anymore, do you"

Don't Play with Me	**What It Means:** If you're joking around, please stop (can be used to express joy or anger) **How to Use It:** "Don't play with me. Did you really get me the PS5?"
Everybody Eats	**What It Means:** We're going to make sure that everybody is well taken care of / successful **How to Use It:** "As soon as I make it to the NFL, I'm going to make sure that everybody who truly supported me eats"
Fumbled The Bag	**What It Means:** To make a financial mistake or make a decision that causes you to lose a lot of money **How to Use It:** "Damn bro, how you get fired on your day off? You fumbled the bag"
Get It Together	**What It Means:** Pull yourself together **How to Use It:** "Bro, I know you're sad that she left, but you have to get it together and move on
Glow Up	**What It Means:** An expression to describe someone who goes through or has gone through a positive transformation. It can be physical, mental, or emotional (BW + LGBTQ+) **How to Use It:** "I heard he's been working on himself since the last time anyone saw him. He's glowed up since high school and travels all over the world now"
Go Off	**What It Means:** To do whatever you need to, to do a good job **How to Use It:** "As soon as coach puts me in, I'm going to go off and drop like 30 points"
I Feel You	**What It Means:** I understand what you're going through **How to Use It:** "I feel you, bro, I know how much it sucks getting turned down by the person you like"

I Know That's Right	**What It Means:** Used as a response to agree with what someone is saying (BW + LGBTQ+) **How to Use It:** "I know that's right! You finally kicked that deadbeat to the curb"
I See You	**What It Means:** I am aware of something positive that's happened to you and I'm praising/gassing you up for it **How to Use It:** "Oh you got a new whip? I see you!"
I'm Crying	**What It Means:** Something was so funny that I've been moved to tears. Can also be used a response to something funny **How to Use It:** "I'm crying, I can't believe you just said that
I'm Dead / Deceased	**What It Means:** Something was so funny or outrageous that I laughed so much it made me dead (of course, not literally dead, lol). Can also be used as a response to something funny or outrageous **How to Use It:** "That's so funny, I'm dead"
I'm Not the One	**What It Means:** You should stop trying to insult/disrespect me. You don't know where I'm from or what I'm capable of doing if you make me upset enough **How to Use It:** "You better stop disrespecting me, I'm not the one"
I'm Weak	**What It Means:** Something was so funny that my body is weak **How to Use It:** "OMG, I can't believe you just said that, I'm weak"
Invited To the Cookout	**What It Means:** Usually used towards a non-Black person. You understand to a certain degree and sympathize with the Black plight in America. You are officially cool to me and possibly other Black people. You still can't say nigga, but you can come hang out

	with us
	How to Use It: "Because you stood up for what was right, you're invited to the cookout"
It's Hitting	What It Means: Usually used in reference to food being delicious
	How to Use It: "Yo, this meal you just made is hitting"
Jesus Take the Wheel	What It Means: There are so many things going wrong right now that I just need Jesus to take control of everything and set things back on the right track for me (BW + LGBTQ+)
	How to Use It: "Jesus, take the wheel; I just got fired"
Left No Crumbs	What It Means: Similar to the "Ate it up" expression. Basically, to do a really good job at something (BW + LGBTQ+)
	How to Use It: "She killed her presentation! She left no crumbs"
Make It Make Sense	What It Means: What you're telling me isn't adding up, and now I'm questioning the validity of everything you just said.
	How to Use It: "You said you didn't go to Chick-fil-A without me, but I found the bag under your seat! Make it make sense"
On God	What It Means: Pretty much just saying "I swear to God"
	How to Use It: "On God, our kids better not have thrown a party while we were gone or they're grounded for the rest of the year"
On The Money	What It Means: Something that was precise. Pretty much another way of saying on point or was impressive
	How to Use It: "This meal you just made was on the money"
Put Me On	What It Means: Requesting help from someone with

	a situation that you know they can help you with
	How to Use It: "I think your friend at the party last night was really cute. Can you put me on"
Say Less	**What It Means**: I understand what you need from me and agree to help. You don't have to keep talking. (Not meant, and very rarely used in a disrespectful way)
	How to Use It: "Oh you need my help putting you on with my friend from the party last night? Say less
Secure The Bag	**What It Means**: Doing something that has led or will lead to financial success
	How to Use It: "Please tell your friends to buy this book so that I can secure the bag (lol but seriously though 😊)
Shoot Your Shot	**What It Means**: Doing something that can be potentially risky. Usually used in reference to flirting
	How to Use It: "Oh, you want to ask her out? Shoot your shot!"
Square Up	**What It Means**: I'm upset at you and want to fight you
	How to Use It: "Oh you think I'm a bitch? Square up"
Talk To Me Nice	**What It Means**: Give me my due respect for something that I do / did / just did
	How to Use It: Basketball player makes the game winning shot "Talk to me nice!"
Tell Me Why	**What It Means**: Gather around; I have some tea to spill with you
	How to Use It: "Tell me why I was in Cabo and saw you know who with another girl!"
Understood The Assignment	**What It Means**: You successfully and perfectly executed on a task
	How to Use It: "The little girl clearly understood the

	assignment because she had us all giving her a standing ovation when she was done with her dance routine"
We Love To See It	**What It Means:** I'm happy for the good news / blessings/ success that you've just recently had **How to Use It:** "You just started a new business? Yessss, we love to see it"
Whew Chile	**What It Means:** Used to express a myriad of emotions when involved in or witnessing a messing situation **How to Use It:** "Whew Chile, does his girlfriend know that he was in Cabo with another girl? She must still think he was on a business trip"
Who You Telling	**What It Means:** I completely agree **How to Use It:** "Who you telling, I also saw you know who in Cabo with that same girl!
Won't He Do It	**What It Means:** God is good **How to Use It:** "You're not sick anymore!? Won't he do it"
You Better Work	**What It Means:** You better do whatever you need to (legal of course) to be successful. Can be used in pretty much any situation that requires someone to work hard **How to Use It:** "Oh you have tryouts this weekend? You better work"
You Got Money	**What It Means:** You've done things / bought things to show that you're financially well off and I applaud you **How to Use It:** "This is your car? Oh, you got money"
You Put A Foot In This	**What It Means:** You did an amazing job with this **How to Use It:** "Grandma put her foot in this apple pie, because yo, it was bussin'''"

You Straight

What It Means:

Definition 1: Don't worry about it, it's okay

Definition 2: Are you okay?

How to Use It:

Example 1: "Don't even worry about the scratch you put on my car, you straight"

Definition 2: Hey man, you look a little sick, you straight?

Giving Credit Where Credit Is Due

"Credit is one of the easiest things to give"

- Tunde

Throughout this book, I have continuously said it's okay to engage with, interact with, and adopt most aspects of Black culture as long as you're giving credit where credit is due. But exactly how do you give credit? Well, once again, in true consultant fashion, the answer is "**it depends.**" Really, though, it depends on the context of exactly what aspect of Black culture you're interacting with, engaging with, or adopting, where you're doing it, how you're doing it, who's around you when you're doing it, and even when you're doing it, will impact exactly how you will need to give credit. Before I go into exactly how to give credit, let's talk about exactly why you need to give credit and why giving credit is important.

In an increasingly interconnected and diverse world, the importance of giving credit to Black creators is more important now than ever. The Black community's impact across various fields, from art, music, science, and literature, to politics, sports, and technology – has been far-reaching and long-lasting. However, many of these contributions have been obscured, erased, downplayed, stolen, or outright ignored by a society that has often failed to address its inherent biases. You can't change the past, but you can change the future. Actively giving credit to Black creators is a vital step towards fostering inclusion, correcting historical narratives, and creating a more equitable world.

But giving credit is not just about saying a name or tagging a source; it's about understanding the bigger picture, too. When discussing the accomplishments of Black people, it's important to contextualize our achievements within the broader social and historical context. By recognizing the barriers and obstacles Black people face, we shed light on the resilience and strength that allows us to succeed despite adversity. Acknowledging the systemic racism and discrimination we navigate underscores the significance of our achievements and emphasizes the importance of continued efforts to combat inequality. Also, representation matters! Elevating voices from the Black community and promoting diverse perspectives helps counter the erasure of our contributions. In media, literature, and art, highlighting Black creators and their stories helps create a more accurate portrayal of the richness that is our collective human experience. By amplifying the works of Black creators, we not only honor their creativity but also pave the way for a more inclusive cultural landscape.

Listening and learning are also fundamental. Taking the time to understand our experiences - listening to the stories of Black creators will be more eye-opening than you can possibly imagine. We can all learn so much from each other, and that's how we grow as individuals and as a society. So, be curious, ask questions, and, most importantly, be a good listener. It's all part of showing respect and giving credit where credit is due.

So, exactly how do you give credit? Well, giving credit is as easy as being forthcoming about the source of whatever it is you're giving credit for. If you learn a TikTok dance, credit the creator; it's as easy as tagging them in your caption. If you get a certain hairstyle/haircut, let people know who the hair stylist/barber is. If you wear an outfit, credit the designer when people ask you about who it is. If, in general, you make a social media post about anything you're leveraging from a Black content creator or the Black community, tag the source. Giving credit is literally just knowing the source of what it is you're leveraging from us (Black people) and telling people who or what the source is. Just so we're all on the same page, a source can be a person, place, or thing -- yes, your source can be a noun, lol. So, this means that your source can be a:

- Influencer / Person You Know (family, friends, co-workers, classmates, ex, etc.)
- Church / Restaurant / Bar / Academic Institution / Museum
- Movie / TV Show / Clip / Interview
- Song
- Social Media Account / Page
- A Tweet
- A Book 😊

...I mean, the list goes on and on. So just give the credit where the credit is due. You'll have peace of mind by doing it, and everybody will be happier because of it. You can't really engage in cultural appreciation without it anyway. Besides, you may be surprised by what doors will open for you when you do.

Lastly, teamwork makes the dream work. Collaboration and partnerships are great ways to give credit where credit is due. Engaging in joint projects, sharing platforms, and collaborating across different spaces and industries can amplify the impact of the works of Black creators and provide a platform for recognition. Recognizing Black expertise and actively seeking opportunities for collaboration also demonstrates a commitment to inclusion and shared progress.

In conclusion (lol... that's such a high school way to end a paragraph), giving credit to people from the Black community is not just about acknowledging individual accomplishments; it's about acknowledging history, confronting systemic biases, and fostering a more inclusive society. By properly giving credit, you help play a part in reshaping the narrative of human achievement. Giving credit to people from the Black community isn't just a good thing to do – it's a public statement. It's a way of saying, "You matter, your work matters, and the impact that you're making is seen and noticed." So, let's all do our part in creating a more equitable world where we recognize and uplift the voices and stories that have long been marginalized. Thanks.

Afterword

"Thank you for coming to my TED talk. I've enjoyed talking to you all, and I hope you were able to learn something new and/or interesting"

- Tunde

I know some people may be upset with me that I wrote this book, and that's okay; not everyone is going to like everything you do. That's just something we all have to learn to be okay with. Had I let my 'what would people say' fears prevail, I never would have finished this book. I've realized the two general schools of thought that exist within the Black community when discussing with non-Black people many of the topics that we discussed in this book are:

(A) Fuck it, it's not our job, nor should it be our burden to educate people on the same topics and issues we've been talking about for decades now. People should just know by now, and if they don't know, then they haven't been listening or paying attention. I think that this is a fair statement.

OR

(B) Let's have these conversations; it's a burden, yes, but I would rather do it with you in a safe, informative, and understanding way than simply tell you to figure it out on your own. You're still going to have to do your own work, but I'm at least willing to point you in the right direction. If we can change just one person's opinion about us positively, that is one more ally for us who will then spread what we've taught them to other people they know. It will eventually cause a positive domino effect... or is it a ripple effect?

While I understand the (A) school of thought, I obviously support the (B) school of thought, and that is partly why I wrote this book. I believe we can only tell people "to just know" and "to go figure it out on their own" for so long before they eventually stop trying to learn and, ultimately, stop caring. The way I see it, interracial interactions between Black people and White people, Black people and Asian people, Black people and Latinx people, Black people, and any combination of ethnicities that exists in the world is unnecessarily overcomplicated. Before skin tone, before nationality, before cultural heritage, before traditions and beliefs, before sexual orientation, before religion, before gender, before age, and before anything else, we're all people first. Irrespective of anything that makes up our own individual, unique, and complex identities, we are all humans, and we are all collectively having a human experience. We all have dreams, ambitions, fears, and concerns. If we looked at the world from an absolute objective point of view, there really is never an 'us vs. them.' It's really just an 'us vs. us.' None of us really 'win' when a group of us is suffering. Across the globe, there are people going through terrible things, and there are way more important things we can and should be worried about than the color of someone's skin. As a society, it's sad that we're still not beyond this one form of identification to determine the value someone has or not. We're so busy fighting each other all the time that we're neglecting the fact we are killing our world and, by extension, each other. It really is simple. Let's just treat everybody, regardless of how complex and unique their identity is, with an equal amount of respect. Let's be kind to one another and just be decent human beings.

We all bleed red, we all need to eat, we all need to sleep, and we all need to breathe. Yes, we are all different, but our differences shouldn't set us apart but should bring us together. It's only by working together that we can achieve an equal and equitable world for all. I wrote this book because I wanted to do my own part in whatever way I could to mend the broken bridges that currently exist.

So please, let's all be better, do better, and treat each other, no matter what, with an equal amount of respect.

Author's Note

I originally wrote this book as a challenge to myself, and it's one that I'm glad paid off. I've challenged myself mentally, creatively, financially, spiritually, and, at times, physically to put this book together. This shit was hard, lol, but I couldn't be any prouder of myself even if I tried. No matter what levels of success this book reaches (or not) in the future, no one can ever take this accomplishment away from me. What started as a possible idea turned into a book and turned me into an author. Who would have thought? I've never written a book before, nor have I ever aspired to be an author before, but hey, here we are. This book was just an idea in my head over three years ago, and now, it's something that is real, and it's in your hands. You're somewhere in the world reading this book right now, and that very thought is sometimes mind-blowing to me.

Personally, I love entrepreneurship, so this is my personal message to anybody with any kind of aspiration or passion. If there is anything in this world you love to do or are passionate about, make sure you do it with everything you have. The successes and growth you will find will be yours and yours alone, and that is something no one can ever take away from you. I want you to always be able to look back and, at the very worst, say, "You know what, I tried it, I did my absolute best, and I have no regrets," or at best, say, "I'm so glad I did it." I don't want any of you to ever look back and say, "I wish I could have, or I should have." It's not always going to be easy, but that is just part of the process. I want to share a quote that sometimes kept me going as I was in the process of writing this book. I first heard it from motivational speaker Eric Thomas, The Hip Hop Preacher, and later by Les Brown: "The graveyard is the richest place on Earth because it is here that you will find all the hopes and dreams

354

that were never fulfilled, the books that were never written, the songs that were never sung, the inventions that were never shared, the cures that were never discovered, all because someone was too afraid to take that first step, keep with the problem, or determined to carry out their dream."

Well, allow me to let you in on a little secret: I put way more effort into this book than any other personal project I've ever done in my life. This book is an accumulation of the last 29 years of my experiences, skills, interests, and talents. I sometimes read back some of the things I wrote and put together and have no idea how I did it. I'm thankful for everything that happened during the writing process, and I'm so glad to be done. Now for a tiny little break before I'm off to my next project.

To my friends who supported me throughout the entire process of writing this book, thank you. Thank you for humoring me, thank you for giving me your suggestions, thank you for giving me your perspectives on things, thank you for pushing back on ideas I had, thank you for helping me gut-check things, thank you for reading this book before it even got printed, and giving me your most objective and critical advice, and most of all, thank you for just being there. I love you all.

To my family, thank you for your prayers. I know that you all pray for me every day, and I believe and know that it was only through God I was able to put all of this together. Thank you for your support emotionally, spiritually, mentally, and financially. I love you more than words can ever describe.

Lastly, with all due respect to whatever religion you may practice or not,

I would like to thank God for everything. To God Be the Glory, Always and Forever.

1 Chronicles 16:34

I hope you've enjoyed this book and all the conversations we had together. We talked about many things and touched on many different but very important topics. If you would like to learn more, please visit any of the following pages.

Website: TalkingtoBlackPeople.com

YouTube: @TalkingtoBlackPeople

Instagram: @T2BPBook

Facebook: @T2BPBook

Twitter: @T2BPBook

TikTok: @T2BPBook

Tunde, Out

Endnotes

We're Not All The Same

1. DW News. (2019, February 26). *Hollywood Movies: Stereotypes and Prejudice - Data Analysis*. *DW*. https://www.dw.com/en/hollywood-movies-stereotypes-prejudice-data-analysis/a-47561660
2. Just Security. (n.d.). How News Media Talk About Terrorism: What the Evidence Shows. https://www.justsecurity.org/63499/how-news-media-talk-about-terrorism-what-the-evidence-shows/
3. https://doi.org/DOI
4. The Washington Post. (2017, August 31). Almost All News Coverage of the Barcelona Attack Mentioned Terrorism; Very Little Coverage of Charlottesville Did. https://www.washingtonpost.com/news/monkey-cage/wp/2017/08/31/almost-all-news-coverage-of-the-barcelona-attack-mentioned-terrorism-very-little-coverage-of-charlottesville-did/?noredirect=on
5. NPR. (2021, September 10). When Should We Label Something Terrorism? https://www.npr.org/sections/codeswitch/2021/09/10/176167881/when-should-we-label-something-terrorism
6. American Friends Service Committee (AFSC). (n.d.). The Problem with Labeling Violence as Domestic Terrorism. https://www.afsc.org/blogs/news-and-commentary/problem-labeling-violence-domestic-terrorism
7. Federal Bureau of Investigation (FBI). (2005). Terrorism 2002-2005. https://www.fbi.gov/stats-services/publications/terrorism-2002-2005
8. White House. (2021). National Strategy for Countering Domestic Terrorism. https://www.whitehouse.gov/wp-content/uploads/2021/06/National-Strategy-for-Countering-Domestic-Terrorism.pdf
9. White House. (2021, June 15). Fact Sheet: National Strategy for Countering Domestic Terrorism. https://www.whitehouse.gov/briefing-room/statements-releases/2021/06/15/fact-sheet-national-strategy-for-countering-domestic-terrorism/
10. History.com. (n.d.). Ku Klux Klan. https://www.history.com/topics/reconstruction/ku-klux-klan
11. Public Police Record. (n.d.). Josue Acosta Inmate Profile. https://www.publicpolicerecord.com/texas/elpaso-jail/ACOSTA_JOSUE/9596346
12. Al Jazeera. (2018, October 18). Arsonist Gets 24 Years in Jail for Texas Mosque Fire. https://www.aljazeera.com/news/2018/10/18/arsonist-gets-24-years-in-jail-for-texas-mosque-fire
13. Federal Bureau of Investigation (FBI). (n.d.). Famous Cases - Baptist Street Church Bombing. https://www.fbi.gov/history/famous-cases/baptist-street-church-bombing
14. Center for American Progress. (2020, October 30). 4 First Steps for Congress to Address White Supremacist Terrorism.

https://www.americanprogress.org/issues/security/reports/2020/10/30/492095/4-first-steps-congress-address-white-supremacist-terrorism/

15. USA Today. (2020, November 16). Biden Must Lead the Fight Against the White Supremacist Terror Threat. https://www.usatoday.com/story/opinion/2020/11/16/biden-lead-fight-against-white-supremacist-terror-threat-column/6263293002/

16. Human Rights Watch. (2020, May 12). COVID-19 Fueling Anti-Asian Racism and Xenophobia Worldwide. https://www.hrw.org/news/2020/05/12/covid-19-fueling-anti-asian-racism-and-xenophobia-worldwide

17. Harvard Gazette. (2021, March). A Long History of Bigotry Against Asian Americans. https://news.harvard.edu/gazette/story/2021/03/a-long-history-of-bigotry-against-asian-americans/

18. Pew Research Center. (2021, April 21). One-Third of Asian Americans Fear Threats, Physical Attacks, and Most Say Violence Against Them Is Rising. https://www.pewresearch.org/fact-tank/2021/04/21/one-third-of-asian-americans-fear-threats-physical-attacks-and-most-say-violence-against-them-is-rising/

19. Fast Company. (n.d.). We Need to Talk About How Media and Creatives Portray Black People. https://www.fastcompany.com/90512750/we-need-to-talk-about-how-media-and-creatives-portray-black-people

20. The Opportunity Agenda. (n.d.). Media Representations Impact Black Men. https://www.opportunityagenda.org/explore/resources-publications/media-representations-impact-black-men/media-portrayals

21. Color Of Change. (n.d.). Dangerous Distortion: The Impact of the Media's Mischaracterization of Black Families and Black-Authored Content. https://colorofchange.org/dangerousdistortion/#report

22. Centers for Disease Control and Prevention (CDC). (n.d.). Health, United States, 2019. https://www.cdc.gov/nchs/data/nhsr/nhsr071.pdf

23. ISD Network. (n.d.). What Is Diversity? https://www.isdnetwork.org/what-is-diversity.html

24. Northwestern University. (n.d.). Social Identities: Definitions & Concepts. https://www.northwestern.edu/searle/initiatives/diversity-equity-inclusion/social-identities.html

Do I Say Black, African American or Person of Color?

1. **Smithsonian National Museum of Natural History.** (n.d.). Introduction to Human Evolution. Retrieved from https://humanorigins.si.edu/education/introduction-human-evolution#:~:text=Humans%20first%20evolved%20in%20Africa,ago%20come%20entirely%20from%20Africa.

2. **The Moxie Exchange.** (n.d.). African American or Black: Which Term Should You Use? Retrieved from https://themoxieexchange.com/blog/african-american-or-black-which-term-should-you-use/

3. **University of South Carolina Aiken - Diversity Initiatives.** (n.d.). Guide to Inclusive Language. Retrieved from https://www.usca.edu/diversity-initiatives/training-resources/guide-to-inclusive-language/inclusive-language-guide/file

4. **University of Alabama in Huntsville - Diversity, Equity, and Inclusion.** (n.d.). Which Is the Correct Terminology: Black, African American, or People of Color? Retrieved from https://www.uah.edu/diversity/news/15567-which-is-the-correct-terminology-black-african-american-or-people-of-color

5. **CBS News.** (n.d.). Not All Black People Are African American: What Is the Difference? Retrieved from https://www.cbsnews.com/news/not-all-black-people-are-african-american-what-is-the-difference/

6. **The Undefeated.** (n.d.). Does It Make a Difference If You're Called Black, African American, Melanated, or Any Other Term? Retrieved from https://theundefeated.com/you-got-99-words/does-it-make-a-difference-if-youre-called-black-african-american-melanated-or-any-other-term/

7. **Living Cities.** (n.d.). Operationalize Racial Equity. Just Say Black. Retrieved from https://livingcities.org/blog/operationalize-racial-equity/just-say-black/

8. **Politico.** (2013, April). An African American or a Black? Retrieved from https://www.politico.com/blogs/media/2013/04/an-african-american-or-a-black-160773

9. **Pew Research Center.** (2021, March 25). The Growing Diversity of Black America. Retrieved from https://www.pewresearch.org/social-trends/2021/03/25/the-growing-diversity-of-black-america/

10. **KARE 11.** (n.d.). African American or Black: Which Term Should You Use? Retrieved from https://www.kare11.com/article/news/local/breaking-the-news/african-american-or-black-which-term-should-you-use/89-0364644d-3896-4e8b-91b1-7c28c039353f

How To Talk To Black People

1. Merriam-Webster. (n.d.). *Microaggression*. https://www.merriam-webster.com/dictionary/microaggression

2. https://www.vox.com/2015/2/16/8031073/what-are-microaggressions

3. Verywell Mind. (n.d.). *What Are Microaggressions?*. https://www.verywellmind.com/what-are-microaggressions-4843519

4. Healthline. (n.d.). *Microaggressions: Definition, Examples, and Impact*. https://www.healthline.com/health/microaggressions#takeaway

5. The Washington Post. (2020, December 4). *Racial Microaggressions: A Constant Burden for Black Americans*.

https://www.washingtonpost.com/business/2020/12/04/racial-microaggressions-black-americans/
6. Medical News Today. (n.d.). *How to Respond to Racial Microaggressions*. https://www.medicalnewstoday.com/articles/how-to-respond-to-racial-microaggressions#health-and-mental-health
7. https://cehs.unl.edu/images/EdPsych/nicpp/NICPP_microaggression_presentation_2015-06-02.pdf
8. https://www.cpedv.org/sites/main/files/file-attachments/how_to_be_an_effective_ally-lessons_learned_microaggressions.pdf
9. NPR. (2020, June 8). *Microaggressions Are a Big Deal: How to Talk Them Out and When to Walk Away*. https://www.npr.org/2020/06/08/872371063/microaggressions-are-a-big-deal-how-to-talk-them-out-and-when-to-walk-away
10. https://medium.com/age-of-awareness/some-of-the-microaggressions-black-people-face-everyday-214b3ea39998

Karen

1. BBC News. (2020, July 30). *What Is a 'Karen'?* https://www.bbc.com/news/world-53588201
2. https://www.insider.com/karen-meme-origin-the-history-of-calling-women-karen-white-2020-5
3. Dictionary.com. (n.d.). *Karen*. https://www.dictionary.com/e/slang/karen/
4. The New York Times. (2020, July 31). *The History of 'Karen,' the Internet's Favorite Derogatory Term*. https://www.nytimes.com/2020/07/31/style/karen-name-meme-history.html
5. New York Post. (n.d.). *What Is a 'Karen' Meme? Name Meaning Explained*. https://nypost.com/article/what-is-a-karen-meme-name-meaning-explained/
6. CNN. (2020, May 30). *Why 'Karen' Is Being Used to Describe Women Who Request Managers*. https://www.cnn.com/2020/05/30/us/karen-meme-trnd/index.html
7. https://www.youtube.com/watch?v=SSXoBtmtypg
8. The Guardian. (2020, May 13). *Karen: the Anti-Vaxxer Suburban Mum Who Became a Coronavirus Conspiracy Theorist*. https://www.theguardian.com/lifeandstyle/2020/may/13/karen-meme-what-does-it-mean
9. The Atlantic. (2020, May 15). *The Coronavirus Memes Are Here*. https://www.theatlantic.com/technology/archive/2020/05/coronavirus-karen-memes-reddit-twitter-carolyn-goodman/611104/
10. The Atlantic. (2020, August 1). *The Revenge of 'Karen'*. https://www.theatlantic.com/international/archive/2020/08/karen-meme-coronavirus/615355/
11. Time. (2020, July 29). *The History and Meaning of the Karen Meme*. https://time.com/5857023/karen-meme-history-meaning/

12. The Guardian. (2020, April 13). *The Karen Meme Is Everywhere – and It Has Become Mired in Sexism.* https://www.theguardian.com/fashion/2020/apr/13/the-karen-meme-is-everywhere-and-it-has-become-mired-in-sexism
13. The Conversation. (2020, June 30). *How 'Karen' Went From a Popular Baby Name to a Stand-In for White Entitlement.* https://theconversation.com/how-karen-went-from-a-popular-baby-name-to-a-stand-in-for-white-entitlement-139644
14. NPR. (2020, July 14). *What's in a 'Karen'?.* https://www.npr.org/2020/07/14/891177904/whats-in-a-karen
15. Parade. (n.d.). *What Is a 'Karen'? The History and Origins of the Popular Nickname.* https://parade.com/1111328/stephanieosmanski/what-is-a-karen/
16. Los Angeles Times. (2020, July 8). *Lawmaker Proposes 'CAREN Act' Making Racially Biased 911 Calls Illegal.* https://www.latimes.com/california/story/2020-07-08/lawmaker-proposes-caren-act-making-racially-biased-911-calls-illegal
17. The Guardian. (2020, October 20). *'CAREN Act' Proposed in San Francisco to Outlaw Racist 911 Calls.* https://www.theguardian.com/us-news/2020/oct/20/caren-act-san-francisco-racist-911-calls
18. Don't Worry Girlfriend. (n.d.). *How to Not Be a Karen.* https://dontworrygirlfriend.com/how-to-not-be-a-karen/

~~Nigga~~

1. The Washington Post. (2021, May 7). *Should You Say the N-Word? No, Especially if You're Not Black.* Retrieved from https://www.washingtonpost.com/opinions/2021/05/07/should-you-say-n-word-no-especially-if-youre-not-black/
2. CNN. (2020, August 10). *The Debate Over Who Can Use the N-Word.* Retrieved from https://www.cnn.com/videos/us/2020/08/10/race-n-word-white-black-zw-orig.cnn
3. https://www.learningforjustice.org/magazine/fall-2011/straight-talk-about-the-nword
4. The Atlantic. (2019, August 15). *When Whites Just Don't Get It.* Retrieved from https://www.theatlantic.com/ideas/archive/2019/08/whites-refer-to-the-n-word/596872/
5. University at Buffalo Spectrum. (2021, March 12). *Why Are Non-Black People Still Saying the N-Word?.* Retrieved from https://www.ubspectrum.com/article/2021/03/why-are-non-black-people-still-saying-the-n-word
6. The Panther. (2020, September 22). *Dueling Column: Non-Blacks Shouldn't Use the N-Word Under Any Circumstances.* Retrieved from http://panthernow.com/2020/09/22/dueling-column-non-blacks-shouldnt-use-the-n-word-under-any-circumstances/
7. NewsOne. (n.d.). *Why White People Want to Say the N-Word.* Retrieved from https://newsone.com/4098396/why-white-people-want-to-say-n-word/

8. Everyday Feminism. (2014, March 10). *White People Can't Use the N-Word – And No, It's Not the Same as Black People Using It*. Retrieved from https://everydayfeminism.com/2014/03/white-people-cant-use-the-n-word/
9. Complex. (2020, March 30). *Joe Exotic Rants About Why He Can't Say the N-Word (Video)*. Retrieved from https://www.complex.com/pop-culture/2020/03/joe-exotic-rants-about-why-he-cant-say-the-n-word-video
10. UD Review. (n.d.). *No, You Can't Say the N-Word*. Retrieved from http://udreview.com/no-you-cant-say-the-n-word/
11. Medium. (n.d.). *How to Explain to My Fellow Whites Why We Can't Use the N-Word*. Retrieved from https://medium.com/our-human-family/how-to-explain-to-my-fellow-whites-why-we-cant-use-the-n-word-cc56fd3196ec
12. An Injustice Mag. (n.d.). *No, Your Black Friends Can't Give You Permission to Say the N-Word*. Retrieved from https://aninjusticemag.com/no-your-black-friends-cant-give-you-permission-to-say-the-n-word-5690b1172495
13. NME. (2015, March 5). *Kendrick Lamar Explains "Negus" Freestyle on To Pimp a Butterfly*. Retrieved from https://www.nme.com/news/music/kendrick-lamar-51-1227080
14. HipHopDX. (2015, March 18). *Kendrick Lamar Explains "Negus" Freestyle on "To Pimp a Butterfly"*. Retrieved from https://hiphopdx.com/news/id.33224/title.kendrick-lamar-explains-negus-freestyle-on-to-pimp-a-butterfly#
15. Merriam-Webster. (n.d.). *Negus*. Retrieved from https://www.merriam-webster.com/dictionary/negus

Dating A Black Person When You're Not Black

1. Insider. (2020, July 14). *4 Tips on How to Address Race in an Interracial Relationship*. Retrieved from https://www.insider.com/4-tips-on-how-to-address-race-in-interracial-relationship-2020-7
2. https://medium.com/@PriceOfSoul/dearproblackpeople-interracialdating-21d09810328e
3. U.S. Census Bureau. (n.d.). *QuickFacts: United States*. Retrieved from https://www.census.gov/quickfacts/fact/table/US/SEX255221
4. https://www.governing.com/archive/gov-black-men-gender-imbalance-population.html
5. Black Demographics. (n.d.). *Black Male Statistics*. Retrieved from https://blackdemographics.com/population/black-male-statistics/amp/
6. Black Demographics. (n.d.). *Marriage in Black America*. Retrieved from https://blackdemographics.com/households/marriage-in-black-america/amp/
7. Pew Research Center. (2017, May 18). *Intermarriage in the U.S.: 50 Years After Loving v. Virginia*. Retrieved from https://www.pewresearch.org/social-trends/2017/05/18/intermarriage-in-the-u-s-50-years-after-loving-v-virginia/

8. Bureau of Labor Statistics. (2018). *Race and Ethnicity in the 21st Century: Workplace Trends*. Retrieved from https://www.bls.gov/opub/reports/race-and-ethnicity/2018/home.htm

9. Pew Research Center. (2016, June 27). *On Views of Race and Inequality, Blacks and Whites Are Worlds Apart*. Retrieved from https://www.pewresearch.org/social-trends/2016/06/27/on-views-of-race-and-inequality-blacks-and-whites-are-worlds-apart/

10. https://www.jstor.org/stable/24756343
11. https://www.youtube.com/watch?v=qu9fZLdEhSU
12. https://www.youtube.com/watch?v=6pgr9wMkCqs
13. https://www.youtube.com/watch?v=mpCVQ-1fq-4
14. https://www.youtube.com/watch?v=ThHdpBGGFxc
15. https://www.youtube.com/watch?v=JEhJjk6j_NE
16. https://www.youtube.com/watch?v=Xjs0Gw_MbdE
17. https://www.youtube.com/watch?v=UbA6Aajz_R0
18. https://www.youtube.com/watch?v=PgwpJgXkfWU
19. https://www.youtube.com/watch?v=O0APSaqJLTY
20. https://www.youtube.com/watch?v=14ZKBNW1vqQ
21. https://www.youtube.com/watch?v=gAmLuc_Wyal
22. https://www.youtube.com/watch?v=Of3FL4X7mLo
23. https://www.youtube.com/watch?v=SzArb_cujSg

Black Twitter

1. Wikipedia. (n.d.). *Hashtag Activism*. Retrieved from https://en.wikipedia.org/wiki/Hashtag_activism

2. The Washington Post. (2014, January 20). *Black Twitter: A Virtual Community Ready to Hashtag Out a Response to Cultural Issues*. Retrieved from https://www.washingtonpost.com/lifestyle/style/black-twitter-a-virtual-community-ready-to-hashtag-out-a-response-to-cultural-issues/2014/01/20/41ddacf6-7ec5-11e3-9556-4a4bf7bcbd84_story.html

3. Marketplace. (2018, February 16). *Black Twitter: A Conversation Amongst Friends*. Retrieved from https://www.marketplace.org/2018/02/16/black-twitter/

4. The Atlantic. (2015, April 2). *The Truth About Black Twitter*. Retrieved from https://www.theatlantic.com/technology/archive/2015/04/the-truth-about-black-twitter/390120/

5. Pew Research Center. (2018, July 11). *An Analysis of #BlackLivesMatter and Other Twitter Hashtags Related to Political or Social Issues*. Retrieved from https://www.pewresearch.org/internet/2018/07/11/an-analysis-of-blacklivesmatter-and-other-twitter-hashtags-related-to-political-or-social-issues/

6. Pew Research Center. (2016, August 15). *The Hashtag #BlackLivesMatter Emerges: Social Activism on Twitter*. Retrieved from https://www.pewresearch.org/internet/2016/08/15/the-hashtag-blacklivesmatter-emerges-social-activism-on-twitter/

7. EdSurge. (2018, August 23). *#BlackStudentsMatter: Why Digital Activism Is a Voice for Black Students*. Retrieved from https://www.edsurge.com/news/2018-08-23-blackstudentsmatter-why-digital-activism-is-a-voice-for-black-students

8. The Bold Italic. (n.d.). *8 Black Activists in the Bay Area to Follow on Instagram and Twitter*. Retrieved from https://thebolditalic.com/8-black-activists-in-the-bay-area-to-follow-on-instagram-and-twitter-b417f3c4c7ea

9. Wikipedia. (n.d.). *Black Twitter*. Retrieved from https://en.wikipedia.org/wiki/Black_Twitter

10. University of Virginia. (n.d.). *Black Twitter 101: What Is It, Where Did It Originate, and Where Is It Headed?*. Retrieved from https://news.virginia.edu/content/black-twitter-101-what-it-where-did-it-originate-where-it-headed

11. Knight Foundation. (n.d.). *Twitter & Media: Twitter Media*. Retrieved from https://knightfoundation.org/features/twittermedia/

12. https://adage.com/creativity/work/best-2020-no-11-twitter-showcases-black-lives-matter-tweets-billboards-across-country/2264076

13. Slate. (2010, August 24). *How Black People Use Twitter*. Retrieved from https://slate.com/technology/2010/08/how-black-people-use-twitter.html

14. Smithsonian Magazine. (n.d.). *Black Tweets Matter*. Retrieved from https://www.smithsonianmag.com/arts-culture/black-tweets-matter-180960117/

15. The Guardian. (2019, December 23). *Ten Years of Black Twitter: Watchdog, Inspiration, and the Dangers of the Hashtag*. Retrieved from https://www.theguardian.com/technology/2019/dec/23/ten-years-black-twitter-watchdog

16. Level. (n.d.). *The 50 Best Black Twitter Accounts Under 50K Followers*. Retrieved from https://level.medium.com/the-50-best-black-twitter-accounts-under-50k-followers-4c486dcbc0ff

17. Pinterest. (n.d.). *Black Twitter*. Retrieved from https://www.pinterest.com/Rollody/black-twitter/

18. https://repository.upenn.edu/cgi/viewcontent.cgi?article=1802&context=asc_papers

19. The Undefeated. (2020, December 16). *Black Twitter's Superpowers*. Retrieved from https://theundefeated.com/features/a-blessing-and-a-curse-the-rich-history-behind-black-twitter/

20. Revolt TV. (2020, December 16). *Black Twitter's Superpowers: What It Is and What It Isn't*. Retrieved from https://www.revolt.tv/news/2020/12/16/22179164/black-twitter-superpowers-dec-21

21. https://www.youtube.com/watch?v=LT4vGpSkOHw

22. https://www.youtube.com/watch?v=Z42FRPPyu-4

Twerking

1. Refinery29. (2017, March 13). *What Is Twerking? A Look at the Booty-Shaking Dance's Origin and Evolution*. Retrieved from https://www.refinery29.com/en-us/2017/03/147720/what-is-twerking-dance-booty-shaking-black-culture
2. Factinate. (n.d.). *What Is Twerking?*. Retrieved from https://www.factinate.com/editorial/what-is-twerking/
3. Author(s). (2019, March 24). *Decolonizing the Art of Twerking and Other Dances of African Origin*. Retrieved from https://www.jodiminnis.com/gray-area/2019/3/24/decolonizing-the-art-of-twerking-and-other-dances-of-african-origin
4. Cultural Front. (2013, May 6). *The Underground Origins of Twerking*. Retrieved from http://www.culturalfront.org/2013/05/the-underground-origins-of-twerking.html
5. Progressive Pupil. (2013, October 26). *African Origins of Twerking*. Retrieved from https://progressivepupil.wordpress.com/2013/10/26/african-origins-of-twerking/
6. Fuse. (2013, August 28). *A Brief History of Twerking*. Retrieved from https://www.fuse.tv/2013/08/brief-history-of-twerking
7. University of California, San Diego. (2014, August 22). *Twerk Culture: Good or Bad?*. Retrieved from https://quote.ucsd.edu/comm100c/2014/08/22/twerk-culture-good-or-bad/
8. Amodrn. (n.d.). *Why Twerking Is the Ultimate Full-Body Workout*. Retrieved from https://amodrn.com/why-twerking-is-the-ultimate-full-body-workout/
9. Wikipedia. (n.d.). *Twerking*. Retrieved from https://en.wikipedia.org/wiki/Twerking
10. The Sun. (n.d.). *Twerking - Origin, Meaning, Celebrity Videos Performing the Dance Move*. Retrieved from https://www.thesun.co.uk/fabulous/3744666/twerking-origin-meaning-celebrity-videos-performing-dance-move/
11. Merriam-Webster. (n.d.). *Twerking*. Retrieved from https://www.merriam-webster.com/dictionary/twerking
12. Oxford English Dictionary. (n.d.). *Twerking*. Retrieved from https://www.oed.com/view/Entry/36358048?rskey=xk7e2k&result=1&isAdvanced=false#eid
13. Mental Floss. (n.d.). *What Is the Origin of Twerking?*. Retrieved from https://www.mentalfloss.com/article/51365/what-origin-twerking
14. Baltimore City Paper. (2016, June 22). *Twerk: The Dance Move that Took Over Pop Culture*. Retrieved from https://www.baltimoresun.com/citypaper/bcp-062216-feature-twerk-20160621-story.html
15. Science of People. (n.d.). *The Science of Twerking: What Makes This Dance So Irresistible?*. Retrieved from https://www.scienceofpeople.com/science-twerking/
16. Lonely Table. (n.d.). *Twerking: The Issue and What's Really Behind It*. Retrieved from http://lonelytable.net/features-1/2015/twerking-the-issue-and-whats-really-behind-it
17. Business Insider. (2013, December 5). *Don't Know What Twerking Is? Then You Probably Googled It Like Every Other Aussie*. Retrieved from https://www.businessinsider.com.au/dont-know-what-twerking-is-then-you-probably-googled-it-like-every-other-aussie-2013-12

18. Playboy. (n.d.). *An Abridged History of Twerk Culture*. Retrieved from https://www.playboy.com/read/an-abridged-history-of-twerk-culture-1
19. World Belly Dance. (n.d.). *History of Belly Dance*. Retrieved from https://www.worldbellydance.com/history/
20. Go&dance. (n.d.). *Where Does the Kizomba Come From? Origins, Evolution, and Actuality*. Retrieved from https://www.goandance.com/en/blog/kizomba/58-where-does-the-kizomba-come-from-origins-evolution-and-actuality
21. Incognito Dance. (n.d.). *What Is Bachata?*. Retrieved from https://www.incognitodance.com/what-is-bachata-2/
22. Golatindance. (n.d.). *5 Lies You've Been Told About Zouk*. Retrieved from https://golatindance.com/5-lies-youve-been-told-about-zouk/
23. Marquette Wire. (n.d.). *Oversexualization of Black Girls and Women Must Stop*. Retrieved from https://marquettewire.org/4041391/featured/moses-oversexualization-of-black-girls-women-must-stop/
24. Georgetown Law. (2017). *Girlhood Interrupted: The Erasure of Black Girls' Childhood*. Retrieved from https://www.law.georgetown.edu/poverty-inequality-center/wp-content/uploads/sites/14/2017/08/girlhood-interrupted.pdf
25. Sage Journals. (2017). *Girlhood Interrupted: The Erasure of Black Girls' Childhood*. Retrieved from https://journals.sagepub.com/doi/pdf/10.1177/2374623816680622
26. Sage Journals. (2014). *The Impact of Colorism on the Career Aspirations and Career Opportunities of African Americans*. Retrieved from https://journals.sagepub.com/doi/10.1177/0095798411418524
27. African American Policy Forum. (n.d.). *Say Her Name: Resisting Police Brutality Against Black Women*. Retrieved from https://aapf.org/sayhername
28. Springer. (2017). *The Intersection of #SayHerName: Cybervigilantism and Violence Against Black Women*. Retrieved from https://link.springer.com/article/10.1007/s10964-017-0695-3
29. American Psychological Association. (2008). *Girls of Color and the School-to-Prison Pipeline*. Retrieved from https://www.apa.org/pi/women/programs/girls/report-full.pdf
30. American Journal of Public Health. (2009). *Girlhood Interrupted: The Erasure of Black Girls' Childhood*. Retrieved from https://ajph.aphapublications.org/doi/10.2105/AJPH.2008.144279
31. American Sociological Review. (2015). *Stereotypes and the Achievement Gap: Stereotype Threat Prior to Test-Taking*. Retrieved from https://www.asanet.org/sites/default/files/savvy/journals/ASR/Dec15ASRFeature.pdf
32. Springer. (2017). *#BlackLivesMatter: A Longitudinal Test of the Ferguson Effect on Fatal Police Shootings of African Americans*. Retrieved from https://link.springer.com/article/10.1007/s11199-007-9278-1
33. Springer. (2016). *Disproportionate Use of Lethal Force in Policing: A Preliminary Analysis of Justifiable Homicides*. Retrieved from https://journals.sagepub.com/doi/full/10.1177/2056305116672485

34. Springer. (2010). *Race, Stress, and Social Support in the Prediction of Job Stress and Burnout*. Retrieved from https://link.springer.com/article/10.1007/s11199-009-9683-8
35. https://www.youtube.com/watch?v=jYG3s6Iu-SI
36. https://www.youtube.com/watch?v=Glw__yfBr8E

The Black-Guy's Handshake

1. NBC Sports. (n.d.). *Warriors Explain Why the Dap Is Much More Than a Handshake in NBA Culture*. Retrieved from https://www.nbcsports.com/bayarea/warriors/warriors-explain-why-dap-much-more-handshake-nba-culture
2. HuffPost. (n.d.). *Key & Peele: We Witnessed Obama's Black Handshake*. Retrieved from https://www.huffpost.com/entry/key-peele-we-witnessed-obamas-black-handshake_n_5b579e9ee4b00e8c8eb76177
3. African American Intellectual History Society. (n.d.). *Diasporic Salutations and the West African Origins of the Dap*. Retrieved from https://www.aaihs.org/diasporic-salutations-and-the-west-african-origins-of-the-dap/
4. Smithsonian Folklife. (2014, May 19). *Five on the Black Hand Side: Origins and Evolutions of the Dap*. Retrieved from https://folklife.si.edu/talkstory/2014/five-on-the-black-hand-sideorigins-and-evolutions-of-the-dap
5. Columbia Festival of the Arts. (n.d.). *Black Vietnam: Into the Light*. Retrieved from https://columbiafestival.org/project/black-vietnam-into-the-light/
6. https://www.youtube.com/watch?v=9aXc1a9RhTw
7. https://www.youtube.com/watch?v=ZT0kYLeKgl0
8. https://www.youtube.com/watch?v=Hip870_tJMw
9. https://www.youtube.com/watch?v=nopWOC4SRm4
10. https://www.youtube.com/watch?v=J5bXj22pmVY
11. https://www.youtube.com/watch?v=DLCTKmwCeaI
12. https://www.youtube.com/watch?v=AjB-AXwLsZE
13. https://www.youtube.com/watch?v=Z3lPkhcJtqY
14. https://www.youtube.com/watch?v=8MadE_caRBk
15. https://www.youtube.com/watch?v=chrhOaNx9mE
16. https://www.youtube.com/watch?v=HufHIqfiW2s

Black Fashion

1. Kuwala. (n.d.). *African Fabrics 101: Dashiki*. Retrieved from https://kuwala.co/blogs/news/173604679-african-fabrics-101-dashiki
2. Wikipedia. (n.d.). *Dashiki*. Retrieved from https://en.wikipedia.org/wiki/Dashiki#:~:text=The%20dashiki%20is%20a%20colorful%

20garment%20worn%20mostly%20in%20West%20Africa.&text=The%20name%20das
hiki%20or%20%22dyshque,outer%20garment%2C%20babban%20riga).

3. The Culture Trip. (n.d.). *How the Dashiki from West Africa Became Cool Again*.
Retrieved from https://theculturetrip.com/africa/articles/how-the-dashiki-from-west-
africa-became-cool-again/

4. Essence. (n.d.). *11 2000s Fashion Trends Made Popular by Black Culture*. Retrieved
from https://www.essence.com/fashion/2000s-fashion-trends-made-popular-by-
black-culture/#525671

5. Zenerations. (2020). *7 Fashion Trends That Originated from Black Culture*. Retrieved
from https://zenerations.org/2020/07/26/7-fashion-trends-that-originated-from-
black-culture/

6. The Tempest. (2020). *A Close Look at 5 Fashion Trends Started by Black People*.
Retrieved from https://thetempest.co/2020/06/30/style/a-close-look-at-5-fashion-
trends-started-by-black-people/

7. 9 Magazine. (n.d.). *Black Influence on Fashion*. Retrieved from http://9-
magazine.com/artsandculture/black-influence-on-fashion/

8. PureWow. (n.d.). *11 Fashion Trends We Owe to Black Culture*. Retrieved from
https://www.purewow.com/fashion/fashion-trends-by-black-culture

9. College Fashionista. (n.d.). *The Origins: The African American's Influence on Fashion*.
Retrieved from https://www.collegefashionista.com/origins-the-african-americans-
influence-on-fashion/

10. nss magazine. (n.d.). *Street Trends and Styles Originated and Made Popular by Black
Culture Throughout History*. Retrieved from
https://www.nssmag.com/en/fashion/17600/op-ed-street-trends-and-styles-
originated-and-made-popular-by-black-culture-throughout-history

11. The Tab. (2020). *All the Trends You Didn't Realize Originated from Black Culture*.
Retrieved from https://thetab.com/uk/2020/07/03/all-the-trends-you-didnt-realise-
originated-from-black-culture-164635

12. My Black Clothing. (n.d.). *90s Hip-Hop Fashion*. Retrieved from
https://www.myblackclothing.com/blogs/my-black-stoop/90s-hip-hop-fashion

13. Highsnobiety. (n.d.). *How Black Culture Has Influenced the World of Streetwear*.
Retrieved from https://www.highsnobiety.com/p/90s-hip-hop-fashion/

14. Bricks Magazine. (2020). *Black Culture in Fashion: A Brief History of Trends That
Originated from Black Communities*. Retrieved from
https://bricksmagazine.co.uk/2020/06/29/black-culture-in-fashion-a-brief-history-of-
trends-that-originated-from-black-communities/

15. Toothology Dental. (n.d.). *The History of Grills in Hip-Hop Culture*. Retrieved from
https://www.toothologydental.com/grills-
history/#:~:text=Hip%20hop%20and%20rap%20artists,edge%20of%20hip%2Dhop%20
culture.

16. The Delite. (n.d.). *31 Celebs Rocking Grillz: Photos of Celebrities Wearing Grills*.
Retrieved from https://www.thedelite.com/celebrity-grills-photos-celebs-wearing-
grills/31/

17. Body Art Guru. (n.d.). *20 Rappers Who Wear Teeth Grills: Famous Celebrities with Grillz*. Retrieved from https://bodyartguru.com/rappers-who-wear-teeth-grills/
18. Verywell Mind. (n.d.). *What Is Cultural Appropriation?*. Retrieved from https://www.verywellmind.com/what-is-cultural-appropriation-5070458#:~:text=Cultural%20appropriation%20refers%20to%20the,stereotypes%20or%20contributes%20to%20oppression.
19. Everyday Feminism. (2015). *Cultural Appropriation: 9 Harmful Ways People Commonly Misunderstand It*. Retrieved from https://everydayfeminism.com/2015/06/cultural-appropriation-wrong/
20. ReachOut Australia. (n.d.). *Why Cultural Appropriation Isn't Cool*. Retrieved from https://au.reachout.com/articles/why-cultural-appropriation-isnt-cool
21. The Accent - Austin Community College Student Newspaper. (n.d.). *Cultural Appreciation vs. Cultural Appropriation: Why It Matters*. Retrieved from http://sites.austincc.edu/accent/cultural-appreciation-vs-cultural-appropriation-why-it-matters/
22. Preemptive Love. (n.d.). *What Is Cultural Appreciation?*. Retrieved from https://preemptivelove.org/blog/what-is-cultural-appreciation/
23. Ditto. (n.d.). *10 Black-Owned Eyewear Brands We Love*. Retrieved from https://ditto.com/blog/10-black-owned-eyewear-brands-we-love/
24. Travel Babe Collective. (n.d.). *Black-Owned Eyewear Brands*. Retrieved from https://www.travelbabecollective.com/post/black-owned-eyewear-brands
25. PopSugar. (n.d.). *18 Black-Owned Sunglass Brands to Put on Your Radar*. Retrieved from https://www.popsugar.com/fashion/best-black-owned-sunglass-brands-47767605?stream_view=1#photo-47767642

Black Hair

1. Waukeearrowhead.com. (n.d.). *Can Hair Be Cultural Appropriation?* Retrieved from https://waukeearrowhead.com/15088/student-life/can-hair-be-cultural-appropriation/
2. HuffPost. (n.d.). *Here's How Non-Black Minorities Can Avoid Appropriation*. Retrieved from https://www.huffpost.com/entry/non-black-minorities-appropriation_l_5d974be7e4b0f5bf797372ba
3. Uhai Hair. (n.d.). *Hair History: A Short Story on the Evolution of Hair in the African American Community*. Retrieved from https://uhaihair.com/blogs/news/hair-history-a-short-story-on-the-evolution-of-hair-in-the-african-american-community
4. Thirsty Roots. (n.d.). *Discovering Our Roots: Do I Hate My Hair?* Retrieved from https://thirstyroots.com/black-hair-history/discovering-our-roots-do-i-hate-my-hair
5. Stylist. (n.d.). *Black Hair History: Definitive Historic Moments*. Retrieved from https://www.stylist.co.uk/beauty/hair/black-hair-history-definitive-historic-moments/437183

6. History.com. (n.d.). *Black Hairstyles: A Visual History in Photos*. Retrieved from https://www.history.com/news/black-hairstyles-visual-history-in-photos

7. Refinery29. (n.d.). *A Visual History Of African American Hair*. Retrieved from https://www.refinery29.com/en-us/black-hair-history#slide-10

8. Aaregistry.org. (n.d.). *Black Hair Care and Culture: A Story*. Retrieved from https://aaregistry.org/story/black-hair-care-and-culture-a-story/

9. Byrdie. (n.d.). *8 Myths About Natural Black Hair to Stop Believing*. Retrieved from https://www.byrdie.com/myths-about-natural-black-hair-400343

10. Mash-Up Americans. (n.d.). *8 Things You Always Wanted to Know About Black Women's Hair*. Retrieved from http://www.mashupamericans.com/issues/8-things-always-wanted-know-black-womens-hair/

11. Glamour. (n.d.). *Black Hair: An Offensive Timeline*. Retrieved from https://www.glamour.com/story/black-hair-offensive-timeline

12. JSTOR Daily. (n.d.). *How Natural Black Hair at Work Became a Civil Rights Issue*. Retrieved from https://daily.jstor.org/how-natural-black-hair-at-work-became-a-civil-rights-issue/

13. Teen Vogue. (n.d.). *A Brief History of Black Hair Politics and Discrimination*. Retrieved from https://www.teenvogue.com/story/a-brief-history-of-black-hair-politics-and-discrimination

14. The New York Times. (2019). *New York to Ban Discrimination Based on Hairstyles*. Retrieved from https://www.nytimes.com/2019/02/21/nyregion/black-hair-decriminalization-ny.html

15. The Washington Post. (2019). *More States Are Trying to Protect Black Employees Who Want to Wear Natural Hairstyles at Work*. Retrieved from https://www.washingtonpost.com/business/2019/09/19/more-states-are-trying-protect-black-employees-who-want-wear-natural-hairstyles-work/

16. Afrocks. (n.d.). *10 Things You Didn't Know About Afro Hair*. Retrieved from https://afrocks.com/blog/10-things-you-didnt-know-about-afro-hair/

17. The List. (n.d.). *8 Truths About Natural Hair That No One Understands*. Retrieved from https://www.thelist.com/35749/8-truths-natural-hair-one-understands/

18. The Odyssey Online. (n.d.). *20 Things Black Girls Want You to Know About Their Hair*. Retrieved from https://www.theodysseyonline.com/20-things-black-girls-hair

19. Who What Wear. (n.d.). *The Ultimate Black Hair Guide*. Retrieved from https://www.whowhatwear.com/black-hair-guide/slide28

20. Good Housekeeping. (n.d.). *40 Beautiful Natural Hairstyles for Black Women*. Retrieved from https://www.goodhousekeeping.com/beauty/hair/g3536/natural-hairstyles/?slide=35

21. The Trend Spotter. (n.d.). *40 African American Hairstyles & Haircuts*. Retrieved from https://www.thetrendspotter.net/african-american-hairstyles-haircuts/

22. USA Today. (2019). *Laws Passed to Stop Natural Hair Discrimination Across the U.S.* Retrieved from https://www.usatoday.com/story/news/nation/2019/10/14/black-hair-laws-passed-stop-natural-hair-discrimination-across-us/3850402002/

23. Men's Hairstyles Today. (n.d.). *35 Cool Hairstyles for Black Men*. Retrieved from https://www.menshairstylestoday.com/hairstyles-for-black-men/

24. Haircut Inspiration. (n.d.). *30 Haircuts for Black Men (2022 Update)*. Retrieved from https://haircutinspiration.com/haircuts-for-black-men/

25. Men's Hairstyle Trends. (n.d.). *27 Haircuts for Black Men (2022 Styles)*. Retrieved from https://www.menshairstyletrends.com/haircuts-for-black-men/

26. The Modest Man. (n.d.). *27 Best Black Men's Hairstyles*. Retrieved from https://www.themodestman.com/best-black-mens-hairstyles/

27. PopSugar. (n.d.). *What's My Natural Hair Type?* Retrieved from https://www.popsugar.com/beauty/What-My-Natural-Hair-Type-36337831?stream_view=1#photo-36337844

28. Rotten Tomatoes. (n.d.). *Good Hair*. Retrieved from https://www.rottentomatoes.com/m/good_hair

29. IMDb. (n.d.). *Good Hair (2009) - Plot Summary*. Retrieved from https://www.imdb.com/title/tt0441779/plotsummary?ref_=tt_ov_pl

30. Rotten Tomatoes. (n.d.). *Da 5 Bloods*. Retrieved from https://www.rottentomatoes.com/m/da_5_bloods

31. The Root. (2021). *Army Adopts More Inclusive Grooming Standards for Black Troops*. Retrieved from https://www.theroot.com/army-adopts-more-inclusive-grooming-standards-for-black-1846144519

32. Natural Club. (n.d.). *Why Is It Called Natural Hair?* Retrieved from https://naturallclub.com/blogs/the-naturall-club-blog/why-is-it-called-natural-hair

33. Wigs.com. (n.d.). *What Is a Lace Front Wig?* Retrieved from https://www.wigs.com/blogs/news/what-is-a-lace-front-wig

34. YouTube. (n.d.). *Good Hair - Official Trailer*. Retrieved from https://www.youtube.com/watch?v=d0Ta0XKlisg

35. YouTube. (n.d.). *Chris Rock - Good Hair - The Dollar Weave Club*. Retrieved from https://www.youtube.com/watch?v=U48565qmqUk

36. YouTube. (n.d.). *Good Hair - India Weave*. Retrieved from https://www.youtube.com/watch?v=dN5DXQMxWCY

37. YouTube. (n.d.). *Good Hair - The Hair Cream*. Retrieved from https://www.youtube.com/watch?v=J4QKBcydqMY

Black Inventions

1. Friendshipcharlotte.org. (2017). *Black Inventors List*. Retrieved from http://www.friendshipcharlotte.org/wp-content/uploads/2017/09/Black-Inventors-List.pdf

2. BlackPast. (n.d.). *Black Inventors and Inventions*. Retrieved from https://www.blackpast.org/black-inventors-and-inventions/#1613494035505-5fed4fcf-98b8

3. FOX 2 Detroit. (n.d.). *8 Everyday Items That You Probably Didn't Know Were Invented by Black People*. Retrieved from https://www.fox2detroit.com/news/8-everyday-items-that-you-probably-didnt-know-were-invented-by-black-people

4. History.com. (n.d.). *8 Black Inventors You Should Know About*. Retrieved from https://www.history.com/news/8-black-inventors-african-american

5. HowStuffWorks. (n.d.). *10 Inventions by African Americans*. Retrieved from https://science.howstuffworks.com/innovation/inventions/10-inventions-by-african-americans.htm

6. Think Growth. (n.d.). *14 Black Inventors You Probably Didn't Know About*. Retrieved from https://thinkgrowth.org/14-black-inventors-you-probably-didnt-know-about-3c0702cc63d2

7. CW33. (n.d.). *30 Inventions You Can Thank a Black Person For*. Retrieved from https://cw33.com/watercooler/30-inventions-you-can-thank-a-black-person-for/

8. WorldRemit. (n.d.). *Celebrating Black Inventors: Their Impact and Legacy*. Retrieved from https://www.worldremit.com/en/stories/story/2019/10/28/black-inventors

9. Daily Hive. (n.d.). *Inventions by Black People That Changed the World*. Retrieved from https://dailyhive.com/seattle/inventions-by-black-people

Systemic Racism

1. Verywell Mind. (n.d.). *What Is Prejudice?*. Retrieved from https://www.verywellmind.com/what-is-prejudice-5092657

2. Verywell Mind. (n.d.). *Implicit Bias Overview*. Retrieved from https://www.verywellmind.com/implicit-bias-overview-4178401

3. Perception.org. (n.d.). *Implicit Bias*. Retrieved from https://perception.org/research/implicit-bias/

4. Simply Psychology. (n.d.). *Katz and Braly (1933) - Stereotype Study*. Retrieved from https://simple.wikipedia.org/wiki/Stereotype

5. ThoughtCo. (n.d.). *Stereotype: Definition and Examples*. Retrieved from https://www.thoughtco.com/what-is-the-meaning-of-stereotype-2834956

6. Ontario Human Rights Commission. (n.d.). *Examples of Racial Discrimination*. Retrieved from http://www.ohrc.on.ca/en/examples-racial-discrimination-fact-sheet

7. Smithsonian Magazine. (n.d.). *158 Resources on Understanding Systemic Racism in America*. Retrieved from https://www.smithsonianmag.com/history/158-resources-understanding-systemic-racism-america-180975029/

8. Ontario Human Rights Commission. (n.d.). *What Is Racial Profiling?*. Retrieved from http://www.ohrc.on.ca/en/what-racial-profiling-fact-sheet

9. American Bar Association. (n.d.). *Racial Profiling: Past, Present, and Future*. Retrieved from https://www.americanbar.org/groups/criminal_justice/publications/criminal-justice-magazine/2020/winter/racial-profiling-past-present-and-future/

10. Common Bond Collaborative. (n.d.). *Interpersonal Racism*. Retrieved from https://commonbondz.org/resources-1/interpersonal-racism

11. Center for Assessment and Policy Development. (n.d.). *Four Levels of Racism*. Retrieved from https://www.cacgrants.org/assets/ce/Documents/2019/FourLevelsOfRacism.pdf

12. Frank Porter Graham Child Development Institute. (n.d.). *What Racism Looks Like*. Retrieved from https://fpg.unc.edu/sites/fpg.unc.edu/files/resources/other-resources/What%20Racism%20Looks%20Like.pdf

13. United Nations Human Rights Council. (n.d.). *The Impact of Systemic Racism on the Full Enjoyment of Human Rights by African Americans*. Retrieved from https://www.ohchr.org/Documents/Issues/Racism/smd.shahid.pdf

14. History. (n.d.). *New Deal*. Retrieved from https://www.history.com/topics/great-depression/new-deal

15. History. (n.d.). *FDR's Fireside Chats: The Role of Eleanor Roosevelt and Crucial New Dealers*. Retrieved from https://www.history.com/event/fdr-fireside-chats

16. U.S. Equal Employment Opportunity Commission. (n.d.). *Overview of the EEOC*. Retrieved from https://www.eeoc.gov/overview

17. Human Rights Watch. (n.d.). *Racial Disparities in the United States*. Retrieved from https://www.hrw.org/reports/2000/uslabor/USLBR008-08.htm

18. Race Forward. (n.d.). *Systemic Racism*. Retrieved from https://www.raceforward.org/videos/systemic-racism

19. Black Excellence. (n.d.). *Black Incarceration Rates*. Retrieved from https://blackexcellence.com/black-incarceration-rates/

20. The Century Foundation. (n.d.). *Racism, Inequality, and Health Care for African Americans*. Retrieved from https://tcf.org/content/report/racism-inequality-health-care-african-americans/?session=1

21. Centers for Disease Control and Prevention. (n.d.). *Health Disparities in HIV/AIDS, Viral Hepatitis, STDs, and TB*. Retrieved from https://www.cdc.gov/media/releases/2017/p0502-aa-health.html

22. Centers for Disease Control and Prevention. (n.d.). *Racial and Ethnic Disparities Continue in Pregnancy-Related Deaths*. Retrieved from https://www.cdc.gov/mmwr/volumes/68/wr/mm6835a3.htm?s_cid=mm6835a3_w

23. U.S. Department of Health and Human Services, Office of Minority Health. (n.d.). *Health Disparities: What Are They?*. Retrieved from https://minorityhealth.hhs.gov/omh/browse.aspx?lvl=4&lvlid=23

24. National Center for Health Statistics. (n.d.). *Deaths: Leading Causes for 2018*. Retrieved from https://www.cdc.gov/nchs/data/nvsr/nvsr69/NVSR-69-7-508.pdf

25. American Bar Association. (n.d.). *Racial Disparities in Health Care*. Retrieved from https://www.americanbar.org/groups/crsj/publications/human_rights_magazine_home/the-state-of-healthcare-in-the-united-states/racial-disparities-in-health-care/

26. Medical News Today. (n.d.). *Racism in Healthcare: What You Need to Know*. Retrieved from https://www.medicalnewstoday.com/articles/racism-in-healthcare#how-racism-impacts-health

27. Stanford Open Policing Project. (n.d.). *Findings*. Retrieved from https://openpolicing.stanford.edu/findings/

28. Pew Research Center. (n.d.). *10 Things We Know About Race and Policing in the U.S.* Retrieved from https://www.pewresearch.org/short-reads/2020/06/03/10-things-we-know-about-race-and-policing-in-the-u-s/
29. https://www.youtube.com/watch?v=DBxfnXql0oo
30. https://www.youtube.com/watch?v=p7Rq78jFiJg
31. https://www.youtube.com/watch?v=-4lgvs4piFs
32. https://www.youtube.com/watch?v=fTcSVQJ2h8g

Is Reverse Racism Really A Myth?

1. Business Insider. (2016, April 6). Here's Why Reverse Racism Doesn't Actually Exist in the U.S. Retrieved from https://www.businessinsider.com/heres-why-reverse-racism-doesnt-actually-exist-in-the-us-2016-4
2. Ka Leo O Hawai'i. (n.d.). Busting the Myth of Reverse Racism. Retrieved from https://www.manoanow.org/busting-the-myth-of-reverse-racism/article_c25c9c7a-a7fb-11e3-9a07-001a4bcf6878.html
3. The Atlantic. (2017, August 28). The Myth of Reverse Racism. Retrieved from https://www.theatlantic.com/education/archive/2017/08/myth-of-reverse-racism/535689/
4. HuffPost. (2014, November 12). Discrimination: A New Tool. Retrieved from https://www.huffpost.com/entry/discrimination-race-religion_n_5833761ee4b099512f845bba
5. Financial Aid Information Page. (n.d.). Retrieved from https://finaid.org/
6. The Anti-Racist Educator. (n.d.). Reverse Racism. Retrieved from https://www.theantiracisteducator.com/reverseracism
7. Minnesota Daily. (n.d.). Op-Ed: Reverse Racism. Retrieved from https://mndaily.com/233763/opinion/op-reverseracism2/
8. Alberta Civil Liberties Research Centre. (n.d.). Myth of Reverse Racism. Retrieved from https://www.aclrc.com/myth-of-reverse-racism
9. Medium. (n.d.). Why Reverse Racism Is a Myth. Retrieved from https://momentum.medium.com/why-reverse-racism-is-a-myth-c2374b8837af
10. TODAY. (2020, June 19). What Is Reverse Racism? Experts Weigh in on the Term. Retrieved from https://www.today.com/tmrw/what-reverse-racism-experts-weigh-term-t184580
11. Harvard Business School. (n.d.). Whites See Racism as a Zero-Sum Game That They Are Now Losing. Retrieved from https://www.hbs.edu/ris/Publication%20Files/norton%20sommers%20whites%20see%20racism_ca92b4be-cab9-491d-8a87-cf1c6ff244ad.pdf
12. Connecticut State Department of Administrative Services. (2007, November 8). Myths and Facts about Affirmative Action. Retrieved from https://portal.ct.gov/-/media/DAS/Commissioners-Office/Myths-and-Facts-11082007.pdf

13. University of South Florida, Office of Diversity, Inclusion, and Equal Opportunity. (n.d.). Ten Myths About Affirmative Action. Retrieved from https://www.usf.edu/compliance-ethics/equal-opportunity/ten-myths-about-affirmative-action.aspx
14. Understanding Prejudice. (n.d.). Affirmative Action: Myths and Misconceptions. Retrieved from https://secure.understandingprejudice.org/readroom/articles/affirm.htm
15. FiveThirtyEight. (2018, July 30). Here's What Happens When You Ban Affirmative Action in College Admissions. Retrieved from https://fivethirtyeight.com/features/heres-what-happens-when-you-ban-affirmative-action-in-college-admissions/

What's Up with Black Lives Matter

1. **Newsweek.** (n.d.). Black Lives Matter. Retrieved from https://www.newsweek.com/topic/black-lives-matter
2. **Black Lives Matter.** (n.d.). About. Retrieved from https://blacklivesmatter.com/about/?__cf_chl_jschl_tk__=pmd_L2UKG0ncwtoyurNSl3fHro6tnCjUuniPrpL5mrZuHyM-1634770059-0-gqNtZGzNAlCjcnBszQrR
3. **The Conversation.** (n.d.). Black Lives Matter: How Far Has the Movement Come? Retrieved from https://theconversation.com/black-lives-matter-how-far-has-the-movement-come-165492
4. **BBC News.** (n.d.). Black Lives Matter: What is the movement about? Retrieved from https://www.bbc.com/news/explainers-53337780
5. **Encyclopedia Britannica.** (n.d.). Black Lives Matter. Retrieved from https://www.britannica.com/topic/Black-Lives-Matter
6. **NBC News.** (n.d.). Movement, Slogan, Rallying Cry: How Black Lives Matter Changed America. Retrieved from https://www.nbcnews.com/news/nbcblk/movement-slogan-rallying-cry-how-black-lives-matter-changed-america-n1252434
7. **Black Lives Matter.** (n.d.). Herstory. Retrieved from https://blacklivesmatter.com/herstory/
8. **Black Lives Matter Los Angeles.** (n.d.). Retrieved from https://www.blmla.org/
9. **People's Budget LA.** (n.d.). Retrieved from https://peoplesbudgetla.com/
10. **Politico Magazine.** (2020, June 9). The Short, Fraught History of the Thin Blue Line American Flag. Retrieved from https://www.politico.com/news/magazine/2020/06/09/the-short-fraught-history-of-the-thin-blue-line-american-flag-309767
11. **DocumentCloud.** (n.d.). Retrieved from https://www.documentcloud.org/documents/6936539-2020-PQ-Ambushes-1.html

What is Juneteenth & How Do I Celebrate It

1. **History.com.** (n.d.). What Is Juneteenth? Retrieved from https://www.history.com/news/what-is-juneteenth
2. **National Museum of African American History and Culture.** (n.d.). The Historical Legacy of Juneteenth. Retrieved from https://nmaahc.si.edu/blog-post/historical-legacy-juneteenth
3. **Juneteenth.com.** (n.d.). Juneteenth World Wide Celebration. Retrieved from https://www.juneteenth.com/
4. **The New York Times.** (n.d.). Juneteenth: A Day of Celebration. Retrieved from https://www.nytimes.com/article/juneteenth-day-celebration.html
5. **PBS: African Americans: Many Rivers to Cross.** (n.d.). What Is Juneteenth? Retrieved from https://www.pbs.org/wnet/african-americans-many-rivers-to-cross/history/what-is-juneteenth/
6. **The White House.** (2021, June 18). A Proclamation on Juneteenth Day of Observance, 2021. Retrieved from https://www.whitehouse.gov/briefing-room/presidential-actions/2021/06/18/a-proclamation-on-juneteenth-day-of-observance-2021/
7. **NPR.** (2021, June 17). Juneteenth: What Is Its Origin and Observation? Retrieved from https://www.npr.org/2021/06/17/1007315228/juneteenth-what-is-origin-observation

What Do I Do If I Get Invited To A Black BBQ

1. Deadspin. (2015, September 15). The Caucasians' Guide to Black Barbecues. Retrieved from https://deadspin.com/the-caucasians-guide-to-black-barbecues-1730865233
2. The Root. (2017, August 4). Five Rules for Black Cookouts and Life. Retrieved from https://www.theroot.com/five-rules-for-black-cookouts-and-life-1798706295

How Can I Be An Ally To Black People & Other Marginalized Groups

1. **Harvard Business Review.** (2020, November). Be a Better Ally. Retrieved from https://hbr.org/2020/11/be-a-better-ally
2. **YWCA Harrisburg.** (n.d.). 10 Things Allies Can Do. Retrieved from http://www.ywcahbg.org/sites/default/files/manager/10%20Things%20Allies%20Can%20Do.pdf
3. **Today.** (n.d.). How to Be a Good Ally. Retrieved from https://www.today.com/tmrw/how-be-good-ally-t184330
4. **Guide to Allyship.** (n.d.). Retrieved from https://guidetoallyship.com/
5. **BetterUp.** (n.d.). 5 Powerful Steps to Becoming a Better Ally. Retrieved from https://www.betterup.com/blog/5-powerful-steps-to-becoming-a-better-ally

6. **Community Toolbox.** (n.d.). Be an Ally. Retrieved from https://ctb.ku.edu/en/table-of-contents/culture/cultural-competence/be-an-ally/main
7. **Indeed.** (n.d.). Become a Better Ally at Work. Retrieved from https://www.indeed.com/career-advice/career-development/become-a-better-ally-at-work
8. **GLAAD.** (n.d.). Ally. Retrieved from https://www.glaad.org/resources/ally/2
9. **Blueprint for All.** (n.d.). How Can I Be an Ally? Retrieved from https://www.blueprintforall.org/how-can-i-be-an-ally/
10. **Learning for Justice.** (2018, Spring). How to Be an Ally. Retrieved from https://www.learningforjustice.org/magazine/spring-2018/how-to-be-an-ally
11. **The Muse.** (n.d.). What Is an Ally? 7 Examples. Retrieved from https://www.themuse.com/advice/what-is-an-ally-7-examples
12. **BuzzFeed.** (n.d.). How to Be an Ally: A Guide. Retrieved from https://www.buzzfeed.com/victoriagasparowicz/how-to-be-an-ally-guide
13. **Women of Color for Progress.** (n.d.). Ally Guide. Retrieved from https://www.womenofcolorforprogress.org/allyguide
14. **Syracuse University News.** (2020, October 14). 8 Ways to Be a Better Ally. Retrieved from https://news.syr.edu/the-peel/2020/10/14/8-ways-to-be-a-better-ally/

Additional Reading

1. Kendi, I. X. (2019). *How to Be an Antiracist*.
2. DiAngelo, R. (2018). *White Fragility: Why It's So Hard for White People to Talk About Racism*.
3. Acho, E. (2020). *Uncomfortable Conversations with a Black Man*.
4. Eberhardt, J. L. (2019). *Biased: Uncovering the Hidden Prejudice That Shapes What We See, Think, and Do*.
5. Alexander, M. (2020). *The New Jim Crow: Mass Incarceration in the Age of Colorblindness*.
6. Rothstein, R. (2017). *The Color of Law: A Forgotten History of How Our Government Segregated America*.
7. Austin, I. (2021). *Not All Black Kids Sit Together in the Cafeteria: And Other Conversations about Race*.
8. Austin, I. (2021). *You Want to Talk About Race: An Indigenous Peoples' Perspective*.
9. Oluo, I. (2019). *So You Want to Talk About Race*.
10. Fleming, C. E. (2018). *How to Be Less Stupid About Race: On Racism, White Supremacy, and the Racial Divide*.

Recommended Black Social Media Meme Pages to

1. https://www.instagram.com/
2. https://www.youtube.com/
3. https://twitter.com/home
4. https://www.facebook.com/
5. https://www.tiktok.com/en

Recommended Black Social Media News Outlets

1. The Minority Eye. (n.d.). *The Top 50 Black-Owned Websites*. https://theminorityeye.com/the-top-50-black-owned-websites/
2. Black Freelance. (n.d.). *Black Media Outlets*. https://blackfreelance.com/black-media-outlets/
3. Black Excellence. (n.d.). *7 Websites to Get Black News the Mainstream Media Ignores*. https://blackexcellence.com/7-websites-to-get-black-news-the-mainstream-media-ignores/
4. Cision. (2019, February). *Top African American News Sites*. https://www.cision.com/2019/02/top-african-american-news-sites/
5. Feedspot. (n.d.). *Top 100 Black Magazines & Publications To Follow in 2021*. https://blog.feedspot.com/black_magazines/
6. Blavity. (n.d.). *Blavity - Creative Minds Think Alike* [Category: Interviews]. https://blavity.com/cmta-brand?category1=interviews
7. Bossip. (n.d.). *About Bossip*. https://bossip.com/about/
8. HotNewHipHop. (n.d.). *About Us*. https://www.hotnewhiphop.com/about.htm

Author Recommended Black Movies

1. **IMDb**. (n.d.). Retrieved from https://www.imdb.com/?ref_=nv_home
2. **Rotten Tomatoes**. (n.d.). Retrieved from https://www.rottentomatoes.com/
3. **Complex**. (n.d.). *The Best Black Movies of the Last 30 Years*. Retrieved from https://www.complex.com/pop-culture/the-best-black-movies-of-the-last-30-years/friday
4. **Tom's Guide**. (n.d.). *Best Black Movies*. Retrieved from https://www.tomsguide.com/round-up/best-black-movies
5. **IMDb**. (n.d.). *Top 100 Greatest African American Movies*. Retrieved from https://www.imdb.com/list/ls054431555/
6. **List Challenges**. (n.d.). *100 Must-See African American Films*. Retrieved from https://www.listchallenges.com/100-must-see-african-american-films

Author Recommended Black Shows

1. IMDb. (n.d.). [IMDb homepage]. IMDb. https://www.imdb.com/?ref_=nv_home
2. Rotten Tomatoes. (n.d.). [Rotten Tomatoes homepage]. Rotten Tomatoes. https://www.rottentomatoes.com/
3. Complex. (n.d.). The 30 Best Black Sitcoms of All Time. Complex. https://www.complex.com/pop-culture/best-black-sitcoms/cosby-show
4. IMDb. (n.d.). [List of Black TV Shows]. IMDb. https://www.imdb.com/list/ls054341449/
5. IndieWire. (2020, June 8). 40 Black TV Shows to Watch Right Now. IndieWire. https://www.indiewire.com/2020/06/black-tv-shows-to-watch-1202238005/
6. Screen Rant. (n.d.). 10 Iconic Culture-Defining Black TV Shows of All Time. Screen Rant. https://screenrant.com/black-tv-shows-iconic-culture-defining/

Author Recommended Black Hosted Podcasts

1. **TuneIn**. (n.d.). *Stream Black Culture*. Retrieved from https://tunein.com/radio/Stream-Black-Culture-g262/
2. **Mashable**. (n.d.). *Podcasts With Black Hosts Cover Pop Culture, True Crime, Politics, History*. Retrieved from https://mashable.com/article/podcasts-black-hosts-pop-culture-true-crime-politics-history
3. **BestColleges**. (n.d.). *The Best Black Podcasts*. Retrieved from https://www.bestcolleges.com/blog/black-podcasts/
4. **BU Today**. (2021). *Nine Movies, Podcasts, and Books to Check Out for Black History Month and Beyond*. Retrieved from https://www.bu.edu/articles/2021/nine-movies-podcasts-and-books-to-check-out-for-black-history-month-and-beyond/
5. **Mic**. (n.d.). *The 9 Best Black Podcasts That Will Get You Laughing, Thinking, Thriving*. Retrieved from https://www.mic.com/p/the-9-best-black-podcasts-that-will-get-you-laughing-thinking-thriving-82831637
6. **Black Enterprise**. (n.d.). *35 Black Podcasts You Need to Tune Into and Download*. Retrieved from https://www.blackenterprise.com/35-black-podcasts-you-need-to-tune-into-and-download/?test=prebid
7. **HelloGiggles**. (n.d.). *11 Black Podcasts to Subscribe to Right Now*. Retrieved from https://hellogiggles.com/lifestyle/black-podcasts/
8. **Revolt TV**. (2020). *13 Hip-Hop Podcasts*. Retrieved from https://www.revolt.tv/2020/5/7/21197888/13-hip-hop-podcasts
9. **Vox Magazine**. (n.d.). *Top Five Podcasts for Hip-Hop Enthusiasts*. Retrieved from https://www.voxmagazine.com/music/top-five-podcasts-for-hip-hop-enthusiasts/article_d2a9ca72-dfb9-11e7-a832-7bbfe32f3223.html
10. **Apple Podcasts**. (n.d.). Retrieved from https://www.apple.com/apple-podcasts/
11. **Spotify**. (n.d.). Retrieved from https://open.spotify.com/genre/podcasts-web

12. **The Stoop**. (n.d.). *About*. Retrieved from https://www.thestoop.org/aboutthestoop
13. **Podchaser**. (n.d.). *The Nod Podcast*. Retrieved from https://www.podchaser.com/podcasts/the-nod-534068

Author Recommended Black (Hip Hop) Radio Stations By City

1. Urban One. (n.d.). [Urban One Radio]. Urban One. https://urban1.com/radio-one/
2. Cision. (2012, June 12). Top 10 African American-Influenced Radio Stations. Cision. https://www.cision.com/2012/06/top-10-african-american-influenced-radio-stations/
3. iHeartMedia. (n.d.). [iHeartMedia Stations - Hip Hop and R&B]. iHeartMedia. https://www.iheartmedia.com/stations?genre=Hip+Hop+and+R%26B
4. IndiePanda. (n.d.). [Best Radio Stations for Rap]. IndiePanda. https://indiepanda.net/best-radio-stations-for-rap/
5. Wikipedia. (n.d.). List of Urban-Format Radio Stations in the United States. Wikipedia. https://en.wikipedia.org/wiki/List_of_urban-format_radio_stations_in_the_United_States#New_York_City
6. TuneIn. (n.d.). [Hip-Hop Music - Free Internet Radio]. TuneIn. https://tunein.com/radio/Hip-Hop-Music--Free-Internet-Radio--TuneIn-c57942/
7. All USA Radio Station. (n.d.). [All USA Radio Station]. All USA Radio Station. http://allusaradiostation.e-monsite.com

Popular Black Dance Moves

1. For Harriet. (2013, February). 18 Black Dances That Still Belong to Us. http://www.forharriet.com/2013/02/18-black-dances-that-still-belong-to-us.html
2. Soul In Stereo. (2019, March). 17 Songs That Launched the Blackest Dance Crazes. http://www.soulinstereo.com/2019/03/17-songs-that-launched-the-blackest-dance-crazes.html
3. Ebony. (n.d.). Music: The Black Family Reunion. https://www.ebony.com/life/music-black-family-reunion/
4. YouTube. (n.d.). https://www.youtube.com/

Ebonics / Black Slang

1. Linguistic Society of America. (n.d.). [African American Vernacular English (AAVE)]. https://www.linguisticsociety.org/sites/default/files/Ebonics.pdf
2. Commonwealth Times. (2021, February 18). AAVE Is Not Your Internet Slang, It Is Black Culture. https://commonwealthtimes.org/2021/02/18/aave-is-not-your-internet-slang-it-is-black-culture/
3. North Texas Daily. (n.d.). Internet Slang Is Rooted in the Appropriation of Black Culture. https://www.ntdaily.com/internet-slang-is-rooted-in-the-appropriation-of-black-culture/
4. Zenerations. (2021, February 10). Dear Gen Z: AAVE Is Not Internet Slang. https://zenerations.org/2021/02/10/dear-gen-z-aave-is-not-internet-slang/
5. Feminuity. (n.d.). Using BVE as a Non-Black Person Is Appropriation. https://www.feminuity.org/blog-posts/using-bve-as-a-non-black-person-is-appropriation
6. Oprah Daily. (n.d.). [Slang Words with Surprising Meanings]. https://www.oprahdaily.com/entertainment/g23603568/slang-words-meaning/?slide=40
7. Refinery29. (n.d.). [Black Slang & AAVE Words Meanings History]. https://www.refinery29.com/en-us/2018/02/142047/black-slang-words-meanings-history#slide-6
8. Stacker. (n.d.). [America's Most Common Slang Words Explained]. https://stacker.com/stories/3361/americas-most-common-slang-words-explained
9. Insider. (n.d.). [24 Slang Words Teens Are Using in 2020 and What They Mean]. https://www.insider.com/24-slang-words-teens-are-using-2020-what-they-mean-2020-12
10. FreedomCare. (n.d.). [New York Slang: Words to Know in the Big Apple]. https://www.freedomcareny.com/posts/new-york-slang
11. Oprah Daily. (n.d.). [Queer Cultural Appropriation: Definition & Examples]. https://www.oprahdaily.com/life/a23601818/queer-cultural-appropriation-definition/

www.ingramcontent.com/pod-product-compliance
Lightning Source LLC
Chambersburg PA
CBHW052014030426
42335CB00026B/3143